Toward a Science of Human Nature
Essays on the Psychologies of
Mill, Hegel, Wundt, and James

Toward
a Science of
Human Nature

Essays on
the Psychologies of
Mill, Hegel, Wundt, and James

DANIEL N. ROBINSON

New York   Columbia University Press   *1982*

Library of Congress Cataloging in Publication Data
Robinson, Daniel N., 1937–
Toward a science of human nature.
Includes bibliographical references and index.
1. Psychology—History—19th century.   2. Mill, John
Stuart, 1806–1873.   3. Hegel, Georg Wilhelm Friedrich,
1770–1831.   4. Wundt, Wilhelm Max, 1832–1920.   5. James,
William, 1842–1910.   I. Title.
BF103.R62   150'.92'2   81-38458
ISBN 0-231-05174-3   AACR2

Columbia University Press

New York   Guildford, Surrey

Copyright © 1982 Columbia University Press
All rights reserved
Printed in the United States of America

*Clothbound editions of Columbia University Press books
are Smyth-sewn and printed on permanent and
durable acid-free paper.*

To
Francine
and
in memory of my grandmother,
Mary Elizabeth Burke

CONTENTS

PREFACE

The present collection of essays is intended to provide the broader conceptual framework within which four of the nineteenth century's most influential writers on psychology developed their views. It has not been my purpose to join their specific notions to some issue of contemporary favor. Writers of the previous century had no way of knowing what would engage today's scholars, and the latter have consistently displayed an often heroic indifference to the older views. My aim, therefore, has not been to make twentieth-century Psychology more intelligible or inevitable, but to examine how the last century understood the issues and the mission of the discipline, at least as this understanding emerges from the works of J.S. Mill, G.W.F. Hegel, Wilhelm Wundt, and William James.

In choosing four luminaries about whom so much has been written by philosophers and historians of Psychology, I have assumed the burden of saying something different, if not original, regarding the psychological dimensions of their published works. This, of course, is a burden an author accepts only when persuaded that the available literature is incomplete or defective. Without going too deeply into the matter, I should say something about what I find lacking in the more accessible treatments of the four.

J.S. Mill, as he is generally known to students of Psychology, is the great patron of inductive science, the modern "father" of experimental method, the formidable defender of associationism, and the man who brought David Hume's powerful and original views to bear upon the broadest range of problems in individual and social psychology. What is less clear in the accounts that focus on these accomplishments is what Mill had to say about competing perspectives; how he understood them and how consistent and effective he was in criticizing them. It is particularly true of the Mill passed on by histories of Psychology that one is hard pressed to discover the internal connections among his associationistic psychology, his phenomenalistic theory of knowledge, his utilitarian theory of morals, and his libertarian school of politics. Nor is it any clearer how each and all of these proceeded from and, at the same time, supported his often radically inductive logic. The effect, then, is that the delivered Mill arrives trailing a collection of maxims and prescriptions about how science, the mind, society, and the world ought to be understood. What we so seldom come to perceive in the Mill thus assembled are those programmatic aspects of his work which, taken together, attempt to be nothing less than a system of Psychology. And it is just this system, when examined as such, that finally locates what is flawed and unfinished in his program. It is not enough to discover how Mill may have aided our own century as it goes about the business of erecting a science of human nature. We must study how Mill and *his* century considered this science. If in some way it makes sense to say that he solved some of our problems, we are still obliged to determine how well he settled his own, those of his age.

Hegel presents a very different dilemma, for he has not been discussed enough in histories of Psychology, despite the fact that *Hegelianism* has probably influenced modern Psychology more widely and deeply than has Mill. The English-speaking historians of Psychology have been rather laconic with respect to this influence, but for reasons that warrant some sympathy. No major philosopher is as difficult to summarize or even to understand in his own language as is Hegel, and English translations do nothing to lighten the load. Moreover, Hegel's "psychology" is not of the narrow disciplinary sort that lends itself easily to comparisons with other schools and systems. It is not surprising, therefore, that it is discussed peripherally in connection with Marxism or Phenomenology or "idealistic" tendencies in nineteenth-century German psychology. Although this treatment is understandable, it has led to an utterly artificial depiction of Psychology's foundations in the nineteenth century. Indeed, in failing to consider just what Hegel set out to do and how his efforts were perceived, assimilated, and criticized by his contemporaries and immediate successors, we are unable to make complete sense of the psychological works of Mill or Wilhelm Wundt. This is why, in the present volume, I have ignored chronology and have inserted Hegel between Mill and Wundt; after Mill, because the modern reader's best introduction to Hegel is to be found in Mill's less than successful refutation of "the Absolute"; and before Wundt because it is only through Hegelian prisms that Wundt's retreats from materialism and *scientism* become plausible, even necessary.

The tendency to treat Wundt's massive effort in *Völkerpsychologie* as something of an afterthought—a late-life alternative to the hard work of experimentation—has been all but eliminated by recent scholarship. Students now know that the cultural and social dimensions of consciousness were recognized as salient even in Wundt's earliest writings, as was his recognition that these could not be incorporated into the experimental and physiological psychology that was his *psychology*. But why not? Why was J. S. Mill so confident that his *ethology* would come to rest on precisely that inductive foundation already supporting the mental science of the individual, whereas Wundt was equally confident that the two spheres of being could never be collapsed into each other? It is not enough to answer this by pointing to Mill's empiricism—for Wundt was unflinching in his empiricism—or to a mere difference of opinion. Rather, we must alert ourselves to that tradition launched by Kant and refined by Fichte, Herbart, Schelling, and, most of all, Hegel; the tradition that installed an immovable wedge between the *causal* realm of natural science and the *rational* realm of human science. Wundt's achievement, though incomplete, was to preserve as much of Mill's science for Psychology as the evidence would support, but to add as much of Hegelian metaphysics as the discipline clearly warranted.

And then there is William James, the most influential psychologist America was to produce; the scholar who could be as comfortable with neurophysiology as with mysticism and psychics. Every history of Psychology reserves pages for him, but it is perhaps not too unfair to notice how quickly he slips off these pages. Was he an empiricist? Yes, a radical one. And did he anticipate so much that would come to animate both gestalt psychology and behaviorism? Did he ground American psychology in the fertile soil of the biological sciences and evolutionary theory? Did he, simultaneously, liberate Psychology from the impositions of biology and evolutionary theory? Again, the answers are in the affirmative. We are told that his "school" was *Functionalism* and that his "method" was *Pragmatism*; that he said much about the "stream of consciousness," and that he was a modern father of "scientific" psychology; that he lectured on the biological correlates of mind, but that he maintained a stubbornly dualistic position on the mind/body problem. But what, finally, was James' *psychology*? And to what was it a response?

The chapters on these four architects of modern thought are bracketed by a general introduction to the intellectual climate of their century and a concluding chapter examining the debts owed to them by our own. Together, the six chapters should be taken as interpretive essays fleshing out the revised edition of my *An Intellectual History of Psychology* and as introductions to more rigorous studies of the philosophical psychologies developed by Mill, Hegel, Wundt, and James. Theirs were *philosophical* psychologies in that neither Wundt nor James will be remembered for specific experiments or technical theories, and neither Mill nor Hegel experimented at all. What the four bequeathed were ways of thinking about Psychology and ways of doing it. Although none of the four can now claim the allegiance of a contemporary audience of professional psychologists, each of them cut a different but clear path to so much of what now presents itself as Psychology. The modern psychologist honors their accomplishments as much by furthering what was valuable in their writings as by sharing their unique confusions.

1. THE NINETEENTH CENTURY

Has an age ever seemed more remote from its immediate successor than the nineteenth century seems to us? The characters of Dickens, for all their vividness, might just as well have been crafted on some distant planet. The prose of the period, read under the harsh light of contemporary expression, could have come from Cicero's Rome. Or, again, consider Nelson at the battle of Trafalgar, signaling from his flagship, "England expects that every man will do his duty," and repeating over and over, as he lay dying, "Thank God I have done my duty." To the modern ear such words have an ancient ring and call up something deep in the recesses of history.

Unlike historians, history itself does not partition its significant developments into neat frames each precisely one hundred years long. Yet, there is something entirely whole about the nineteenth century or at least about that epoch that took shape soon after the French Revolution and kept its shape until the eve of the First World War. Under its great variety of enthusiasms, false starts, shifting loyalties, and celebrated paradoxes, we find a central core of truths about this period; a signature, as it were, that dates and defines every work that bears it.

The nineteenth century perceived itself in genuinely historical terms. It was, perhaps, the most self-conscious century of all. The commentators of the Renaissance charm us with their vanities and arouse envy with their confident sense of triumph but we soon discover that they were not finally impelled as much by history as by myth. The Florentines of the fifteenth century took ancient Rome and Athens for their ancestry, regarding the intervening ages as merely "Dark" or "Middle." In theology they were as much at home with the ancient pagans as with the Christian Fathers. In philosophy they were cheerful, if superficial, and in science they displayed somewhat more eagerness than competence, more superstition than objective detachment. The Renaissance world really did not know where it came from and had a nearly theatrical view of where it was going. If it had strength and genius, it also had innocence. But with the nineteenth century, matters are entirely different. Here we find an age thoroughly cognizant of its immediate past and its debt to that past; an age that correctly perceives itself as transitional and that wonders aloud about how it will affect the future. It laments its failures and is fearful of its successes. It worries without pause over its justice, its virtue, its science, and its faith. When it permits itself the luxury of optimism, nearly invariably it looks to a future time, a future race unlike itself. But even in these moments, the joy is restrained, for the nineteenth century saw not only itself, it saw us. I refer here not to an act of prophesy but to one of inference. It was in the nineteenth century that the machine replaced the hand and public opinion replaced both prince and prophet. This was the century that faced the moral tensions between populism and individualism, freedom and democracy, utility and natural law, Nature and Spirit. "Truly may we say with the Philosopher," wrote Carlyle in 1829, "'the deep meaning of the Laws of Mechanism lies heavy on us'; and in the closet, in the Marketplace, in the temple, by the social hearth, encumbers the whole movement of our mind, and over our noblest faculties is spreading a nightmare sleep."[1]

It would be convenient to divide up so productive and various an age into smaller temporal fragments, but it would also be something of a contradiction, for the nineteenth century displays not only uncommon continuities but presents itself as a veritable religion of progress. Its chief spokesmen, throughout the century, thought of themselves as carrying on the political and intellectual programs of the eighteenth-century Enlightenment. For many of them, the French Revolution and its aftermath constituted a substantial laboratory within which the fundamental premises of psychology and moral and political philosophy were tested. Thus, to separate the century into pre-Victorian and Victorian categories—a separation that would allow a more tidy discussion of art, architecture, and manners—would be to introduce an utterly arbitrary barrier into an otherwise continuous stream of social criticism, scientific enterprise, and philosophical reflection. If we adopt the metaphor of the research program, we might say that the Enlightenment had developed the principal hypotheses and the nineteenth century had set about to conduct the tests. Put another way, what the Enlightenment had erected as an *ism*, the nineteenth century sought to transform into a *system* or, in other hands, to reduce to rubbish. Let us briefly examine the several *isms* bequeathed by the Enlightenment.

Mechanistic Materialism and Romantic Idealism

A recurring theme in nineteenth-century thought addresses the limits of philosophical materialism. Thus, Tennyson, in stanza 120 of *In Memoriam*, gives us one verdict:

> I trust I have not wasted breath:
> I think we are not wholly brain,

> Magnetic mockeries; not in vain,
> Like Paul with beasts, I fought with death;
>
> Not only cunning casts in clay:
>   Let science prove we are, and then
>   What matters Science unto men,
> At least to me? I would not stay.
>
> Let him, the wiser man who springs
>   Hereafter, up from childhood shape
>   His actions like the greater ape,
> But I was *born* to other things.

And the same is handed down by Carlyle again, with more thunder if no greater light, as he estimates the worthiness of Pierre Cabanis' biological theory of mind:

> The metaphysical philosophy of this last inquirer is certainly no shadowy or unsubstantial one. He fairly lays open our moral structure with his dissecting-knives and real metal probes; and exhibits it to the inspection of mankind, by Leuwenhoeck microscopes, and inflation with the anatomical blowpipe. Thought, he is inclined to hold, is still secreted by the brain; but then Poetry and Religion (and it is really worth knowing) are "a product of the smaller intestines!" We have the greatest admiration for this learned doctor: with what scientific stoicism he walks through the land of wonders, unwondering.[2]

The issue is, of course, still with us, although it has been largely absorbed by the more technical branches of philosophy, psychology, and the neural sciences. But in the nineteenth century issues of this sort were taken to be in the general province of intellect and were considered as vital to the affairs of men and State. That is, how one finally decided to settle a matter of this kind *mattered*. It was not something to be relegated to the schoolhouse.

Clearly, neither Tennyson's poetic idiom nor Carlyle's polemical flourishes decided the issue one way or the other. It would be a grave underestimation of both to suggest that they themselves thought otherwise. Instead, we can glean from these excerpts the impatience with "metaphysical" speculation that was to characterize the entire century. In this regard, the fact that both Tennyson and Carlyle spoke for the side of Romanticism is less important than that they both spoke against pure theory-spinning.

But terms such as *romanticism* and *materialism* often say too much by not saying enough, permitting detractors to discover fatal flaws of their own manufacture. Equally often, they tend to convey irreconcilable differences between perspectives enjoying a fair measure of kinship. Even in its rather superficial Enlightenment form, *materialism* was not confined to a small set of maxims claiming the allegiance of all who would call themselves materialists. Cabanis surely did not relegate poetry and religion to "the smaller intestines," nor did his immediate intellectual parents, d'Holbach and Diderot. French materialism was a creation of the seventeenth century, a world-view fashioned out of the achievements of Descartes, Galileo, and Newton. None of the three would qualify for the rebuke Carlyle heaped on Cabanis, nor for that matter did Cabanis. Note that materialism, as a metaphysical system or bias, is but one of the more obvious inferences drawn from a larger *naturalism* which seeks and finds those laws by which the world's phenomena become succinctly described and faithfully predicted. At the grossest level, the phenomena all answer to the designation, "matter in motion." The question then becomes one of deciding whether there is something about humanity that resists this designation, or whether man, too, is subject to similar laws because man, too, is merely "matter in motion."[3]

The first direct and sustained approach to the question in modern times was Descartes'. In seeking to establish the biological sciences on the same sure footing that Kepler and Galileo had given to the physical sciences, Descartes inquired into the principles of sensation, action, emotion, and intellect. He satisfied himself that a wide range of biological and psychological phenomena could be understood in purely mechanical terms, at least to the extent that experience and behavior bore a direct relationship to impinging stimulation. The animal body was conceived of as an elaborate collection of interconnected pathways through which environmental energies could activate the organs of sense and the latter could activate the mechanisms of motion.

Although Descartes could find little in the behavior of animals to suggest any but a mechanical principle of action, he was persuaded that certain facts of human life could not be explained in the same manner. He argued that there would always be a way of distinguishing between a perfectly constructed automaton and a genuine human being: The former would not possess the capacity for abstract thought and would never engage creatively in the use of language.[4] Descartes' position on this was neither mere opinion nor the gift of religious conviction, but the inescapable deduction of his larger philosophy of mind. He was not able to reconcile the human grasp of abstract and universal propositions to an empiricistic epistemology which would ground all knowledge in (sensory) experience. Everyone schooled in arithmetic knows that no number is so great that it cannot be increased, but no one reaches this conclusion through "experience" or by induction. Although he explicitly rejected the theory of "innate ideas" imputed to him, he concluded nevertheless that there were aspects of human cognition which could not be accounted for in terms of sensation, memory, or experience and which, therefore, had to be understood as irreducibly *mental* attributes.[5] On the strength of this conclusion, Descartes entered himself for all time as the textbook "dualist." Still, his most ardent critics would scarcely dub him a "romantic idealist," and this is enough to establish that there are more than two metaphysical categories into which one's ideas may be placed.

Descartes, the man who invented a method of doubt so that he might discover certainty, was willing to let matters rest, if awkwardly, in a consistent dualism. The eighteenth century, however, was rather less tolerant of ambiguity and, in France at any rate, more inclined to treat metaphysical disputes as battles unto the death. With historic irony, the gentle and Christian Newton, the retiring Cambridge don who had served out his years as keeper of the mint, had now become the idol of the salon, the victor over "Cartesianism," the rallying point for that cadre of *philosophes* gaily assaulting Crown and Cross. With relentless if not entirely convincing logic, a rigorous naturalism and physicalism were promoted by the leading figures of the Enlightenment—promoted in their essays and letters, in their famous *Encyclopaedie*, even in their dramas and poems. Against the venerable theory of man's free will, Voltaire mockingly noted: "It would be very strange that all the planets should obey fixed and eternal laws, and that a little creature, five feet tall, should act as he pleased, solely according to his own caprice."[6] Against the claim that intellect and matter have nothing in common, La Mettrie issued his *l'Homme Machine* (1748) containing a variety of medical and anecdotal "proofs" of the complete dependence of the alleged functions of the soul on the processes and organization of the body and especially the brain.[7] With equal dispatch, Baron d'Holbach would put it this way: "The distinction that has so often been made betwixt the *physical* and the *moral* man is evidently an abuse. Man is a being purely physical; the moral man is only this physical being considered under a certain point of view; that is to say, relatively to some of his modes of action owing to his particular organization."[8] And some two decades later, in the Preface to his *Memoirs*, Pierre Cabanis would echo and reinforce this same perspective:

"Man has certain needs: he possesses faculties in order to satisfy these needs; and both needs and faculties are directly dependent on his physical constitution."[9]

Yet, the radical materialism of La Mettrie and Holbach was more the exception than the rule among the *philosophes*. The commoner position was one of a general faith in the ability of science to establish the precise connection between mind and body, and a devout conviction that, in any case, the question was entirely beyond the capabilities of the metaphysician. Locke had set the tone for French intellectuals when, almost as an aside, he turned the issue over to the anatomists.[10] Thus, what drew the *philosophes* together was not a unified position on the Mind/Body problem, but an uncompromisingly naturalistic world-view and a commitment to the prescriptions set forth in the scientific writings of Francis Bacon. They were opposed to an authoritarianism that had for so long controlled the subjects and methods of European inquiry, and they thought their objections had been vindicated by the superiority of Newtonian (English) over Cartesian (French) physics and Lockean (English) over Cartesian (French) psychology. Their anglophilia grew to nothing less than anglomania. Voltaire, for example, seems to have been convinced that a causal link united the Elizabethan war on Catholicism and Scholasticism and Newton's later scientific accomplishments. We see, then, that the glorification of Newton and Locke was at least in part an element of that grander social and political mission to which the *philosophes* were so tirelessly committed. In this connection, it was less important for them to "prove" that man is merely matter in motion than for them to be able to argue cogently against traditional and "official" views to the contrary.

In the very process of celebrating *naturalism*, however, the major spokesmen of the Enlightenment were unwittingly (and, in the case of Rousseau, wittingly) laying the foundations for the next century's Romantic Idealism. It is useful to recognize at this juncture that the differences and conflicts between the political philosophies of Hobbes, Locke, Hume, and Rousseau tend to become minor against the background of their shared naturalism. Hobbes' *Leviathan* spins political organization and monarchy out of the common citizen's fear of violence and out ot the relatively equal capacities of men to plunder and harm one another. The resulting social "machine" that is the State is thus recognized as the inevitable outcome of human fears and competition; the outcome of a less than noble and ruthlessly natural instinct to survive. By a different route, Locke arrived at much the same place: "The great and chief end, therefore, of men's uniting into commonwealths, and putting themselves under government, is the preservation of their property; to which in the state of nature there are many things wanting."[11] And both the Hume who discredited the theory of the "social contract" and the Rousseau who embraced it grounded their arguments in what was taken to be man's basic nature.[12]

What we discover in such widely divergent political writings is the abandonment of biblical and logico-deductive justifications for government and the substitution of historical and psychological lines of evidence. At the heart of these theories is an estimation of the nature of human nature and the accompanying insistence that the ultimate sanctions available to any social or political institution arise from the natural inclinations and necessities of human life. Accordingly, the traditional theological and rationalistic defenses give way to an analysis of the human passions and desires. It is to these that Hume would constantly refer in his analysis of morals, and it is to the same that Adam Smith would refer in seeking the foundations of economics.

The slide from this cast of mind to "romanticism" is neither steep nor thorny. What, after all, do we mean by "romanticism" if not the installation of passion, intuition, and natural instinct as the ultimate arbiters of things human? Is this not precisely what Wordsworth counsels when he assures us that "Nature never did forsake the heart that loved her"? But for the fuller sense of Romantic *idealism*, it is better to consult not the poet's work but his theory of that work. In part 1 of *A Defense of Poetry* (1819), Shelley set the theory forth this way:

A poem is the very image of life expressed in its eternal truth. There is this difference between a story and a poem, that a story is a catalogue of detached facts, which have no other bond of connexion than time, place, circumstance, cause and effect; the other is the creation of actions according to the unchangeable forms of human nature, as existing in the mind of the creator, which is itself the image of all other minds.[13]

The passage cannot, of course, be taken as the last word on the views of those early nineteenth-century writers with whom the term "romantic idealism" is most often associated, but it does contain two axioms that animate their major creations: that there is a universal principle of consciousness whose activity in the affairs of human life is entirely indifferent to time and place; and that the poetic *imagination*—the artist's *genius*—is the agency of its discovery. Wordsworth, Coleridge, Shelley, Goethe, Schiller, and the lesser luminaries of the Romantic movement saw no real distinction between art and philosophy. When, in his *Preface to Lyrical Ballads*, Wordsworth explains his choice of rural scenes and rustic persons, he does so in terms of the need to locate the uncorrupted and undisguised connections between thought and feeling, believing that a true philosophy of man must be based upon the philosophies of true men as these are revealed in their cares, their customs, and their language.

We see, then, that the "idealism" of the first generation of Romantics was not mystic transcendentalism but a search for the elementary and universal laws of psychology with which to comprehend what makes life *human* life, what makes feeling *human* feeling. This is apparent in the uncritical adoption by Coleridge and Wordsworth of the associationistic theory of ideas which had been present in Locke's educational writings and which was central to the philosophical psychologies developed by Hume and by David Hartley.[14] Turning again to the *Preface to Lyrical Ballads*, we find Wordsworth repeating his famous definition of poetry as the "spontaneous overflow of powerful feelings," but pressing on to account for the manner in which this comes to work on the psychology of the reader:

For our continued influxes of feeling are modified and directed by our thoughts, which are indeed the representatives of all our past feelings; and, as by contemplating the relation of these general representatives to each other we discover what is really important to men, so, by the repetition and continuance of this act, our feelings will be connected with important subjects, till at length, if we be originally possessed of much sensibility, such habits of mind will be produced, that, by obeying blindly and mechanically the impulses of those habits, we shall describe objects, and utter sentiments, of such a nature and in such connection with each other, that the understanding of the being to whom we address ourselves, if he be in a healthful state of association, must necessarily be in some degree enlightened, and his affections ameliorated. (*Ibid.*)

We can forgive the author for one of the longest sentences in the English language, for in it he has derived an entire theory of art from what he takes to be a fundamental law of human psychology. Wordsworth here calls upon the poet to consult his own feelings as these are later represented in thought. Then the poet must examine how these "representatives" are related to each other or, in other words, how the associational chains of ideas are formed. Achieving this, the poet now knows "what is really important to men," because he now knows how the record of personal experience comes to be stored in human consciousness. Through practice and his own native sensibility, the poet comes to acquire the ability to reflect in his works the natural connection that exists between experience and feeling. He is able, at last, to impart this automatically in his works and thus to instruct and to relieve his readers. The poem, by displaying the interdependencies among experience, reflection, and emotion, awakens the reader to the principles of his own constitution, his own psychological organization. It puts his mind at ease—enlightens it—by holding up before it the laws by which it is governed. This is as much psychology as it is esthetics, and even if it fails as a materialistic theory of mind, it is surely *mechanistic*. Wordsworth would stand behind Tennyson's conviction that "we are not wholly brain," but he would still describe the poet's mission in the language of naturalism, and even a mechanistic version of it.

Where then are we to locate the angry separation of mechanistic materialism and Romantic idealism? The answer, or course, is in the excesses of both. The scientific community of the nineteenth century came to organize itself around a number of metaphysical systems—positivism, determinism, "monism"—only tangentially related to the actual scientific achievements of the period. What began as a loose if instructive collection of methodological recommendations in the eighteenth century now took shape as an ironclad philosophy of science. To obey its canons was to be a scientist. To disobey was to engage in nonsense or, what was worse, "metaphysics."

For its own part, and especially in its German manifestations, Romanticism sounded equally strident battle cries. England's Lake Poets had their counterparts and models in the similarly rustic and little outpost of Weimar, whose resident genius was Goethe. He, too, through his *Sorrows of Young Werther,* his *Wilhelm Meister,* his *Faust*—not to mention his letters and poetry—claimed to reveal what was universally operative in significant human affairs; the triumph of love over reason, of heart over head. As much as any scientist, he strived to uncover the fundamental principles of nature, but was steadfast in his conviction that this discovery must be forever partial and always the gift of *intuition*. And here it was the intuition of the true artist that linked human freedom to the determined laws of nature; the true artist who, in revering "art for the sake of art," gave expression to the universal human need for evolution and freedom. The science of numbers and gadgets was useless here as were the logical niceties of the philosophers. Led in his thinking by a somewhat eccentric reading of Spinoza, Goethe found a consistent Christianity in a form of pantheistic naturalism.

The debt of German Romantic idealism to Kant is a curious one, and certainly one that Kant himself would be loath to acknowledge. In the present context, it is enough to point to a few of the Kantian themes that recur during the first decades of the German idealistic movement. First, on the specific issue of mechanistic materialism, there was Kant's own explicit rejection. In his immensely influential *Critique of Pure Reason*, he weighs the possibility that the "pure categories of the understanding" are the result of man's unique biological organization. He dismisses the possibility on this ground: The pure categories are *necessary*, whereas the laws of human biology are only *contingent*. Thus, the former cannot be explained by appeals to the latter.[15] The point might be illustrated this way. Take the "pure category" of *modality* which includes the concept of "necessarily true." An example of this concept is our recognition of the relationship between true premises and the truth of a conclusion deduced from them. If all men are mortal and if Socrates is a man, that Socrates is mortal is *necessarily true*. Yet, nothing in the realm of experience is *necessarily* true, so the concept cannot be grounded in our experience. Thus, the concept of necessity is something prior to experience (*a priori*) and constitutes one of the features of thought by which a given perception (e.g., the death of Socrates) is seen to be necessary. Unless we grant the concept of necessity *a priori*, some of our knowledge claims are logically impossible, literally inconceivable. But on Kant's reckoning, none of this could be so if the "pure categories" were no more than an expression of biological operations, for nothing in the purely contingent realm can transport the concept of *necessarily true*.

This philosophical aside is offered not to suggest that Romantic idealists arrived at their beliefs through painstaking Kantian analyses, but to indicate the *psychological* immaterialism they judged to be sanctioned by Kantian metaphysics. Then, too, there was that very critique of pure reason by which Kant had sought to establish the boundaries of the knowable. In setting out to address the skepticism defended in Hume's *Treatise*, Kant seemed to some to have erected an invincible skepticism of his own. He had partitioned the universe into the merely *phenomenal* realm of purely subjective experience and the ever concealed realm of true, objective, *noumenal* being; the realm of *objects as in themselves they really are*. It thereupon became the artist's task, if not his conceit, to discover this noumenal realm by consulting his own intuitions, his own genius. What science could not discover, trapped as it is by the inescapably subjective "facts" of observation, art can provide through intuitions that transcend experience. The first part of Book 1 of the *Critique* is devoted to the *Transcendental Aesthetic* which Kant defined as "The science of all principles of *a priori* sensibility."[16] These are the principles that we discover when we strip experience of its cognitive and its sensory overlay, "so that nothing may remain save pure intuition and the mere form of appearances"[17] But this was not to be the sense of "transcendentalism" that would attach to Romantic idealism. In Kant's sense, the "transcendental aesthetic" pertained to the conditions under which phenomenal, not noumenal, knowledge must take place. What Kant's analysis did achieve in this regard was the removal of space and time from the domain of objective reality and their transportation into the domain of thought; more specifically, their establishment as the very conditions of experience rather than objects of experience. The artist who would escape from the narrow channels of appearance would have to abandon the time-locked and space-locked sphere of common experience. He would have to search beyond both reason and sense for that noumenal reality which is *absolute, timeless, transcendent*. And if anything in the body of Kantian metaphysics spoke unequivocally of this reality, it was the concept of *freedom*, that which "posits itself" and is *unconditioned*. For the Romantics, this freedom was an unbounded playground of the imagination in which the genius discovered the universal ideals. As William Hazlitt put it, "There is no place for genius but in the indefinite and unknown."[18]

As the opening years of the nineteenth century passed, a wedge was placed between science and art, between science and philosophy. The hopeful naturalism of the Enlightenment was taking shape now as a war between schools. The scientists turned to the laboratory, the artists to their private visions. With each claim and finding emerging from the laboratory and the clinic, a counterclaim was registered by the "metaphysician." In opposition to a psychology of matter in motion, the Romantics offered the Absolute Idea. Biological determinism was countered with the claim of moral freedom. And scientific method was decried as a poor and deceiving alternative to intuitive genius.

Freedom, however, as the French Revolution had so clearly shown, exposes more than one side of human nature, and the Romantic movement was not indifferent to the implications contained in the most recent record of depravity, the grim animality of the mob. Perhaps it was Edmund Burke, the philosophical statesman, who brought this into focus at the earliest date when he identified the *sublime* in art as that which is "soever fitted . . . to excite the ideas of pain and danger, that is to say, whatever is in any sort terrible."[19] In this, the most famous enemy of the French Revolution anticipated by some forty years what so many would find arresting in the thuggish villainies of Robespierre. In any case, the art of the late eighteenth and early nineteenth century moved daringly away from classical forms and themes and toward the macabre, the awful, the grotesque—nature uncensored and unclothed. Together, the Gothic novel, the ultrarealistic paintings, and the Gothic revival in architecture reflect the general disaffection toward rationalism and the mounting suspicion that human endeavor is impelled by forces far darker than the Englightenment had been willing to notice. The emerging picture is captured by Goya's *Giant* (figure 1) a figure of naked power and distracted intelligence, scarcely aware of the cosmic engines controlling his destiny. In this *irrationalism* of the Romantics the scientists of the nineteenth century found but another reason to reject what was removed from the immediate arena of common experience, and were fortified in their conviction that the scientific outlook was civilization's last great hope. If mechanistic materialism did not answer all important questions, it at least settled some of them; it at least stated its case in a manner permitting test and refutation; it at least resisted that fashionable charlatanism which the Romantics called genius.

The Struggle for Epistemological Authority

The legacy of the Enlightenment as regards epistemology is one of the least ambiguous records of eighteenth-century thought. It is not enough to call it "empiricism" or

Goya **The Giant**

to describe it as a renewed confidence in the power of observation. It was at once a metaphysics, a sociology of knowledge, a theory of government, and a guide for the perplexed. Thus, in his *Preliminary Discourse* to the 1751 edition of Diderot's *Encyclopedia*, d'Alembert would write: "Nothing is more indisputable than the existence of our sensations. Thus, in order to prove that they are the principle of all our knowledge, it suffices to show that they can be."[20]

Newton, as has been noted, was the patron saint of the Enlightenment, and Locke was accepted as his chief disciple on psychological and political matters. The Newtonian conception of corpuscular interactions governed by unfailing mechanical laws was applied generously to the widest range of social, ethical, and governmental concerns. More modestly, Locke had fashioned his psychology around just such principles, and had passed on a *sensationistic* theory of knowledge grounded in alleged compatibilities between the material world and the organs of perception. Locke, however, was not a radical empiricist. In analyzing the sources of human knowledge, he added the *demonstrative* and the *intuitive* to that of perception. Thus it is intuitively that we know the Law of Contradiction and demonstratively that we know the relationship between the hypotenuse and the sides of a rectilinear triangle. Nonetheless, when Locke examined the basis upon which we come to have a factual comprehension of things and events in the material world, he concluded that our minds were furnished completely by *experience*.

Of the many attempts to repair and to complete Locke's psychology, the most original and influential was David Hume's *Treatise*.[21] It was in this work that a scientific psychology was grounded in the laws of association. Briefly summarized, the theory proposed that the contents of the mind resolve themselves into *impressions* and *ideas*, the latter being less vivid "copies" of the former. The Humean

impressions included not only sensations but also emotional feelings, whereas the ideas were made up of those
mental elements corresponding to thought and reason.

These ideas form the atomic or corpuscular furniture
of the mind, but they do not behave in a random or an
erratic manner. Rather, they enter into combinations according to fundamental laws, and these turn out to be the
laws or principles of association. The three advanced by
Hume are those of *contiguity, resemblance,* and *cause and
effect.* All other considerations kept constant, ideas A and
B will be associated when A and B are spatially and
temporally close together or contiguous. Moreover, A
and B will more readily enter into associational relation
when the two are similar. Finally, it is a fixed feature of
the mind to regard as a *cause* any event which reliably
precedes and is always "conjoined" with another event
which the mind then takes to be the *effect.* Indeed, the
idea of causality is nothing but this constant conjunction
between two events narrowly separated in time. The
irresistible conclusion, of course, is that "any thing may
produce any thing" provided the *psychological* criteria of
constant conjunction and reliable succession are met.[22]

Even in this hasty review we recognize the powerful
simplicity and formidable skepticism achieved by the *Treatise.* It tells us that it would be a manifest contradiction to
assert knowledge of that of which we have no idea, and it
then limits *idea* to sensory impressions and their residual
traces. In a bold stroke, it proceeds to restrict all the
interactions that might take place among these ideas to
those allowed by the laws of association. And, of our most
vaunted theological and metaphysical claims—our claim,
for example, that we know the "causes" of things or even
that they are caused—the *Treatise* insists that nothing is
contained in such knowledge except a reflection of the
mind's own habits. Were we to live in a world in which, for
whatever reason, rain always followed immediately when-

ever dogs barked, we would be forced by the very constitution of our minds to conclude that barking dogs "cause" the rain.

Of the several momentous consequences of the Humean outlook, the one that most directly concerns us here was the tendency to reserve final epistemological authority to the experiences and ideas of the individual. The differences between the thoughts and judgments of different persons could be understood only in terms of their respective histories of "impressions"—the impressions of sensation and the impressions of reflection. To determine more precisely how the principles of association operate, the observer must consult his own mind and inquire into the sequences and patterns of his own thoughts. The recommended method then, at least implitcitly, was *introspection*.

Regarding morals, the *Treatise* was similarly unsettling to theologians and traditional rationalists, for Hume could discover no foundation for morality other than the pleasures and pains, the happiness and misery regularly associated with events and circumstances of a certain kind. Far from being a tidy collection of proscriptions deducible from a small set of first principles, the moral realm was occupied by the pains and passions of self-serving beings. Nor was Hume alone in this view; he had the entire record of the British "sentamentalist" philosophers behind him,[23] and his century would end with Jeremy Bentham's *utilitarianism* standing firmly in support of his position. "Pleasure," wrote Bentham, "is in *itself* a good ... the only good; pain is in itself an evil; and, indeed, without any exception, the only evil."[24]

There was in these eighteenth-century analyses a foreshadowing of those bleaker Romantic themes already noted. In their empiricistic epistemologies, the philosophers of the Enlightenment were presenting man as something of a passive witness, a spectator in the crowded and cluttered world of his own sensations; a pleasure-seeking, pain-avoiding survivor finding rude solace in the chimerical productions of his own imagination; a luckless truth-seeker whose triumphs turned out to be no more than the mirror-image of his own sensations and feelings; a solitary being driven to society by considerations no more noble than fear, no more elevated than self-interest.

On the specific matter of a scientific psychology, the eighteenth century ended by taking back with its Kantian hand what it had extended with its Humean hand. In several cogent passages, the *Critique of Pure Reason* shattered all prospects of a genuinely Newtonian psychology, a psychology grounded in observation, experiment, and general laws. The mind, in the very act of observing itself, alters itself. It does not stay in place or retain its contents with the constancy a science would require. Even the idea of a Rational Psychology is shown by Kant to be one of the "paralogisms" of pure reason. Such a psychology would take the "soul" to be the object of its science, but in this soul, "everything is in continual flux and there is nothing abiding except (if we must so express ourselves) the 'I,' which is simple solely because its representation has no content."[25]

But Kant also left an opening for a kind of psychology and for the revival of issues skeptical empiricism and utilitarianism sought to dissolve. At the very foundation of Kantian "rationalism" are the *a priori categories of the pure understanding*; those *necessary* conditions of mind in which experience itself is grounded. Through his own sort of conceptual analysis, Kant had demonstrated that a *tabula rasa* psychology was self-contradictory, for unless certain rational categories are posited *a priori*, neither "experience" nor "mental association" is even possible. The former takes place *in space*, the latter *in time*, and neither space nor time is itself an object of experience. To use the modern idiom, we might say that Kant required a cognitive psychology as the precondition for an empirical psychology. Even more, he drew attention to the structural or formal dimensions of thought which must be understood if sense is to be made of the contents of thought.

Similarly, in the domain of morals Kant's analysis convinced many that a purely hedonistic theory was either provably false or conceptually incoherent. The famous inscription on his tombstone instructs us quite economically in Kant's moral philosophy: "The starry sky above him, the moral law within him." He had recognized that the essential feature of all moral discourse is the concept of "ought," and that such a concept could not arise out of experience, passion, feeling, or even pure selfishness. It is in the very nature of moral "oughts" that they are indifferent to time and place, that they do not attach to objects or even actions, but only to intentions. Thus, they can be posited only by a being that is moral *as such*, and necessarily such a being is rational. We see, therefore, that Kantian epistemology and Kantian moral philosophy both raised telling objections against empiricism. Both also left room for a skepticism quite different from the one contained in Hume's analysis. The latter, with its focus on the purely contingent and uncertain nature of perception, left the field of knowledge littered with the half-truths of opinion and feeling, and given shape by little more than the lucky similarity of judgments formed by a community of percipients. Kant, however, in accepting much of the Humean thesis, showed how it finally depended upon the fixed and rationally coherent laws of thought, themselves unconditioned and logically binding. Thought itself, though inaccessible to the methods of experimental science, was on Kant's construal accessible to rational analysis and to "scientific" description in the enlarged as opposed to the technical sense of the term.

Note, then, that as the nineteenth century began its progress, the councils of wisdom were faced with competing claims from the several schools established a century earlier. One of these, under the noble banner of Naturalism, proclaimed the authority of immediate experience and insisted that the final test of every factual allegation is conducted in the private arena of each man's mind; that the final test of every moral or political allegation is conducted in the private arena of each man's pleasures, pains, and sentiments. In the end, all such allegations can carry no more weight than a certain probability of truth, a degree of plausibility which may be enhanced or diminished by further and different experiences.

Another claim, flying the flag of Rationalism (but stripped of its theological markings), promised more than shifting probabilities and offered evidence that human existence—its genius, its moral freedom, its rationality— could not be subordinated to the laws governing the inanimate or merely animate realms. It may be illuminated through physiological or naturalistic inquiry, but never *explained* thereby. In the known universe, man alone presents unambiguous proof of reason, will, and moral concern. His actions are grounded not in the laws of gravitation or the principles of mechanics; these apply only to his *re*actions. As an intending agent, as a bona fide moral actor, he can be understood only in the language of reasons. Accordingly, in regard to what makes him uniquely human, he is essentially immune to the methods and perspectives of natural science.

To Rationalism and Naturalism must also be added Fundamentalism which, throughout the nineteenth century, was the court of last recourse at least in the popular imagination. Whether in its Reformist or its severe Calvinist variety, its Roman or Puritan form, official Christendom had that one great book of truths and a thousand years of philosophical study with which to stave off those who might challenge its authority. Its own exquisite history had made it the repository of all metaphysical systems. Its disciples and saints included many of the most celebrated rationalists, empiricists, materialists, and even skeptics. Thus, during much of the nineteenth century, the secular debates were conducted for clerical approval. At least on the surface, science and faith would remain partners until the Darwinian revolution. And when the schism came, it was deepened less by the biological and geological aspects of evolutionary theory than by it *psychology*.

It is important to appreciate the source of Christianity's flexibility during this century of seige. Too often the religionist's approval of the scientific world-view is seen as a kind of defensive maneuver, an afterthought, an ex post facto rationalization. The fact, however, is that by the nineteenth century the major Christian sects had long since adopted an essentially naturalistic outlook that was as congenial to Enlightenment progressivism as it was hostile to Enlightenment atheism. The more renowned salons of Paris were seldom without a priest in the group, and it was not at all uncommon for clerics to take a leading part in pleading the virtues of science before a contented orthodoxy. At least as early as the sixteenth century, religious philosophy became distinctly "naturalistic." Thus, there was no intrinsic tension between churchmen and those who would describe humanity in terms of progressive liberation achieved through competition and strife; morality in terms of instinctive "sentiments" and founded on the universal desire for pleasure; nature in terms of a continuous series of forms, each adapted to its surroundings, and with man standing as the culmination of nature's genius.

It is tempting to think of the Anglican ministers who ranted against Darwin as inquisitors on leave from the court that was still taking testimony from Galileo. But nearly two and a half centuries separated these events, and both of them depended as much upon the narrow righteousness of the clergy as upon the excessive generalizations of the scientist. But in important respects, the independence of science had already been won by Darwin's time, and the issue was now not one of heresy but validity. It is worth mentioning that some of the most technical and scientifically informed criticism directed at the Darwinists came from the clergy. Indeed, it is a measure of the standing science had earned by the second half of the eighteenth century that this immense issue was addressed primarily in the language of science.

On the matter of epistemological authority, Psychology had a central part to play in more than one way. There was, of course, its part as the object of the debate: What is the proper method by which to develop a science of human nature? More subtly, however, it was also the subject of the debate by virtue of those philosophical systems that took individual experience as the last word on matters of truth. And mixed in with these considerations were the momentous political and social movements of the time; movements defended or attacked on grounds that were principally "psychological," as they had been throughout the Enlightenment.

It is useful to recognize also that the nineteenth century did not harbor as uniform and uncritical a view of "science" as the one held by the majority of our contemporaries. The search for a *science* of human nature occupied the Romantics as much as it did those who worked in clinics, in laboratories, or in the wilds. Note that the German distinction between *Naturwissenschaft* and *Geisteswissenshaft* pertains to the subject of inquiry, not to the sort of understanding yielded by the inquiry. In both cases— whether it is "mind" or "nature"—the subject is finally to be comprehended by a set of universal principles accounting for the elements and arrangements that define the realm of mind or the realm of matter. We see, then, that the struggle for epistemological authority was not so much a contest between scientists and nonscientists. The struggle would enter this phase only relatively late in the nineteenth century. Instead, it was a struggle between competing methods of inquiry, where the principal contestants were logic, experiment, natural observation, and self-examination, and where each of these borrowed liberally from the discoveries of the others. The Romantics, for example, may be grouped according to their general allegiance to the artistic productions and the universal sentiments of the human race; productions and sentiments clearly indicative of a being whose salient need is the need for freedom and whose salient attribute is moral evolution. On this view of the subject, a science of human nature can only be retarded by an examination of those human characteristics which are common in nature; e.g., matter or tissue or even brains. Rather, a developed science—a scientific understanding of the human race—must begin with what is exceptional in the subject, what makes the subject a thing apart. Only when recognized in this light can the Romantic movement be understood as one of the worthier vessels on the long voyage, and not as some makeshift and woeful little skiff pitching about aimlessly in the main currents of serious scientific inquiry.

In the same light, it becomes clearer why so many of the naturalists of the period, some of them writing decades before Darwin's *Origin of Species*, served up numerous tomes which described the art, architecture, military operations, superstititions, systems of justice, and developed sciences of ants, spiders, flies, dogs, monkeys, and birds. Indeed, as the record of the accomplishments of the "lower orders" increasingly approximated the sorts of things traditionally confined to human genius, the Romantics became somewhat more profligate in their attributions, leaping from the modest Cartesian "cogito" to the Hegelian *Absolute*. Carlyle shows us this side of Romanticism in his *Journal* entry for February 1, 1833: "The philosophers went far wrong. . . . (I)nstead of raising the natural to the supernatural, they strove to sink the supernatural to the natural. The gist of my whole way of thought is to do not the latter but the *former*."[26]

Rationalism, too, had its Romantic side as it sought to deduce the Great Plan of nature. As Fichte saw it, this Plan was finally man's quest for total freedom according to the dictates of reason. Governed and moved by this universal law, the human race passes through successive stages of moral enlightenment. That he judged the stage his own early nineteenth-century Prussia had attained to be that of "perfected wickedness" is a common conclusion reached by the spokesmen of the period.[27] So, also, is the Fichtean theory of moral evolution, a theory bequeathed by the Enlightenment and reaching the status of a religion in the philosophies of Fichte, Feuerbach, Hegel, and their disciples. The point, however, is that all of them were persuaded that their systems were quintessentially *scientific*, if for no other reason than that they were logically required deductions from first principles. The essence of science, on this construal, is its axiomatic and geometric form, not the ragged hodgepodge of unconnected observations; much less is it those laboratory undertakings which seek to understand nature by denying its complexities.

There is, to be sure, the uppercase Rationalism and the lowercase rationalism. Science was never at war with the latter, of course, and its contempt for the former came about only when Rationalism emerged as the Idealism of the neo-Hegelians. John Stuart Mill, thought of by his countrymen as "the saint of reason," was but one of many nineteenth-century patrons of science who expected politics, psychology, social science, and society itself to be *rationally* understood through the methods of science. Across the metaphysical and ideological boards, then, rationalism was the controlling passion of the entire century and its short bridge to the philosophers of the Enlightenment.

The Individual and the Aggregate

Disputes between hereditarians and environmentalists are among the oldest in intellectual history, occupying a central place in such Socratic dialogues as *Meno* and *Republic* and serving to divide such otherwise likeminded *philosophes* as Diderot and Helvetius. Radical environmentalism is always embarassed by the facts of individual differences, and radical hereditarianism by the striking ease with which many of these differences surrender to nurturance by a solicitous society.

The nineteenth century, as all periods of heightened intellectual energy, had to contend with this issue, but it also had to contend with the privileges and burdens of colonialism, the rise of nation-states, the sudden growth of immensely populous cities, the equally sudden growth of a new class of new wealth. A *science* of human nature, by the optimistic standards of the last century, was obliged to explain the economic and social realities of the human condition; to unearth the principles and laws by which these realities come into being. Recall that, as the century began, Napoleon was warring to reestablish the "natural boundaries" of France and that by "natural" he meant nothing less than the Gaul commemorated by Julius Caesar! Similarly, as Fichte reviewed the Prussia laid waste and humiliated by Napoleon, he would find the cause in the failure of the German people to remain connected to their own ancient traditions and loyal to their uniquely German destiny.* And then, too, there was the need to understand—if not justify—the imperial hegemony exercised by the great powers, the slavery so ruthlessly practiced in the New World, the increase of criminality and insanity in the world's centers of civilization and high

---

* This is made fearsomely clear in his *Address to the German Nation*, misunderstood by many to be a kind of Hitlerian call to arms.

culture. Were these and related phenomena to be understood in terms of a grand (and rationally deducible) design? Were they the inevitable outcome of purely natural forces, including those that guarantee that some will survive and others perish, some will prosper as others suffer? Or were they the consequence of purely local (historical, social, political) practices and therefore amenable to solution with the tools of a "social science"? Is the ultimate purpose of the State the securing of its citizens' happiness, as utilitarianism would have it, or the promotion of moral virtue, as the "transcendental nationalists" (e.g., Fichte) would have it? Put more simply, does the State exist for the individual or vice versa?

What is so distinctive about the manner in which the nineteenth century addressed such issues was the commitment to base conclusions and recommendations on "scientific" grounds, whether these were unearthed by the tines of logic, or were derived from naturalistic observations, or were revealed by a correct reading of scripture, or were ordained by the inexorable laws of history. On each of these separate constructions, the linchpin of the argument was an implicit or, more typically, an explicit theory of human psychology. In some cases, this was a theory of *national* psychology, though not always of the hereditarian stripe. In some cases it was a theory that took the psychology of the individual to be merely prototypic of the human race as a whole; a theory which would make of "social psychology" no more than the multiplication of individual characteristics, and of the individual no more than one cog in the larger machinery of a species evolving.

In the following chapters, the solutions and recommendations of only a handful of nineteenth-century thinkers are reviewed. They are not, however, simply representatives of the age, but leaders of thought; men whose works would impart to the psychology of our age many if not most of its defining features. In each chapter, the focus is on not only the principal teachings of each author but also his immediate and more remote disciples. The objective here is to clarify the nature of the debt we owe as well as the not so distant sources of our reigning confusions.

2. JOHN STUART MILL

The Larger Context

In his unsigned eulogy which appeared in the *Fortnightly Review* for June 1873, John Morley observed:

Much will one day have to be said as to the precise value of Mr. Mill's philosophical principles, the more or less of his triumphs as a dialectician, his skill as a critic and an explorer, and his originality as a discoverer. However this trial may go, we shall at any rate be sure that with his reputation will stand or fall the intellectual repute of a whole generation of his countrymen.[1]

The passage comes from the pen of one of Mill's close friends and admirers, but it could have been written by any number of eminent Victorians critical of Mill's philosophy and his politics. So manifest were his powers of mind, so thoughtful and fair were his criticisms of competing views, that he enjoyed the rare distinction of being respected as much by his opponents as by his friends and disciples. For two decades, his essays were an obligatory feature of an Oxford education. And, as Morley went on to say: "He is the only writer in the world whose treatises on highly abstract subjects have been printed during his lifetime in editions for the people, and sold at the price of railway novels."[2]

He was the most articulate and persuasive advocate of *individualism* and libertarian ethics in modern times; the most skillful and relentless proponent of empiricism since Hume; one of the few philosophers of the first rank who may be said to have directly achieved political and social reforms in their own day. Since he did much to transform our very modes of thought, it follows that he has inscribed his signature on that range of inquiries which have since taken shape as academic psychology.

But our present purpose is to examine Psychology's debt to John Stuart Mill, and since his *Autobiography* is both widely cited and frequently supplemented, only a few relevant details of his life need be mentioned. His formal education, as is well known, was rigorous but privately conducted, chiefly by his father, James Mill. The elder Mill, who was also of "radical" political persuasion, did much to promote the teachings of Jeremy Bentham. It was primarily through his father's influence that John Stuart Mill embraced the associationistic theory of mind and those rudiments of Benthamism which, in his mature years, he would recast as Utilitarianism.[3] Through his father also he was immersed early in that veritable school of Scottish radicalism sired by Hume and Adam Smith and nurtured by Bentham, David Ricardo, and James Mill himself. In his biography of James Mill, Alexander Bain recalls that the French Revolution was only a year old when James Mill entered Edinburgh University and that by 1793 the events in France had created in England an "excitement . . . at fever heat."

On the 30th August this year (1793), occurred the memorable trial of Thomas Muir, who was sentenced to 14 years' transportation for sedition, as the mildest form of political agitation was then called. Cockburn tells us that Jeffrey and Sir Samuel Romilly were present. "Neither of them ever forgot it. Jeffrey never mentioned it without horror." Next January, 1794, occurred the trial and banishment of the other Edinburgh political martyrs. These atrocities would affect Mill no less than they did Jeffrey and Romilly.[4]

It was in these same years that the "rights of man" literature emanating from France and America was capturing much of the British imagination, and when Tom Paine had as great a readership in England as he did at home.

To be raised and tutored by a man who did so much to reform the laws of a nation—a man to whom passage of the first Reform Acts (1832) was greatly beholden—would still not be enough to guarantee a lifelong commitment to libertarianism, let alone associationistic psychology. Here as elsewhere the liabilities of "psychohistory" overrun its few and arguable assets. A mind as powerful and agile as John Stuart Mill's would not have passively assimilated a father's beliefs, thereupon to repeat them with monotonous fidelity throughout the remaining years of activity. But the son had an avenue of independence nearly as wide as his own intelligence paved for him by the academic regimen his father established; a regimen balanced equally between classics and science, politics and ethics, the practical and the abstract. That it was confined too much to the head at the expense of the heart we learn from Mill's *Autobiography* but it was surely not shaped to foster a narrow ideology or to summon allegiance to one school of thought by concealing its defects.[5] Those who, in Morley's words, do "the work of the world" inherit nothing less than the world's history. Thus, if J. S. Mill's broad goals and accomplishments are to be comprehended, we must look less to his father's beliefs than to those historical influences which both of them identified, felt, and shared.

In the most general terms, these influences were of the same sort that had driven Socrates and his circle to examine the idea of government and to do so within the context of a broad theory of human nature and human knowledge. The decisive historical event for the Socratics was the Spartan defeat of Athens; for James Mill and his fellow radicals, the French and American revolutions. This, of course, is a common theme in the history of ideas and is

illustrated, to choose only a few examples, by Hobbes'
Leviathan, by Rousseau's *Social Contract*, and by Locke's
Second Treatise of Civil Government. In each of these—and
illustrations can be multiplied into the dozens—we find
the philosopher discovering in the social turmoil the need
to reassess any number of traditional convictions and
maxims adopted uncritically by the masses and now found
to be the source of the trouble.

The American Revolution had many friends in England,
as it had quite a few enemies in the colonies. Of the
former, we need only consider Dr. Richard Price
(1723–1791), who preached and wrote often and in the
most glowing terms of the freedom-loving colonists, and
who found in their defiance the same spirit that had
impelled England's "Glorious Revolution" of 1688.[6] Price's
dissenting congregation—his "Revolution Society"—was
but one of a large number of small groups sprouting up
throughout England in the final decades of the eighteenth
century; groups united, if at all, by a commitment to
religious freedom and to a greater voice in those political
spheres in which their own destinies were forged. But
sympathy for the Americans was not confined to dissenters.
It came from statesmen as well, and especially from one
of Britain's greatest, Edmund Burke, who saw in the
colonial resistance a devotion to those very principles of
freedom and justice that England herself had refined and
promulgated.[7]

The revolution in France, however, was quite another
matter and elicited from the same Edmund Burke a
polemical critique perhaps unmatched in the history of
that genre.[8] Where the colonists had fought relentlessly
for no more than justice in the face of hypocritical and
tyrannical authority, the French had deposed a legitimate
and an accommodating monarch for little more than the
comforts of anarchy. On Burke's account, they had sacri-

ficed the accumulated wisdom of the nation and replaced
it with an unnatural philosophy:

> We are not the converts of Rousseau; we are not the disciples of
> Voltaire; Helvetius has made no progress amongst us. Atheists
> are not our preachers; madmen are not our lawgivers. We know
> that *we* have made no discoveries, and we think that no discoveries
> are to be made, in morality—nor many in the great principles of
> government, nor in the idea of liberty, which were understood
> long before we were born altogether as well as they will be after
> the grave has heaped its mould upon our presumption, and the
> silent tomb shall have imposed its law on our pert loquacity.[9]

Soon after Burke's *Reflections on the Revolution in France*
appeared (1790) Thomas Paine's rousing if often shallow
rebuttals were widely disseminated in France and in England. Part 1 of his *Rights of Man* was published in England
in 1791 and part 2 in the following year, when he was
officially declared persona non grata by the British government. A visitor there at the time, he was forced to flee
to France where he became an honorary member of the
French Convention. In speaking out against the execution
of Louis XVI, however, he suffered the scorn of the
Jacobins and was imprisoned in Paris from 1793 to 1794.
But he had ample time before his friends locked him up
to write a summoning defense of their politics and a
devastating attack on Burke's. It was in *The Rights of Man*
that he carried through the logic of his earlier pamphlet,
Common Sense (1776), in which all governments were taken
to be illegitimate if they were not "representative." Trapped in the fire of his oratory was every form of hereditary
monarchy: "But in whatever manner the separate parts of
a constitution may be arranged, there is one general
principle that distinguishes freedom from slavery, which
is that all *hereditary government over a people is to them a species
of slavery, and representative government is freedom.*"[10]

On every page of *The Rights of Man* Paine reserved some
space to mock and depreciate English customs and practices, fortified in his dismissal of hereditary succession by
the spectacle of George III's well-known psychiatric maladies. The small kernel of truth in his essays was protected
by a thick shell of sophistry and garnished with Lockean
"self-evident" principles. To the new British inclination
toward religious toleration, he responded with indignation.
"Toleration," he insisted, "is not the *opposite* of intoleration,
but is the *counterfeit* of it. Both are despotisms."[11] Needing
far fewer words than Bentham to make a point, he spoke
to the commoner understanding in a language stripped of
metaphysics: "Whatever the apparent cause of any riots
may be, the real one is always want of happiness. . . . But
as a fact is superior to reasoning, the instance of America
presents itself to confirm these observations."[12] And on
the question of a titled class, he was no more forgiving:

Titles are like the circles drawn by the magician's wand to contract
the sphere of man's felicity. He lives immured within the Bastille
of a word and surveys at a distance the envied life of man. . . .
Through all the vocabulary of Adam, there is no such an animal
as a duke or a count; neither can we connect any idea to the
words. Whether they mean strength or weakness, wisdom or
folly, a child or a man, or a rider or a horse, is all equivocal.
What respect then can be paid to that which describes nothing
and which means nothing? . . . There is no occasion to take titles
away, for they take themselves away when society concurs to
ridicule them.[13]

The contrast between Burke and Paine is useful, not
only because both were at the center of revolutionary
crisis, but because both were in the main spokesmen for
the cause of liberty on the eve of libertarian reform. In
important respects, therefore, the conflicts facing first
James Mill and later his son were not between liberalism
and illiberalism, but between various forms of liberalism

and the consequences held out by each. We can comprehend the size and number of these conflicts by listing the
sorts of questions Burke and Paine bequeathed: Can the
"rights of man" prosper in a nation with an official
religion? Is the only just government a representative one?
What is the principle that guides the very methods of
representation? Must every citizen have an equal voice
(share) in the government or are there legitimate grounds
of exclusion? By what means are the true ends of government to be defined? What connection is there between a
"right" and a "duty," and what proof might be adduced to
show that either has real existence? If, as Paine and many
others argued, sovereignty resides in the "people"—that
it is they who bring constitutions and governments into
being and that these continue at the pleasure of the
"people"—can there be any political stability and continuity? And if, as Paine constantly urged, no government
or people can impose restrictions on future generations,
can any constitution outlive its framers and their contemporaries?[14] John Stuart Mill surely would not have needed
James Mill as a father in order to face these questions, for
they had been in the minds and on the lips of his
countrymen since the seventeenth century. In one or
another form, they had occupied the attention of philosophers since the time of Pericles and had been answered
according to principles grounded in an implicit Psychology
of Man.

What is it, then, that sets J. S. Mill apart from that long
intellectual tradition? Primarily, it is the explicit *scientific*
tone of his analysis and his sustained defense of the claim
that questions of this sort are to be settled by a method—
a scientific method that is as aloof to authority as it is
beholden to observable facts.

Mill was not the first philosopher to attempt to establish
political theory on psychological principles. His own father
could be mentioned in this connection were it not for the

scores of thinkers, going back to Greek antiquity, who shared the distinction. By the nineteenth century, it was a commonplace to defend or attack various political theses according to the alleged "nature" of man. The ground had been thoroughly prepared by Bacon and Hobbes, by Descartes, Locke, and Hume, by the small army of French *philosophes*. But in the works of his predecessors, human psychology was more or less taken for granted, its possible scientific status confined chiefly to the method of introspection. Locke, in his educational writings, had taken note of associationistic processes (as had Aristotle), and Hume had gone so far as to reduce them to the principles of contiguity, resemblance, and causality.[15] And at about the same time, David Hartley attempted to ground them further in neurophysiological functions answerable to Newtonian laws.[16] But none of Mill's predecessors had convincingly derived a *social science* from such individual psychologies, and none had attempted to integrate the political, economic, moral, and personal dimensions of social life within a body of scientific principles. Every issue and every principle examined and employed by Mill had been refined in an older kiln, but it was in his factory that the various combinations were tested and the most durable ones assembled. He found his most immediate source of encouragement in the new Positive Philosophy of Auguste Comte, and though his discipleship was brief, the modifed stamp of *positivism* never entirely faded from any of his works. It will be useful to pause here to sketch out the major features of Comte's system before resuming the discussion of Mill's psychology.

The Positive Philosophy

It was not long after the collapse of the French monarchy that the better and more disinterested minds became aware of the size of the moral and social void that slogans and rhetoric could not fill. Neither the colossal episode that was Napoleon nor the restoration of the French throne compensated for the lost traditions, the forever buried culture and order of the *ancien régime*. The *philosophes* of the eighteenth century had promised a rule of reason to guide humanity along the path of continuous progress and liberation, but the promise was more a hope than a program. The giddy optimism of 1789 was all too suddenly silenced by the grim hatefulness of the Jacobins, the Terror of Robespierre, the ultimate and humiliating defeat at Waterloo. By 1815, it would be very difficult for a serious observer to sustain the utopian visions of a Condillac or a Condorcet, let alone the strident and confident republicanism of a Tom Paine. Yet, by 1815 it was also somewhat more plausible to think of the natural sciences and of technology as the surest guides toward a new order. However corrupted the ideals of the Revolution had become, however fickle the destinies had proved to be, the machines worked!

Of those in the first two decades of the nineteenth century who sought to understand and organize the social realm according to the principles of science and the methods of industry, the most original was Claude-Henri de Rouvroy, Comte de Saint-Simon (1760–1825). He founded the journal *L'Industrie* (1816) which permitted him to address a large number of powerful bankers and industrialists. From this and other literary platforms he preached the gospel of *social* science; an approach to governance grounded in the laws of historical evolution and implemented by the techniques and discoveries of the industrial community. The proposed government would be led by a scientific elite rather than a desultory bureaucracy. Organized around purely rational and scientific principles, such a society—such an international community—would have small need for states and would avoid the wars and brutalities fostered by them. Here there is the echo of Paine who had written:

The mutual dependence and reciprocal interest which man has upon man and all parts of a civilized community upon each other create that great chain of connection which holds it (society) together. The landholder, the farmer, the manufacturer, the merchant, the tradesman, and every occupation, prospers by the aid which each receives from the other and from the whole. Common interest regulates their concerns and forms their laws; and the laws which common usage ordains have a greater influence than the laws of government. In fine, society performs for itself almost everything which is ascribed to government.[16]

And here too is the anticipation of the Marxist dream of the elimination of the State.

It was in 1817 that Saint-Simon began a seven-year association with Auguste Comte, whose six-volume *Course of Positive Philosophy* (1830–1842) would come to develop and promulgate "Saint Simonianism."[17] It was Comte who founded *positivism* and who coined the term *sociology* (which Mill would later call a convenient barbarism). As employed by Comte, positivism referred both to a method of study and the final stage of social evolution. His well-known "law of the three stages" was intended as the briefest description of the history of human thought and political organization. According to this law, societies pass through a series of epochs most aptly defined in terms of the shared under-standings, beliefs, and aspirations of their members. In the order of their degree of evolution, these epochs may be called the *superstitious*, the *metaphysical*, and the *positive*. The first is dominated by a fear and reverence rooted in ignorance; the second, by a faith in unseen but rationally and personally authored universal laws; the third by allegiance to the concepts of progress and order and by submission only to the objective facts of the world. What is surrendered in the final stage is the vain hope of perfect

knowledge, the chimera of a completely deduced system
of the world. As he says in *The Catechism of Positive Religion*:

The various essential branches of the study of the world or of
man reveal to us an increasing number of different laws, which
will never be susceptible of being reduced the one under the
other, despite the frivolous hopes inspired at first by our planetary
gravitation. Though for the most part still unknown, and many
ever to remain so, we have made out enough of them to guarantee
against all attacks the fundamental principle of the Positive
doctrine, namely, the subjection of all phenomena whatsoever to
invariable relations. The all-pervading order which is the outcome
of the sum of natural laws bears the general name of *fate* or of
chance, according as the laws are known to us or unknown. . . .
Still we may hope to discover for each of the more important
cases empirical rules which, insufficient from a theoretic point of
view, yet suffice to keep us from disorderly action.[18]

What Comte promised in his social science was not
deductive certainties but reliable guides to political life.
The motto "Progress and Order" (and sometimes "Love,
Progress, and Order") was not intended to suggest the
mindless efficiency of the ant heap but the deepest yearn-
ings of all persons. Comte was convinced in this regard
that his best disciples would be drawn from the working
classes and from the feminine half of humanity; the former
because they "have a clearer sense of that union of reality
with utility by which the Positive spirit is characterized,
than most of our scientific men,"[19] the latter because, "In
the most essential attribute of the human race, the tendency
to place social above personal feeling, she is undoubtedly
superior to man."[20] Thus, the triumph of positivism
awaited the unification of three classes: the philosophers,
the proletariat, and women. The first would establish the
necessary intellectual and scientific principles and methods
of inquiry; the second would guarantee that essential
connection between reality and utility; the third would

impart to the entire program the abiding selflessness and moral resolution so natural to the female constitution.

Throughout his works, Comte's rigorous moralism, his "positive morality," is the centerpiece. He is at pains to show that conversion to positivism will not oblige society to abandon any of the moral benefits conferred by religious or metaphysical systems, but will secure them to the sturdier moorings of science:

> The most willing assent is yielded every day to the rules which mathematicians, astronomers, physicists, chemists, or biologists, have laid down in their respective arts, even in cases where the greatest interests are at stake. And similar assent will certainly be accorded to moral rules when they, like the rest, shall be acknowledged to be susceptible of scientific proof.[21]

We must be clear, however, on what Comte meant by "scientific proof" in the social and moral spheres. He did not, of course, have in mind those axiomatic proofs of the metaphysician, but he also did not have in mind the sorts of evidence gathered in the laboratory. What he was contemplating were the *invariable relations* and *empirical rules* (*vida supra*) disclosed by an objective study of social history. It was just such a study that had already turned up the "law of three stages" and that had established the invariable connection between social attitudes and social utility. The unprejudiced sociologist does not examine the past in order to rebuke it, but to broaden the foundation of evidence supporting that empirical rule by which social phenomena reflect the practical realities of an age.

It would be inviting, especially these days, to "explain" Comte's tolerant discussions of medieval institutions in terms of his own Catholic origins and his conception of the role of women in society as nothing more than the "sexist" credo of the nineteenth century. But we are reviewing the works of a man who allegedly declared himself an atheist at the age of fourteen and whose analysis of medieval society seldom included comments on the validity of Christian beliefs. Comte's respect for feudal organization and its overarching Catholic theology was based upon the judgment that both moved humanity along the path of progress. And his rejection of both was based upon the judgment that the modern world—the world of national divisions and commercialism—simply had outgrown them. They were no longer *useful*, and their vestiges could now have only a paralyzing effect.

There is much in Comte's positivism that would come to be rejected by Mill. In his religion of "love, order, and progress," Comte was contemptuous of the sort of individualism that Mill would ultimately espouse. In his praise of Gall and of Lavater, Comte had associated positivism with physiological principles which, at a later date, Mill judged to be simplistic and even dangerous.[22] And in his emphasis upon a science of human collectives, Comte had given short shrift to that very individual psychology upon which Mill would rest most of his ethical and political principles. But with these considerations set aside, Comte's essential outlook claimed Mill's praise and his loyalty. The outlook was historical, empirical, systematic, progressive, benevolent. It required the philosopher to accept social utility and human happiness as the ultimate standards by which to measure the validity of his own creations. It called upon him to recognize the peculiar properties of *critical* as opposed to *organic* stages of social evolution so that his science might embrace the dynamics of human history. It obliged him to give up once and for all time the comforts of that "geometric" method which seduces the metaphysician by deluding him, and to embrace the *historical* method whose harvest is useful and reliable, even if not exhilarating and eternal. This much of the Comtean outlook was to be a permanent fixture in Mill's own works.

Mill's Program and Its Dilemma

Thus far, I have drawn attention to two otherwise or apparently unconnected influences on Mill's thinking. There was first the larger context of political and social reform within which opinions ranged from anarchism to absolutism. Burke had served as a forceful defender of ancient institutions by connecting them to the collective genius of the English people and their deepest and most natural inclinations. Thus, Burke's celebration of tradition was set on the stage of practical utility. As much as Paine, he pointed to the facts of history and took for granted what history had revealed as the essential nature of man. But what Burke's side never made clear was the difference between a custom originating in human nature and one slavishly supported by nothing more than ignorance and habit. It certainly could not be an original feature of the human frame that it moves toward hereditary monarchies or away from universal suffrage or with diffidence before a House of Lords.

On Paine's side in the dispute there were equally vexing elements. Who, after all, are "the people," and what protection is there—when they are sovereign—against that *tyranny of the majority* that would so worry Tocqueville?[23] To brush aside the institutions of a millenium for no reason other than the predilections of a given generation—for no reason other than their "happiness"—was not a practice to be endorsed by serious persons. Every generation has a covenant with the future, even if it has no debt to the past. To honor this covenant, however, the past must be consulted if its benefits are to be preserved.

The initial appeal of positivism, in league with Bentham's "pleasure principle," was that it provided an objective way of addressing these issues. Through the careful observation of society, both contemporary and historical, a new science can be fashioned—the one Mill labeled *ethology*. No fact of human nature will elude it and no alternative approach will surpass it. But as bequeathed by Comte, positivism simply reformulated the dilemma, it did not remove it. The historical analysis of the place and record of women in society, for example, led Comte to generalities that were not only libelous but that could do no more than sanction the status quo. Similarly, his acceptance of Gall's approach resulted in a theory of human "types" that was not only illiberal in its effects, but that utterly failed to distinguish between environmental and anatomical determinants of conduct. By grounding the moral, intellectual, and sentimental dimensions of man in the eccentricities of his biology, the phrenologist, whether he intends it or not, provides a justification for every form of bigotry, paternalism, and caste.

Then, too, there was a common notion to be found not only in the views of Burke, Paine, and Comte, but among the dominant philosophical schools in England, Germany, and (even) America. I refer to that ensemble of arguments and theses that can been found scattered in such otherwise diverging philosophies as Kant's, Hegel's, and "Common Sense." It is an ensemble that goes by many names—Intuitionism, Transcendentalism, Absolute Idealism—and that serves a variety of purposes, not all philosophical. At base, these philosophies take for granted that knowledge or truths of a certain kind precede experience, or "transcend" it, or make it possible, or give it its characteristic marks and contours. We have seen in the first chapter how Kant went about defending this view. Among Mill's countrymen, however, the authority for it came less from Kantian philosophy than from what was (and has ever since been) loosely called the Scottish Common Sense school, fathered by Thomas Reid (1710–1796) and claiming Dugald Stewart (1753–1828) as its most celebrated disciple.[24] Without attempting a thorough analysis of common sense philosophy, it is important to summarize

Reid's principal claims. It is even more important to be aware of what Reid *did not* claim, for J. S. Mill and Kant were only the most brilliant philosophers of the large number who systematically misunderstood Reid's principles.

If there was a central aim in all of Reid's major works it was to refute the skeptical arguments of Hume and to develop a mental science on the model recommended by Bacon and perfected by Newton.[25] To achieve this aim, Reid attempted to show first that Hume's entire epistemology was fatally flawed by the subtle defects of his psychological theories. Cardinal among the latter was what Reid called the "ideal theory," a vestige of Descartes' philosophy of mind. As Reid understood it, the ideal theory was grounded in a set of neat premises:

1. The mind perceives only its own contents.
2. The contents of the mind are but the images or "copies" or "impressions" of the senses.
3. Only an unknown and even mysterious relationship exists between the world as it really is and our knowledge of it.
4. What passes for human intelligence can, therefore, be no more than these subjective impressions glued together by such principles as contiguity, resemblance, and cause and effect.
5. Our most fundamental convictions—our very *selves*—are merely "bundles of perceptions."

It was Reid's assessment that if 1 and 2 were true, all the rest followed and skepticism with its morbid implications must be adopted. Happily, Reid discovered (at least to his own satisfaction) that 2 was simply false and that, as a result, the whole of the skeptical philosophy crumbled.

In his *Inquiry into the Human Mind on the Principles of Common Sense* (1764)[26] Reid provided a particularly searching analysis of the notion that the mind is furnished with "copies" or "impressions" passed along by the senses. In the chapter titled "The Geometry of Visibles" he compares a *tangible* right-angle triangle (the right-angle triangle as it is felt, for example, by a blind geometer moving his finger around its sides) with a *visible* one.[27] What is interesting about the comparison is that we actually *see* the triangle as having its *felt* properties, even though the visually projected triangle is quite different. Given the shape and the optics of the eye, the visible triangle is projected as if it were painted on the surface of a sphere with the observer placed at the center. The projected figure is no longer rectilinear and, indeed, its angles sum to more than the 180 degrees of the tangible triangle. But what is it that we *see*? What we see is not the spherical triangle but just that right-angle triangle as it is known tangibly. The mind, then, is in possession not of "copies" of sensory impressions but of the objects in the external world. Through this and many similar analyses, Reid rejected Hume's skeptical epistemology and replaced it with what we would now call *direct realism*. According to its tenets, the mind is so constituted that, from the "natural signs" delivered by the senses it is able to move directly to "the thing signified," which is the object itself.

For Reid, the impressionistic ("ideal") theory failed to account for the facts of visual perception, and it was only these that could plausibly be thought of as "copies" or "impressions." How, for example, can an odor be copied or leave an impression of itself? But more than this, the skeptical theory threw into doubt not only the received wisdom of the ages but even the very principles by which the animal kingdom would have to be regulated if survival were to be possible. The theory was quite literally unnatural. Reid often referred in his essays to creatures such as the caterpillar who would roam over hundreds of different leaves until it settled on the one that was compatible with its needs. The creatures of nature—and man as well— have been fitted by "the mint of Nature" to transact their business with the world they live in, the world as it is. They are guided in these transactions by *the principles of common sense* which they "are under a necessity to take for granted" in all the affairs of life.[28]

The controlling term in Reid's theory of common sense is *necessity*, and the failure to appreciate his meaning here has been responsible for all sorts of slanders.* When Reid spoke of the principles of common sense he was referring neither to opinion nor (even) to judgment. Rather, he was proposing those very activities of mind and laws of conduct by which life becomes possible. These principles regulate the thinking as much as the unthinking members of the human race. Even skeptical Hume took for granted that he had sensations, and this not out of choice or opinion but because of a natural *necessity*. He could not think otherwise. Reid is not surprised by this, since he thought it would be very odd if nature had given us one set of faculties (perceptual) that deceived us and another set (cognitive) to expose the deception.

It had also been a central and striking feature of Hume's metaphysics that our notion of *causation* was nothing more than an idea fashioned out of our experiences of events which occur together regularly in time and space. In thus grounding causation in nothing more than particular habits of mind governed by association, Hume was led to the daring claim that, in fact, anything may be the cause of anything else.[29] On this construction, if a man just happened to observe rain every time and only when his neighbor blew a whistle—and if there were no contradictory experiences included—the man would inescapably be led to the conclusion that his neighbor's whistling was the "cause" of rain. This, too, Reid found to be not only

---

* Kant thought of Reid as appealing to nothing loftier than common prejudices and ignorances. Kant, however, could not read English. The translation available to him, anonymously composed, rendered common sense as *gemeine Menschenverstand*, but *gemeine* is the word we would use in speaking of, for example, a *common* criminal.

preposterous but utterly at variance with fact. No two events have ever been more "constantly conjoined" than the rising of the moon and the setting of the sun, noted Reid, and yet no man of ripe reason has ever thought of one as the cause of the other. Moreover, a man who intends a certain action and proceeds to perform it is under no doubts as to the "cause" of his action—even though it is one that neither he nor anyone else ever took before.[30] The cause of the action is the will of the actor, and the cause of the will is the man himself.

Reid was not surprised by the failure of those who subscribed to the "ideal theory" to be able to include the *person* in their philosophies. Having made what Reid took to be a false start in their epistemologies, it was inevitable that their theories of the *self* would be incoherent. Locke, for example, had taken the concept of self to refer to no more than whatever experience had planted in consciousness. Thus, Locke's theory required an essential identity between self and memory. All that the "I" could refer to were those recollections unique to the particular "I." But Reid was quick to note the logical unintelligibility of this thesis once its implications were drawn. Think, for example, of a young officer who recalls having been the child punished for stealing fruit from the orchard. Now consider the decorated general who recalls having been the young officer, but who has no recollection whatever of having been the punished child. With this example Reid demonstrated the futility of the Lockean account. If *self* and *memories* constitute the identity implied by Locke's theory, we can label the child, the young officer, and the decorated General A, B, and C respectively. But what Locke's theory then asserts is,

$$A = B$$
$$B = C$$
$$A \neq C$$

The principle of transitivity, which applies to all formal

identities, is violated and the theory is thus found to be simply contradictory.

Hume's approach to the problem of *self* was more careful than Locke's but not more convincing. Hume specifically rejected the memory-theory and attempted to reduce the self to an ensemble of causal relations obtaining among the impressions furnishing the mind. At root, Hume's theory is but another form of his general associationistic theory designed to account for the connections that form among one's perceptions. When he claims, therefore, that his search for his self turns up nothing but a "bundle of perceptions" he is underscoring his larger claim that a term either refers to something given in experience or it refers to nothing having real existence.

Note that Hume's theory of *self* is not a memory-theory as such but an associationistic theory that limits the meaning of *self* to a collection of causally related perceptions. Thus, Reid's rebuttal of Locke is not quite successful when turned against Hume. However, Reid was convinced that Hume's theory of causation was irremediably flawed and, since this theory is required by the Humean theory of *self*, the latter becomes a fatality in Reid's war on the former. But these analytical details aside, Reid was firmly convinced that any philosopher genuinely skeptical of his own existence was not fit to be reasoned with. For there to be treason, argued Reid, there must be a traitor; and for Hume to look for his self there must be a Hume doing the looking, a Hume distinct from anything that might be found through the search. For Reid's part, it was sufficient to accept *self* as an irreducible entity, the necessary first-term in all possible experience. One must take it for granted even as a condition of doubting it. Reid, we see, took the self to be a *substance* in the older scholastic sense of the term: an immaterial, undetermined agent necessarily implied by the facts of experience and intending actions.

By like reasoning, Reid arrived at the conclusion that the moral and ethical attributes of life originate in the very constitution of man; that he possesses a *moral sense* whose authority is as irresistable as that of the external senses: "The testimony of our moral faculty, like that of the external senses, is the testimony of nature, and we have the same reason to rely on it."[31] That Hume was wrong in grounding all morality in the "passions" is proved by our commitments to "the good on the whole"; that is, by our willingness to forego the pleasures of the moment in order to secure greater but more distant ones. The point here is that such forbearance can only proceed from an act of deliberation, which proves that our moral side is regulated by a rational rather than a purely emotional principle.

Even so hasty a review of Reid's approach and major conclusions brings to light another source of Mill's dilemma. To accept the Reidian critique of Hume was to abandon the linchpin of utilitarian and libertarian politics, for it was to abandon both the *hedonistic* theory of ethics and the *relativistic* theory of knowledge. It required the former because Reid had anchored the moral realm to *reason* and had liberated it from the Humean theory of narrow self-regard based upon pleasure and pain. And then Reid's epistemological *realism* restored human knowledge to respectability by peeling away the impressionistic varnish that skepticism had painted over it. Together, these aspects of the Reidian critique called for a return to confidence in those intuitive certainties that had guided human endeavors since time immemorial. But in this very summons was the implicit rejection of that "radical" program which called for new measures to meet new and different circumstances. In his appeals to human nature—to *the constitution of our nature*—Reid sought to reestablish the primacy of reason in moral matters which were known to be moral matters as a result of a universal but essentially unanalyzable "moral sense." Against the arguments of the skeptic, Reid presented not only the durable evidence of human history but the daily evidence of the natural order. Thus, the traditional verities were to be understood not as the production of metaphysical theory but as an expression of the Creation itself. For each of life's specimens and for each of the challenges it faces, nature has provided the requisite "faculties." The creature that struggles to oppose their dictates is as foolish as it is short-lived. This point will be reexamined later in the chapter.

But in light of Mill's larger objectives, the utter rejection of Reid's philosophy would create still other problems. Surely he could not deny in one breath man's fundamental sense of right and wrong, and appeal in the next to that same sense in attempting to defend the reform of society. Similarly, it would be ludicrous to set about transforming a world which, on his own epistemology, could be nothing but a world of appearances. And how could he formally disregard the habitual inclinations of mankind throughout history while insisting that the *historical method* must animate all political theory? Reid in a whimsical but not unconvincing way, and Kant in his grave and cumbrous manner had readmitted to philosophy a set of intuitive *truths*, and both paved the way for a revival of the absolutistic theories of morality and knowledge that the Enlightenment had temporarily banished. In different ways, both had also defended their systems with a theory of the human mind—with a psychology. Mill's dilemma, then, could be removed only through a superior psychology.

Mill's Psychology

Nearly all of Mill's major works are "psychological" in the sense that they construct arguments out of the alleged

facts of human psychology. Yet, there is no single essay or
text that stands as Mill's *Psychology*. His father's *Analysis of
the Phenomena of the Human Mind* (2d ed., 1869) developed
the associationistic principles which Mill never abandoned
but, as noted, theories of this sort had been seriously
proposed long before the elder Mill began his book (1822)
and had it published (1829). The edition of 1869—only
the second in forty years—probably would not have come
about had any lesser figure than J. S. Mill been its editor
and had not the old associationism been revitalized and
powerfully defended by him.

The temptation that has to be resisted is one that would
bring focus to bear on associationism as a way of seeing
more clearly Mill's psychological system. It was, after all,
among his least original contributions and the one that
inspired the least criticism. He made much of the putative
"laws" of association not so much because others doubted
them but because they were to serve as the defense and
the illustration of a far more controversial position, his
radical *phenomenalism* and its ethical and political implications. This is the heart of Mill's psychology and it is to be
discovered primarily in three of his works: *System of Logic*
(1843), *Utilitarianism* (1863), and the seldom discussed *An
Examination of Sir William Hamilton's Philosophy* (1865).[32]
The last of these contains not only the most thoroughgoing
of his psychological analyses but his ripest reflections on
the principles he had advanced in his earlier writing. The
explicitly psychological portions of the *Logic* are colorfully
defended in the *Examination* against the rebuttals that had
been accumulating since 1843. More than in any of his
other works, the *Examination* names the enemy, as it were,
and acknowledges what is at stake: "The question really at
issue in Sir W. Hamilton's celebrated and striking review . . . is this: Have we, or have we not, an immediate
intuition of God" (p. 34).

Here is a bold declaration of the issue, but it should not

be construed as a theological quibble. Let us recall that Bentham was studiously antireligious and let few opportunities go by for offending clerical sensibilities. Let us also recall that the aftermath of the French Revolution and Napoleonic excesses had led to a restoration of Catholic authority in France; an authority that was now righteously indignant and intolerant. Recent French history had a sobering effect on the already sober British consciousness and this expressed itself in the form of a revived puritanism. These tendencies were hardened by the realistic fear of what happens when the established order is upset. They were further hardened by schools of philosophy and religion which taught that the established order was, alas, the *natural* order known to be so by the common man's intuitive faculties. In the legion of establishmentarians flooding the populace with such reassurances, Sir William Hamilton was of the highest rank. He had edited and commented extensively on new editions of the works of Reid and of Dugald Stewart and had constructed a wide bridge over which Kantian and Hegelian influences could pass into English thought.[33] And so we find Mill saying: "My subject, therefore, is less Sir W. Hamilton, than the questions which Sir W. Hamilton discussed. . . . On all the subjects on which he touched, he is either one of the most powerful allies of what I deem a sound philosophy, or (more frequently) by far its most formidable antagonist" (*Examination*, p. 2).

It is in chapter 9 of *Examination* that Mill distinguishes between what he calls the "introspective" and the "psychological" methods, a distinction that underscores his general theory of mind. As he understands the former, consciousness is to function as the ultimate arbiter of competing psychological claims. To the extent that this is so, the claims of *intuitionism* are protected, but only perversely. To choose one of Mill's examples, we might consider the notion of matter which, as it happens, was one of the

notions Descartes had treated as innate.[34] The argument
for this is straightforward: If all we ever know directly are
the contents of our own minds, and if these can only be
ideas (sensations, perceptions, cognitions, etc.), then we
can never arrive at the notion of an external material world.
That is, there can be nothing in consciousness or experience that will (can) convey or deliver the idea of *matter*, for
there is nothing material about a thought or percept. Yet,
everyone not only has the idea of matter but is abolutely
certain that it is just this matter of which we have ideas.
Accordingly, the idea of matter must be an innate fixture
of the mind or, as the Common Sense philosopher would
say, part of the very constitution of our nature.

By the same logic, it should be clear that a potentially
limitless number of intuitive truths might be proposed
ranging from metaphysical verities (e.g., causation) to
moral imperatives. In each case, the knower is asked to do
no more than consult his own consciousness, to identify an
idea or notion which nothing in the world of perception
conveys, and then to recognize this as the native and
irrefutable gift of the intuitive faculty. The method, then,
is that of *introspection* which, on Mill's account, virtually
guarantees this outcome. Nor is it difficult to discover
why:

We have no means of interrogating consciousness in the only
circumstances in which it is possible for it to give a trustworthy
answer. Could we try the experiment of the first consciousness
in any infant . . . whatever was present in that first consciousness
would be the genuine testimony of Consciousness. . . . But we
have no means of now ascertaining, by direct evidence, whether
we were conscious of outward and extended objects when we
first opened our eyes to the light. That a belief or knowledge of
such objects is in our consciousness now, whenever we use our
eyes or muscles, is no reason for concluding that it was there
from the beginning. . . . If any mode can be pointed out in which
within the compass of possibility it might have been brought in,

the hypothesis must be examined and disproved before we are entitled to conclude that the conviction is an original deliverance of consciousness. (*Examination*, p. 140)

Mill opposes the psychological method to this method of introspection, and applauds Locke for recognizing that a mental science must concern itself with the *origin* of ideas. But

we cannot study the original elements of mind in the facts of our present consciousness. Those original elements can only come to light as residual phaenomena, by a previous study of the modes of generation of the mental facts which are confessedly not original; a study sufficiently thorough to enable us to apply its results to the convictions, beliefs, or supposed intuitions which seem to be original. . . . This mode of ascertaining the original elements of mind I call, for want of a better word, the psychological, as distinguished from the simply introspective mode. It is the known and approved method of physical science, adapted to the necessities of psychology. (*Examination*, p. 141)

Now it is clear, thinks Mill, that the laws of association are sufficient to explain the generation of an immense number of "mental facts," proving that at least these "are confessedly not original." Accordingly, the *onus probandi* falls to those who entertain the intuitionistic hypothesis. Why should we conclude that any fact of mind is original when (a) we can never actually prove as much and when (b) we can show that all of the more recently conscious facts of mind have been acquired?

The side for which Hamilton was spokesman had proposed to examine those facts of mind that were "ultimate and simple" by which was meant that they were neither grounded in nor generalizations from past experience.[35] What was to set such facts apart from our acquired ideas was the property of *necessity*. The notion or idea in question must be of such a nature that its contradictory is unthinkable, inconceivable, incredible. It is on this point that Mill concluded there was no essential difference between the epistemology of Reid and that of Kant.[36] Indeed, what separates Herbert Spencer from the "intuitionists" was Spencer's willingness to grant such cognitive necessities but to explain them as results of either personal or ancestral experience.[37] Mill carefully avoids support from the Lamarckian thesis but stands foursquare behind the empirical one. He rejects the necessitarian theory of intuition on two grounds: first, the very fact that the thesis is being contended proves that it is scarcely impossible for the mind to consider alternatives; second,

even if this incapability extended to all mankind, it might be merely the effect of a strong association. . . . The history of science teems with inconceivabilities which have been conquered, and supposed necessary truths which have first ceased to be thought to be necessary, then to be thought true, and have finally come to be deemed impossible. (*Examination*, p. 145)

In attempting here however to cover all possible objections Mill seems to miss the only ones that really count. In the *Examination* and in several other essays he reveals an unwarranted confidence in the alleged similarity among the philosophies of Reid, Stewart, and Kant, and between them and the philosophy of Sir William Hamilton. The present purposes are not served by attempting to analyze the principled differences among them, but the reader might refer again to the earlier discussion of Reid's use of the concept of necessity in relation to the principles of common sense. When he defined a principle of common sense as one we are under a *necessity* to take for granted in all the affairs of life, Reid was surely not suggesting that philosophers were incapable of disputing the point; only that they were incapable, in the nonspeculative realms of life, to *act* as if such a principle were in doubt. A thirsty man pours a cold drink into a glass and drinks the contents. He is, of course, able to entertain the notion that his actions are in fact under the control of an unknown and external agent; that his belief that he is the author of his own actions is simply a delusion; that the entire episode is in reality but a dream and that there is neither thirst nor beverage in the world. But a race of beings having any likelihood of self-preservation and propagation will and must act in a manner consistent with the belief that their actions have consequences and causes, and that the former include their *intentions* to act.

Note, therefore, that Mill's first objection—that Mill and many others are able to deny the alleged attribute of necessity—is entirely beside the point. The point—at least Reid's point—is that life in the real world, life outside the metaphysician's closet, places us under a necessity to take certain principles for granted; e.g., that the glowing iron rod now near my nose is the cause of the heat I feel and will soon be the cause of irreparable damage to me if I do not get out of the way; or, more generally, that events proceed from causes; that what I now perceive continues to exist when I no longer see it; that a thing cannot simultaneously exist and not exist; that the cause of some of my actions is my will to act. To repeat, the necessity in such cases attaches not to the facts but to our presumptions about facts of a certain kind. Reid is quite clear on this point in the fourth of his *Essays on the Active Powers of the Human Mind*: "And though it were certain, that every event we have had access to observe had a cause, it would not follow that every event must have a cause: for it is contrary to the rules of logic to conclude, that, because a thing has always been, therefore it must be; to reason from what is contingent to what is necessary."[38]

Mill's second objection to intuitionism was also thoroughly anticipated by Reid, as was Mill's alternative hypothesis. What Mill wants to establish, following Hume, is that the universal distribution of a notion is no proof either of its truth or of its intuitive origins. Thus, that all persons believe that every effect has a cause can be explained by the universal operation of the laws of association rather than the universal possession of an intuitive truth. Reid weighs this line of argument in a number of places and makes clear that there is no contradiction entailed in asserting an intuitive principle of mind *and* the effects of learning and experience on it. Again, the notion of causation is illustrative:

Mr Hume . . . endeavours to account for it by the association of ideas. . . . A person who has lived so long in the world, as to observe that nature is governed by fixed laws, may have some rational ground to expect similar events in similar circumstances; but this cannot be the case of the child. His belief therefore is not grounded on evidence. It is the result of his constitution. Nor is it the less so, though it should arise from the association of ideas. For what is called the association of ideas is a law of nature in our constitution; which produces its effects without any operation of reason on our part, and in a manner of which we are entirely ignorant.[39]

Writing on morals he observes:

I am far from thinking instruction in morals unnecessary. Men may, to the end of life, be ignorant of self-evident truths. They may, to the end of life, entertain gross absurdities. . . . The most obvious truths are not perceived without some ripeness of judgment. . . . Our judgment of things is ripened, not by time only, but chiefly by being exercised about things of the same, or of a similar kind.[40]

We see, then, on this side of the dispute Mill did not faithfully project at least the Reidian variety of intuitionism and, more strikingly, did not carefully focus the various impressions aroused by the concept of "common sense." Because of this, he never did confront the Reidian version

of our alleged "immediate intuition of God," an intuition
to which Reid himself devoted rather little space. Steadfast
in his empiricistic psychology, Mill located the sources of
all thought outside the percipient, and attempted to explain all ideas as but the associative combinations of past
and current perceptions. His program, like Hume's, would
rise or fall depending on the validity of this claim. In
different ways, Reid, Stewart, Kant, and Hamilton judged
it to be invalid. The *Examination* was composed to answer
their criticisms but in significant respects the success of
the *Examination* was illusory—which is no more than to
observe that the issues are still alive.

Mill takes as intuitionism's strongest case the concept of
necessity and attempts to interpret it within the framework
of associationistic psychology. His most sustained effort is
found in chapter 14 of the *Examination* in which he applies
the principle of *inseparable association* to the intuitionist's
examples of necessity. "Reid and Stewart," he says, "who
had met with it only in Hartley, thought it needless to take
the trouble of understanding it" (p. 250), so Mill confines
his criticism almost entirely to Hamilton and Mansel.

In the Reidian tradition, but without Reid's range and
depth, Mill's targeted critics contend: (a) that any number
of perfectly reliable conjunctions (e.g., the sun's rising and
the moon's setting) never create in us the idea of a
necessary connection or, for that matter, even of a (con-
tingently) causal one; (b) that ideas formed out of nothing
but experience never rise higher than the level of probability, whereas the idea of necessity carries with it the
attribute of certainty; (c) that we have no trouble conceiving
of, for example, a centaur even though we have never
seen a human head on the body of a horse and, therefore,
have never had occasion to "associate" the two.

These are different kinds of assertions and Mill resorts
to appropriately different counterarguments. On the sun-
moon phenomenon, he notes that the pair of events suffers

from so long a temporal separation as to preclude the formation of that very "inseparable association" which *is* the idea of necessity. For us to come to believe that something about the sun's activity necessarily entails something about the moon's, the two activities would have to be effectively cotemporaneous and exceptionless in their occurrences. Under such conditions, we would not only judge the relationship to be necessary but, of course, one which was *certain*, for on what can the concept of certainty be based if not exceptionless correlations?

Conceptions of centaurs or of stones that float come about by a combination of exceptions to inseparable associations and the process of generalization. Our experiences in time come to include all sorts of combinations, some strange, and alert the mind to the possibility of the improbable. Although we have never seen a stone float, we have seen stonelike objects float. Similarly with the idea of a centaur: "The mere mobility of objects in space is a fact so universal in our experience, that we easily conceive any object whatever occupying the place of any other; we imagine without difficulty a horse with his head removed, and a human head put in its place" (*Examination*, p. 265).

We can move quite easily from this analysis to Mill's theory of thought, which he develops under the headings, "The Doctrine of Concepts, or General Notions" (ch. 17), "Of Judgment" (ch. 18), and "Of Reasoning" (ch. 19). The first of these chapters is devoted to the proof that the mind is not furnished with abstract concepts, but only with *terms* whose meanings are derived from their association with specific attributes of things. The word *horse*, for example, is a class-name or general term which has no signification beyond its associative connection with the perceived attributes of specific horses. What is opposed by this analysis is that Conceptualist theory according to which thought is abstract and is able to frame general concepts. Mill would replace the words *concept*, *judgment*, and *reason-*

ing with *term, proposition,* and *argument* (*Examination,* p. 324). To the extent that the mind deals with anything that is not particular, it is dealing with a *term* devised to signify particular attributes. And to the traditional rationalistic claim that through our cognitive faculty we are able to generate an infinite number of truths, Mill applies the same corrective. First the claim: To know that if A = B and if B = C, then A = C is to know in principle an infinitude of truths certain. Now the corrective:

> When reasoning really leads to the "countless multitudes of truths" not self-evident . . . that is, when the judgments are syntheticall—we learn, not that A is part of C, because A is part of B and B of C, but that A is conjoined with C, because A is conjoined with B, and B with C. The principle of the reasoning is not, a part of the part is a part of the whole, but, a mark of the mark is a mark of the thing marked. . . . It means, that two things which constantly coexist with the same third thing, constantly coexist with one another; the things meant not being our concepts, but the facts of experience on which our concepts ought to be grounded. (*Examination,* p. 345)

To this point, Mill's analysis provides a cognitive psychology that begins with elementary sensations and evolves through their associative combinations and the general terms invented to represent these. A question quickly raised by this sort of analysis has to do with the sort of reductionism defended and required by it. Does the analysis, for example, impose upon Psychology the obligation to trace elementary sensations back to their neural and ultimately biophysical origins? Put another way, is the science of Psychology only the preliminary phase of a discipline that is finally Biology? Then, too, are we to conclude from this theory of the human mind that the evidence of consciousness is somehow ultimate and that, accordingly, all other sciences finally collapse into Psychology?

These questions are dealt with most directly in Mill's *A System of Logic*, where his answers lead him finally to an examination of the methods most suitable to a scientific psychology.[41] The narrow path he must tread is lined by the thorny brush of absolute skepticism on one side and the intoxicating fruits of intuitionism on the other. He is impelled by the conviction that a knowledge of how we come by our beliefs is adequate protection against the reassuring fallacies of the intuitionists: "I must protest against adducing, as evidence of the truth of a fact in external nature, the disposition, however strong or however general, of the human mind to believe it. Belief is not proof, and does not dispense with the necessity of proof" (*Logic*, Book 3, ch. 21, sec. 1).

He knows also that his laws of association seem to come very close to proving that the very concept of causation is native to the mind: How, for example, could the constant conjunction of A and B lead us to conclude that one is the cause of the other, if we did not already possess the notion of causality? "'All men are mortal' is not the proof that Lord Palmerston is mortal; but our past experience of mortality authorises us to infer *both* the general truth and the particular fact. . . . The mortality of Lord Palmerston is not an inference from the mortality of all men, but from the experience which proves the mortality of all men" (sec. 4). All, therefore, is fashioned out of experience and those laws of thought which regulate and give coherence to experience. By this same experience we come to recognize the most general attribute of nature which is *the law of universal causation*. Experience alone is sufficient to confirm this law, and only counterexamples in experience can tell against it. Neither the law nor its proof (or possible disproof) is grounded in intuition.

Mill settles the issue of infinite regression by acknowledging that even the Law of Universal Causation requires qualification, if only because of the limits of experience.

With respect to "the ultimate properties of things" and to "the primary powers of nature," there are *uniformities*, but not *causes* (ch. 22). It is these properties and powers which are the fundamental causes of all the phenomena of nature but which are themselves uncaused and, therefore, not candidates for further (causal) analysis. They are, as it were, just there—the bare facts of the universe, the irreducible first-terms in any causal description of natural phenomena. The limits of a reductionistic analysis are set by the fact that some properties and powers are ultimate.

Regarding reductionism in psychology, however, Mill is less clear. Consistent with his epistemology, he refuses to wade into metaphysical waters to discover what mind is "in itself," preferring to confine his efforts to its *sensible manifestations* (Book 6, ch. 4, sec. 1). Nonetheless, Bain, Spencer, and others have offered compelling arguments in favor of a biological approach to mental science. We see again a very narrow path cut for Mill's psychology; this time between the borders of a purely metaphysical psychology and a purely physical (neurophysiological) one. To reject out of hand the very possibility of a coherent and exhaustive physiological psychology is to embrace, grudgingly or otherwise, a form of *substance* theory of mind which is only a step away from dreaded spiritualism. But to go the whole materialistic route is not so much to establish a scientific psychology as to eliminate psychology altogether. Perceiving no third alternative, Mill will have both:

The immediate antecedent of a sensation is a state of body, but the sensation itself is a state of mind. . . . Whatever opinion we hold respecting the fundamental identity or diversity of matter and mind, in any case the distinction between mental and physical facts, between the internal and the external world, will always remain as a matter of classification; and in that classification, sensations, like all other feelings, must be ranked as mental phenomena. . . . All states of mind are immediately caused either

by other states of mind or by states of body. When a state of
mind is produced by a state of mind, I call the law concerned in
the case a law of Mind. Whan a state of mind is produced directly
by a state of body, the law is a law of Body, and belongs to the
physical sciences. (secs. 1, 2)

In this same place Mill goes on to rebuke Comte for his
phrenological loyalties which, far from making psychology
scientific, threaten to give it the character of astrology.
Mental phenomena display those "uniformities of succession" which are the proper subjects of study, and these
cannot now be deduced from any more general laws of
physiology. Indeed, Mill claims, the science of mind "is in
a considerably more advanced state than the portion of
physiology which corresponds to it" (sec. 2). It can be
further refined without reference to advances in the
biological sciences and without any attention to such distracting metaphysical conundrums as the Mind/Body
problem.

In chapter 5 of Book 6, Mill makes the important
distinction between *empirical* and *causal* laws, assigning
proprietorship of the former to scientific psychology and
the latter to the more general science which he calls
Ethology "or the science of the formation of character."
The first of these sciences is what we would now take to be
individual psychology with special emphasis upon perceptual and cognitive processes; the second, a form of social
psychology: "While, on the one hand, Psychology is altogether, or principally, a science of observation and experiment, Ethology, as I have conceived it, is . . . altogether
deductive. The one ascertains the simple laws of Mind in
general, the other traces their operation in complex combinations of circumstances" (sec. 5). Moreover the former
gives only empirical laws of a correlational nature whereas
the latter seeks genuinely causal laws. It is from the
empirical laws of psychology that a "system of corollaries,"

ethology, is deduced. And, although this is a social psychology, it is still a psychology of the individual whose *character* (rather than merely his mental states) is the object of inquiry. Thus understood, human character may now be studied in its even more complex social, moral, and political manifestations. This is the proper study of social science which arises out of ethology as ethology arises out of psychology. Social science itself cannot be experimental because the participating variables are too numerous, too changing, and too resistant to experimental manipulation and control. Thus, the development of social science depends upon the application of the deductive method (derivations from the laws of Ethology) and that "inverse deductive method" which Mill calls the science of history, so usefully exploited by Comte (chs. 10, 11). What distinguishes these deductive approaches from the "geometric method" of the *a priori* school is the criterion of *verification.* Deductions drawn from the study of history must be tested against observable facts, not the rules of the syllogism.

Mill's vision of the developed human sciences included interdependent fields of special inquiry; one devoted to unearthing the empirical laws of mind; another to the deductive system of the (causal) laws of character; another to the expression and formation of character in society; still another to those trends of human history suggestive of nothing less than the laws of human progress. But here again he faced twin perils: If there are causal laws of character and society, must we not then subscribe to a form of "Asiatic Fatalism?" If, instead, character and social phenomena are not caused, on what basis might we defend the claim that they are amenable to scientific study and explanation? These questions bring us back to the *Examination* and to Mill's theory of character, motivation, and volition.

It is consistent with Mill's entire program to produce arguments favoring the experiential origins of all our ideas, including the idea of "free will." He judges the intuitionistic position as one that claims we have direct consciousness of this freedom and that takes it to be an intuitive certainty. Mill's counter takes a familiar form: "Consciousness tells me what I do or feel. But what I am *able* to do, is not a subject of consciousness. Consciousness is not prophetic. . . . We should not know that we were capable of action at all, if we had never acted. . . . If our so-called consciousness of what we are able to do is not borne out by experience, it is a delusion (*Examination*, p. 449). Our notions of freedom, no less than our notions of justice, arise out of a personal history of actions and consequences knitted together by the laws of association. There is nothing in the idea of "moral wrong" except the connection provided by experience between a certain class of actions and the punishments they nearly invariably receive. The Golden Rule, on this account, is simply a generalization by which we project onto other persons the same self-regarding sentiments we have ourselves, and realize that we should suffer for transgressions against them precisely what we would cause them to suffer for transgressions against us.

The question that naturally arises, of course, has to do with just how far Mill is willing to take determinism in his account of morals. His critics are persuaded that he shares with the Owenites a form of "Asiatic Fatalism" (*Examination*, p. 465), and this calls upon Mill to make distinctions among the various systems of determinism.[42] The Asiatic variety, adopted by Oedipus, for example, is a religious belief that the gods have foreclosed all options and have arranged the future according to their liking. Mill labels this *pure* fatalism, and contrasts it with that Modified Fatalism which "holds that our actions are determined by our will, our will by our desires, and our desires by the joint influence of the motives presented to us and of our individual character; but that, our character having been made for us and not by us, we are not responsible for it, nor for the actions it leads to" (*Examination*, p. 465). However, the "doctrine of Causation" rejects both the pure and the modified versions of fatalism, and asserts "that not only our conduct, but our character, is in part amenable to our will; that we can, by employing the proper means, improve our character. . . . We are under a moral obligation to seek the improvement of our moral character" (*Examination*, p. 466).

This is, to say the least, a less than satisfying "solution" to the ageless tension between free-will and deterministic theories of human action. And it becomes still less convincing when we learn, a few words later, that we will not seek such moral improvement unless our desire to do so is stronger than our aversion to the steps we must take. Our "desire," after all, is on Mill's construction, the product of our history of rewards and punishments and is therefore as *determined* by the great law of causation as anything else residing in consciousness or in feeling. Decades earlier, in his *Logic*, Mill eagerly sought to disconnect determinism from necessitarianism, at least in human affairs, by liberalizing his theory of motivation. Moving a safe distance from Benthamism, he then insisted that "a motive does not mean always, or solely, the anticipation of a pleasure or of a pain" (Book 6, ch. 2, sec. 4). Rather, by long experience, we come to choose the *means* for their own sake. That is, if action A has regularly been associated with pleasing consequences, we will engage in it in time without any attention given to the consequences themselves. Virtue becomes, as the maxim says, its own reward. "It is only when our purposes have become independent of the feelings of pain or pleasure from which they originally took their rise that we are said to have a confirmed character" (sec. 4).

But it is entirely unclear how this line of reasoning immunizes Mill's theory against infection by Modified

Fatalism. It is clearer that it does no such thing. And by the same token, it is not clear that his concessions to the character's self-determination immunizes his theory against infection by the Free Will school. Put in simpler language, an agent is either sometimes in personal control of his actions or he is not. If he is, and if his choices are not completely determined by prior or current external forces, then he is properly said to act freely. If not, he is properly said not to *act* at all, but to *react*. The central question here is an ontological one: *Is there moral freedom in the world?* Any answer that is not exceptionlessly negative is totally affirmative, and if it is neither, it is not an answer but an equivocation.

Mill's desire to avoid Modified Fatalism is quite understandable in this patron of inductive science. If the present is entirely determined by the past, then the future is entirely determined by the present, and things will be what they will be. This is not the sort of conclusion that fires the zeal of the reformer. For all practical purposes, in fact, the distinction between Asiatic and Modified Fatalism would sink to the level of a quibble. We would be left in the moral and social spheres of life in just the same position as Berkeley's metaphysics leaves us in the experiential domain; which is to say, precisely where we are. If the philosopher convinces me that everything I am prepared to say about an external world is actually no more than a description of my own ideas (sensations), and that I have no justification for imputing an independent existence to the former, *nothing changes!* Berkeley admitted as much, and so must anyone who completes the arc of impressionistic metaphysics. And the same conclusion awaits those who complete the arc of deterministic psychologies. If everything I know and think and believe and desire must be understood as the inevitable consequence of past associations, punishments, and rewards, I am left with precisely the same knowledge, conviction, and inclination, including my inclination to accept the theory. The reformer, whatever his cause, wants his audience to promote change; change in their perspective or their conduct or their desires. But if these have been put in place by nothing less than the Law of Universal Causation, how is a speech or a pamphlet to have any effect at all? Only if the reformer leaves room for *self-determination*, for some airy entity known as "character," can he expect to persuade his public that their initiative is something more than a chimera. Without this element, his exhortations fall, as it were, on a collection of broken watches and urge them to change jewelers.

Mill's dilemma in the matter of character, as with all the other dilemmas facing his psychology, was made graver by his commitment to oppose intuitionism in all its forms. The Common Sense school, at least with Thomas Reid as its spokesman, had come down unequivocally on the side of free will; on the side of man as a moral agent whose significant actions are not caused by passions or motives, "but by some cool principle of action, which has authority without any impulsive force: for example, by some interest, which is too distant to raise any passion or emotion; or by some consideration of decency, or of duty."[43]

According to Reid, such significant actions are *caused* by the will of the man who is acting. Indeed, on Reid's account, a so-called motive cannot be the cause of anything, for it possesses no active principle. It should be recalled that Reid's theory of causation was drafted in opposition to Hume's contiguity theory. The latter would permit anything to be the cause of anything else, provided the two events were constantly conjoined and one reliably followed and never preceded the other. Reid judged this to be absurd, as we have seen, and also to be an eccentric use of language. When we think of an effect as something that has been brought about, we ordinarily take for granted that the causal antecedent had the power to produce the effect. This, however, is an inference we make based upon ourselves as causal agents. That is, we impute to the purely physical realm the *active powers* we have as free agents and of which we are conscious as deliberative beings. Yet, if we examine purely natural events with greater comprehension, we will begin to recognize how peculiar it is to speak of "causes" in the inanimate world. As Reid says,

> When an event is produced according to a known law of nature, the law of nature is called the cause of that event. But a law of nature is not the efficient cause of any event. It is only the rule, according to which the efficient cause acts. A law is a thing conceived in the mind of a rational being, not a thing that has a real existence; and, therefore, like a motive, it can neither act nor be acted upon, and consequently cannot be an efficient cause. If there be no being that acts according to the law, it produces no effect.[44]

This is all part of Reid's support for a "first cause" thesis which finally supports the theory of a providential God. Stripped of its theological ornaments, however, it is a thesis regarding the sources of human action and the essentiality of *volition* in any occurrence said to be *caused*. In human affairs, the operative laws are moral laws of nature, not to be confused with physical laws of nature. The latter are immune to human agency whereas the former "respect voluntary and free actions only. . . . There is no impossibility in the violation of the moral laws of nature, nor is such a violation an effect without a cause. The transgressor is the cause, and is justly accountable for it."[45]

Reid's theory of active powers includes a distinction between them and the mechanical principles of causation in the physical world. To say that an agent has it in his *power* to bring something about is to say, among other things, that he can withhold this power. In the physical realm, it is manifestly contradictory to speak of an effect without a cause or a cause with no effect. But no such contradiction is entailed by claiming the existence of a power in the absence of an outcome. Moral agents have the power of voluntary action and, through deliberation or (more typically) their sense of duty, they are able to withhold, direct, exercise, and otherwise manage this power.

In this sketch of Reid's theory of volition we see just what it is that Mill cannot accept. The theory takes the person—the *self*—as an irreducible entity capable of causing its own behavior. This same person, endowed with conscience, expresses his will freely, though cognizant (intuitively) of the moral law. Just as a rock does not learn to fly by being thrown often, the entity living under a moral law does not acquire a conscience, but possesses one as part of his very constitution. It is a "natural faculty" possessed by a rational being. Note, then, that Reid not only ignores those vaunted principles of associationism, but removes morality entirely from the domain of external circumstances and locates it within the agent himself, while leaving ample room for the influence of training and instruction. Mill's recourse to the concept of "character" was to give his psychology and his politics an opportunity for cross-fertilization. Thus, he suspends (or seems to suspend) the "universal" Law of Causation often enough and long enough for men to take some responsibility for their society and their daily lives. Character, as a self-determining feature of the person, warrants Mill's libertarian theory of government or at least does not contradict it. But for character to be self-determining, it must not be completely formed by past associations or hereditary endowments. However, to satisfy these criteria, character comes perilously close to Reid's notion of a free moral agent. This agent, even apart from the embarrassments he causes to the balance of Mill's psychology, raises all sorts of havoc for Mill's Utilitarian theory of ethics. The

morally free being presented by Reid is not constrained by
hedonistic motives or passions; he does not routinely
engage in calculations designed to maximize his own
rewards; he is not simply moved about by threats and
seductions. Thus, he is not the creature conjured up by
Bentham or Hobbes.

Mill was acutely aware of the gaps and exaggerations
punctuating the radically Benthamistic forms of the Utilitarian theory. As he set about to eliminate them, he found
it necessary to dwell upon man's higher purposes and to
distinguish between the fleeting pleasures of the senses
and the enduring happiness of the virtuous and cultivated
life:

Now there is absolutely no reason in the nature of things why an
amount of mental culture sufficient to give an intelligent interest
in these objects of contemplation, should not be the inheritance
of everyone born in a civilized country. As little is there an
inherent necessity that any human being should be a selfish
egotist, devoid of every feeling or care but those which center in
his own miserable individuality.[46]

Accordingly, while he retains *happiness* as the ultimate
standard by which to assess competing courses of action,
the happiness is that of humanity on the whole, and that
variety of happiness available only to morally and rationally
endowed creatures. What is interesting in this liberalization
of Benthamism is Mill's tacit endorsement of Reid's theory
of the social impulses coupled with Mill's official anti-
intuitionism.[47]

But here again success is incomplete and largely apparent. The strong and interesting version of Utilitarianism
proposes to reduce the complexities of social and ethical
conduct to the barest principles of self-regarding motivation. Happiness on this account begins as nothing more
than freedom from pain and access to pleasurable sensations. Through the operation of associational processes,

this elemental happiness is then parlayed into the richer combinations which traditionally go by such names as "virtue," "benevolence," and "moral sense." Had Mill stayed with this version, he might at least have fashioned a coherent and very modern variety of contemporary behaviorism. His failure to do so was not, of course, the result of his simply not thinking of it. Rather, he recognized that a theory of this nature would rapidly become entwined in paradox and in libels against fact. It would lead him first to a defense of some form of materialism or biological psychology which he otherwise found necessary to avoid. It would call upon him to treat man as a purely affective being—except for those rational operations employed in solving the problems of the hedonistic calculus. Innumerable instances of persons striving to achieve "good on the whole" would have to be explained in the argot of a theory which rests on a skeptical attitude toward foresight, deliberation, and other manifestations of rationality. Worst of all, it would summon him to the defense of a set of allegations which would simply replace one metaphysical system with another. And so Mill leaves the camp of radical metaphysics and meets Reid halfway. He expresses his belief that "the moral feelings are not innate, but acquired" but then replaces with one hand what he took away with the other:

If there were not . . . a natural basis of sentiment for utilitarian morality, it might well happen that . . . even after it had been implanted by education, [it] might be analyzed away. But there *is* this basis of powerful natural sentiment. . . . This firm foundation is that of the social feelings of mankind; the desire to be in unity with our fellow-creatures.[48]

He never does make clear why he is willing to accept the evidence of the ages regarding one "natural sentiment" (the desire to be in unity with our fellow-creatures), but unwilling to accept the same evidence regarding our moral feelings. As with so much of his psychology, Mill's utilitarian principles proved to be usefully ambiguous, flexible, and conservative.

Mill's Legacy

Mill's books and essays contributed directly and indirectly to any number of turns Psychology would take toward the end of the nineteenth century. His philosophy of science put the older empiricism of Bacon and Locke on modern footing and lent plausibility to the claim that an *experimental* science of mind was within reach. In this same vein, his sustained defense of the "relativity of knowledge" submitted questions of fact to arbitration by direct experience.[49] His famous definition of matter as "permanent possibilities of sensation" (*Examination*, p. 183) was a refinement of Hume's *phenomenalism* and a bridge to Ernst Mach's version of *positivism*. Indirectly, this line of analysis gave great importance to studies of perception and sensory processes since it tied the limits of human knowledge to the underlying laws of perception.

In developing his principles of *utility* and *association*, Mill anticipated and encouraged the sort of research ordinarily identified as "behavioristic." Utilitarianism includes pleasure and pain as the immediate goads to adaptive behavior, and the "laws" of association when added to these give us at least the skeleton of a drive-reduction model of learning.

Unlike his close and admired friend, Alexander Bain, he avoided the temptation to rush Psychology into scientific status by biologizing it. Perhaps the somewhat sluggish march of British Psychology toward "neuropsychology" might be understood as the lingering influence of Mill's own reservations. This influence, however, is just as apparent in the early works of Watson and Skinner in the behavioristic tradition and, as we shall see, of Wundt in the cognitive tradition. Mill did not so much deny or reject the possibility of causal biological laws of mind as he insisted that mental phenomena would still have to be dealt with in their own terms even were such laws forthcoming.

As we have seen, the door was left open for Psychology to admit a self-determining entity or process—human *character*—and Mill's arguments for it would constitute an authority for studies of personality and individual differences. Between Herbert Spencer's evolutionary environmentalism and Alexander Bain's physiological associationism, Mill's psychology took a middle course and imbued the new discipline with a much needed modesty. At the same time, his tireless critiques of intuitionism, transcendentalism, and idealism freed Psychology from the burden of having to study the ineffable. He left only the smallest space for native faculties and none at all for *a priori* truths—not even in mathematics! More than any other scholar of his time, he drove a wedge between Continental psychology in the Hegelian tradition and what would soon become the distinctive psychology of the Anglo-American world.

Taken as a whole, Mill's psychology must be judged a failure, but an extremely productive and interesting failure. Research over the past two or three decades makes it abundantly clear that all of the advanced species enter the world with far more organizing and biasing equipment than Mill would have expected. Whether this equipment is best described in the Reidian language of "natural faculties" or in more neutral terms is irrelevant. What is beyond dispute are the selective perceptual and cognitive orientations of the newborn, the native formal properties of language, and the inability of associational principles to account for the facts of perception, cognition, language, and thought. Let me not be guilty of an *ipse dixit*. I do not claim that no form of associationistic psychology could possibly absorb these findings; only that such a psychology would look very little like the theories advanced by Mill and his father.

The "happiness" doctrine of Mill's utilitarianism underwent such expansion in Mill's own time as to be a threat to very few traditional accounts of human society and human ethics. He retained the *preference* criterion for weighing the quantity and quality of a given pleasure but left such room for individual and contextual sources of variation as to make the doctrine little more than a *petitio principii*. Whatever force it continues to exert on modern psychology is confined to settings in which only the most rudimentary features of animal and human conduct are examined. Broadened to include such considerations as society's good "on the whole," and enriched to include the happiness we feel when we exercise our most noble "faculties," utilitarianism—like phenomenalism and the universal law of causation—leaves the world just as we found it.

If Mill's psychology did not succeed as a positive contribution, we still must take note of it as a critique of alternative systems and formulations. These were in Mill's day the creations of the "German school." In the next chapter we will examine the most influential representative of this school and will develop a clearer understanding of what Mill was opposing. But before turning to it a distinction must be made between the *intuitionisms* flourishing on the different sides of the English Chanel.[50] Mill, in his eagerness to uproot every trace of the *a priori* psychology, had a habit of grouping theorists who, in fact, held few principles in common. At several places in the *Examination* he pays Hamilton the dubious compliment of sparing his opponents the need to criticize his friends, but one still comes away with the impression that Reid and Hamilton had designed their psychologies from the same blueprints.

It is even fair to say that the rapidly declining influence of the Common Sense school can be traced to Mill's devastating analysis of Hamilton's works, coupled with the incorrect assumption that these works were essentially loyal to the Reidian system. The less than cautious and thorough reader would surely conclude that Mill, in a single stroke, reduced to incoherence the philosophies of Hamilton, Reid, Stewart, Kant, and Hegel.

The fact, of course, is that Mill made ample use of any number of principles generally identified with the Reidian school, and that his celebrated critique of Hamilton left most of the other Reidian arguments untouched. This is quite evident, to choose one example, in Mill's defense of *phenomenalism* and its corollary, the "relativity of knowledge." His rebukes of Hamilton here spring from the valid complaint that Hamilton often shifts his ground, sometimes openly subscribing to a form of phenomenalism and at other times fastening his epistemology to intuitionism. But the complaint cannot be extended to Reid who, in all of his major essays, never deviated from the theory of *direct realism.* And more to the point, Mill's defense of phenomenalism never succeeds in answering Reid's critique of the "ideal theory." All in all, Reid's challenges to Hume are not dulled by the century separating Hume's *Treatise* and Mill's *Logic.* The major strategy adopted by Mill was to avoid the reification of such terms as *impression, sensation,* and *reflection,* but his theory of cognition always remained Humean in its fundamental respects. This is at the base of his defense of the "relativity of knowledge" and his insistence that the mind can possess only those elements and combinations furnished by the senses. That Reid's rebuttal of this theory is less than convincing is a matter beyond the scope of this chapter. But that Mill failed to address this rebuttal in a sustained and coherent fashion is quite evident. As with Mill later, Reid always took such issues to be the proper business of observation and experiment. And since there was complete agreement on this point—and since Mill had no observational or experimental data with which to refute Reid's claims—Mill's defense of phenomenalism simply evaded Reid's version of realism. As Reid so often contended, we have no reason to trust any one of our faculties more or less than the rest. Our senses deliver the facts of the world and we believe that what we see is actually there. Our success in dealing with the world depends not only on this belief but on the validity of this belief. The consistent skeptic sooner or later steps into a "dirty kennel" and bruises his head against a signpost.

The deep and awesome question which Mill judged to be at the bottom of Hamilton's philosophy—whether we have an intuitive knowledge of God—was always a commoner question in Germany than in Scotland. Reid, for example, explained our conception of God as something of an inference from our idea of causation. We know ourselves to be the voluntary authors of our own significant actions, and we are led by this knowledge to the inference that an intelligent will has caused the world. The point here is not that Reid's proposal is sound or compelling, but that it is not one of those *a priori* deductive certainties that Mill was at pains to expose.

Even in his recommendation of the psychological method over the introspective method, Mill was far closer to Reid than he was wont to acknowledge. More than any of his immediate disciples, Reid emphasized the *developmental* course followed by all of the mental and moral faculties, and their dependence on a nurturing environment. What he opposed was the radical environmentalism of, say, a Helvetius. Reid's psychology gave a separate place and a special function to instinct, habit, and reason. The burden that each animal carries is that of adjusting its behavior to the demands of the real world. Many of these demands come too early and too suddenly in the life of the animal for learning or deliberation to be of any use. Thus, nature has endowed the creature with a readier source of adaptation—instinct. It is only when we reach the level of rational beings that futures can be proposed and provision made for them; only when we reach the level of moral beings that good and evil can be sensed. Perhaps a perfectly rational being could calculate the personal gains and losses attached to any given action, but again life does not wait until all such calculations are completed. Thus, nature equips the moral being with a sense of *duty* which serves as a kind of shortcut to those behaviors which are in the best interests of the species as a whole. Note, then, that Reid's moral psychology, as with his cognitive psychology, is naturalistic, developmental, Darwinian. Accordingly, his views are either compatible with Mill's or, when they are not, are more in keeping with today's thinking on the same subjects.

The intuitionism usually associated with the names Kant, Fichte, Schelling, and Hegel is, of course, of a radically different nature and is rather less able to defend itself against the sort of criticism developed in Mill's *Examination* and *Logic*. It is less able to defend itself primarily because it proceeds from entirely different first principles and has as its goal a radically different "science." What Mill accomplished—even as he failed to damage the psychology of the Common Sense school—was the nearly surgical removal of Continental intuitionism from mainstream psychological thought in the English-speaking world. There were and have been flickering signs of a revival, but the definite cast of modern psychology has been Millsian for the better part of a century. Mill was a central figure, perhaps the central figure, in the nineteenth-century search for a science of human nature. In following his counsel, modern psychology has flourished in its experimental and quantitative endeavors. Nonetheless, there is the lingering suspicion that something important has been ignored; something uniquely human, uniquely "psychological." As we shall see in the next chapter, what many judge to be missing in today's psychology is just what Mill's analysis successfully cut away.

3. GEORG WILHELM FRIEDRICH HEGEL

Was Ist Aufklärung?

It is both poignant and subtly ironic that Immanuel Kant (1724–1804) would ask and answer this question, "What is Enlightenment?"[1] In his own life and through his extraordinary works, it was Kant who exemplified the very spirit of the Enlightenment. And it was the same Kant whose *Critique of Pure Reason*, at least on a very popular construal, may be said to have extinguished it. Scholars continue to weigh not only what Kant thought and concluded but also the validity and implications of his most important deductions. There is no attempt, therefore, in this section to set down *the* Kantian position nor to provide a close philosophical analysis. The subject here is more the historical than the philosophical Kantian system; the system as it was understood by contemporaries and immediate successors. Every age, and ours is surely no exception, enjoys the privilege of misunderstanding its intellectual heritage in its own unique way. In the more energetic periods, the misunderstandings tend to be systematic, such that the older authorities come to serve either as foils or apologists for the new orthodoxy. To appreciate the point, one need only consider the diverse and even contradictory missions "Aristotelianism" has served during the centuries of Western thought. "Kantianism" has suffered in kind, if not to the same degree, although few major philosophers have been as systematically misunderstood by their own countrymen as was Kant. Thus, in his case, all the libels cannot be dismissed as problems of "translation."

The first chapter took note of several of the more fundamental features of Kant's epistemology, particularly in relation to Hume's skeptical conclusions. But however one may judge the success of Kant's *Critique* as a reply to radical sensationism, it scarcely served the aims of the Enlightenment rationalists. The issues here are extremely complex, and it is only with hestitation that one might attempt to list them briefly. But the central figure of the present chapter is Hegel, whose influence on modern Psychology must be understood within a Kantian context. Accordingly, and with appropriate caveats, this larger context may be summarized thus:

1. If it was Hume's attempt to establish that human knowledge begins and ends with perception and its various residuals, then it was Kant's achievement to show that perception itself proceeds according to necessary principles which cannot themselves be derived from experience. Stated perhaps somewhat cryptically, the point here is that Kant demonstrated that perception arises out of cognition, and not vice versa.

2. On the question of what it is that we may be said to know *about*, Kant and Hume were in substantial agreement, in that both took experience to be the only means by which we can have knowledge of material reality. Kant's "pure categories of the understanding" in this connection refer not to the contents but to the modes or forms of thought. Similarly, the "pure intuitions" of *space* and *time* constitute the necessary framework of all perception but do not supply perception with specific contents. The "pure categories," then, are not evidence against the empiricist's

argument but are the *a priori* boundary conditions within which empirical philosophy must operate.

3. In light of the foregoing, Kant arrives at very nearly the same *phenomenalism* that is the cornerstone of Hume's epistemology. The real world, as it is represented in consciousness, is mediated by the organs and principles of perception. Our knowledge of this world inescapably bears the imprint of these utterly subjective influences. Thus, we can aspire only to a coherent understanding of *phenomena*, forever bereft of a knowledge of "things-in-themselves" (*noumena*). When we attempt to rise above the level of appearances, we discover other ostensible aspects of reality. But these turn out to be merely rational reconstructions of our own experiences, and not some additional knowledge of reality itself. The reconstructions are universally valid since the rational principles on which they are based are an endemic feature of mind. Thus, Kant's thesis does not lead to solipsism or subjective idealism, nor does it confine epistemology to the realm of mere opinion. It does, however, insert an apparently immovable wedge between things as they are and our knowledge of them. Thus humbled, reason contents itself to labor in its own vineyard.

The analysis standing behind these conclusions seemed to put to rest, once and for all, those heady Enlightenment notions of human perfectibility, the limitless reach of reason, the authority of experience, a true science of man and society. Unlike Hume, who at least left room for a scientific psychology, Kant added the terrible injunction according to which a *science of the mind* was a veritable contradiction in terms. Reason, regulated by the categories, cannot stand outside them and inspect itself. Mind, in the very act of self-reflection, is thereby changed. The Enlightenment Achilles never can catch the Kantian tortoise.

It was when Kant turned to the problem and the nature

of morals that he departed so strikingly from the quasi-Humean position that colors his epistemology. Some interpreters have insisted that his moves here were invalid; others have stubbornly argued that he never really made them; still others have insisted that Kant's moral philosophy bears no coherent relation to his epistemology and is therefore quite literally incoherent. Charges of this sort were not uncommon in Kant's own day and they provided impetus for his *Fundamental Principles of the Metaphysic of Morals.*[2] It is in this brief work that Kant adopts a professorial tone and deliberately instructs his readers as to just what he has said and not said. First, what is a "metaphysic" of morals?

1. Rational knowledge is of two sorts, the *material* and the *formal.* The former pertains to objects which are governed by the laws of nature and embraced by the science of physics. Material knowledge is the subject of *natural philosophy* to the extent that it is confined to the laws of physical nature. *Formal* knowledge pertains only to the forms and modes of understanding and is a purely rational enterprise.

2. Material knowledge, to the extent that it is the gift of experience, is the subject of empirical philosophy. *Pure* philosophy, however, addresses those principles which are given *a priori* and which, accordingly, have experience as neither a source nor a justification. When pure philosophy is confined to the entirely formal aspects of these principles, it is *logic.* When, however, it addresses actual objects of the understanding, it is *metaphysic.*

3. Since material knowledge excludes nothing which may be said to be an object of the understanding, philosophy must consider the entire array of phenomena generally included under the heading *freedom.* The division of philosophy concerned with the *laws of freedom* is moral philosophy whose science is *ethics.* Its mission is to provide a *metaphysic of morals* by which the empirical contents of

moral philosophy are explicable in terms of rational (*a priori*) first principles.

We see that what Kant is searching for in the moral domain is something akin to the "pure categories" of the epistemological domain, namely, the conceptually necessary preconditions for knowledge. If it can be said that experience requires the pure intuitions of space and time, what is it that morality requires? As in the case of experience, it will not do to say that whatever morality requires is provided by experience, if only because there cannot be a *moral* dimension to any natural event unless it is imposed by the percipient. Moreover, the distinguishing features of morality are its universally binding nature and the obligation that attaches to moral truths. But nothing in the purely empirical realm shares these features, just as nothing in the purely empirical realm *is* space or *is* time.

If Kant's epistemology is to be somewhat symmetrical with his moral philosophy, therefore, we should expect two conditions to be satisfied: first, that the empirical side of this philosophy will unfold according to determinative rules or laws (here, the "laws of freedom"); second, that these very rules will be *a priori* in that they will be conditional upon nothing of an empirical nature. As moral laws, they will be *imperatives* to action, and as empirically unconditional, they will be *categorical*. As Kant meant this to be understood, *categorical* imperatives are to be distinguished from *hypothetical* imperatives. The universal goal of happiness supplies any number of hypothetical imperatives: If you wish to be happy, you must do X, Y, or Z. Thus, on the hypothesis that happiness is the goal, certain actions become necessary. However,

there is an imperative which commands a certain conduct immediately, without having as its condition any other purpose to be attained by it. This imperative is *categorical*. It concerns not the matter of the action, or its intended result, but its form and the principle of which it is itself a result; and what is essentially good in it consists in the mental disposition, let the consequence be what it may. This imperative may be called that of *morality*. (*Metaphysic of Morals*, p. 33)

The genuinely moral imperative is, as it were, an end in itself and not a warrant to act *in order that*. Its sanction comes from the very form—the very logic—of moral discourse. Stripped of it, an action may be wise, prudent, successful, and pleasurable, but it cannot be *moral*. Equally significant, such an action cannot proceed from an *autonomous will*:

If the will seeks the law which is to determine it *anywhere else* than in the fitness of its maxims to be universal laws of its own dictation ... [it] does not give itself the law, but it is given by the object through its relation to the will. This relation, whether it rests on inclination or on conceptions of reason, only admits of hypothetical imperatives: *I ought to do something because I wish for something else*. (p. 57)

The pivotal phrase in this quotation is "the fitness of its maxims to be universal laws," for this is Kant's sense of the categorical imperative: Act in such a way that you would have the *maxim of your action* installed as a universal law of nature. No end of confusion has been spawned by this sentence and the other equally pithy versions Kant provided in his moral essays. To some—indeed, even to as astute a critic as J. S. Mill—the imperative seems to license any action which the actor would be happy to universalize. Thus, the pyromaniac can claim to act morally once he truly asserts that he would have everyone burning buildings if he could. To others, the imperative seems to strip nearly every action of moral content, since only philosophers pause to rest actions on such universal principles, and they only in their writings.

Again, this is not the place to undertake a conceptual

analysis of the validity of the categorical imperative as a construct. It is important, however, to liberate it from those thickets of confusion and silliness in which it finds itself all too often. The question facing Kant, once his analysis came to require a *categorical* imperative, pertained to the *formal* properties that must be possessed by any moral maxim not tied to some external goal. That is, what is it about a maxim that would guarantee it was morally *right* in and of itself, independently of any external consequence or mental disposition or empirical hypothesis? As an answer to this question, the categorical imperative is (must be) tied to no particular action and particular purpose. It is a *maxim* of action, not an action itself. As it is (must be) utterly indifferent to external conditions and circumstances, its validity is timeless and spaceless. To the extent that it is valid at all, it is *universally* valid. And to the extent that it is an imperative at all, it is *universally imperative*. Thus, if the actor could give it the force of law, *necessarily* he would install it as a universal law of nature. Were he to restrict it to Thursdays, it would not be categorical, but only conditional, hypothetical, and contingent.

But what, then, of our pyromaniac? To the extent that he sets fires for pleasure, his "imperative" is simply not categorical and so it does not figure in the analysis at all. In a perverse way, his "principle" would sanction his own destruction since it would allow other pyromaniacs to set him ablaze, but this is really beside the point. The categorical imperative can be fleshed out with empirical contents and implications, but it is a *formal* principle that enters into the logic of morals. The specific action which an agent claims to be governed by it must bear a logical connection to it. The mere *act* of setting buildings on fire is not a *maxim*, but proceeds from one. To the extent that the controlling maxim is self-regarding, it is not moral at all—it is amoral, perhaps immoral.

It has also struck some writers as something of an oxymoron to refer to the "laws of freedom," for how can an actor be said to be *free* if his conduct is governed by laws? Kant, too, acknowledged that a kind of circularity infected most of the traditional arguments favoring human freedom but he was confident that his was different. The distinction rested, he thought, on the agent as the efficient cause of his own actions and on the moral imperative as something of the "final cause" or the *end* of those same actions. Each person is able to adopt these two perspectives, recognizing himself as the author of his own conduct but recognizing further that it must proceed according to the provisions of the moral law.

Here also Kant falls back on the epistemological arguments of the *Critique* for illustrations. The thoughtful percipient, for example, comes to be aware of the fact that there is a difference between those *appearances* which are the gift of perception and the actual things (*things in themselves*) of which perception provides the appearances. Equipped with this distinction, we thus become aware of two realms—the realm of sense and the realm of understanding. The former, filled with appearances, is a realm in which different observers may have radically different perceptions of the same thing and in which the same observer's impressions may change abruptly even as he regards the same object. But in the realm of understanding, there is the recognition of a permanence and sameness which, though empirically inaccessible to us, must be posited if only to give meaning to the world of sense. The same is the case in the matter of one's knowledge of self. The *ego* comes to be known in two ways or as two different entities. There is first the *empirical* self, the passive entity receiving stimulation both from the external environment and the internal senses. However, for these utterly empirical transactions to occur, the observer must necessarily suppose something else as their basis, namely, his *ego*, whatever its characteristics in itself may be. Thus in respect to mere perception and receptivity of sensations he must reckon himself as belonging to the *world of sense*; but in respect of whatever there may be of pure activity in him (that which reaches consciousness immediately and not through affecting the senses), he must reckon himself as belonging to the *intellectual world*, of which however he has no further knowledge. (*Metaphysic of Morals*, p. 85)

In coming to appreciate himself as something apart from not only the material world of objects but also the subjective world of appearances, one discovers the faculty of *reason*, which is more fundamental than even the understanding. The latter (*Verstand*), in not going beyond the distinction between appearances and noumenal existence, requires the senses and their impressions just to make this distinction. But reason (*Vernunft*) can stand apart even from understanding, and respect itself as a pure (i.e., nonempirical), spontaneous (i.e., unconditional) activity. The understanding is confined to imposing rules of organization on the data of perception such that the elements of consciousness are united and, as it were, played out on a constant screen. The rules governing the entire procedure are the *pure categories of the understanding* combined with space and time, the categories of "pure intuition." But only reason can distinguish the world of sense from the world of understanding and can thereby transcend those conceptions that depend upon sensibility of any kind. Reason sets limits on the understanding itself.

Given the nature and function of sense, understanding, and reason, a rational being may regard himself from two radically different perspectives. As a sensible being who, to this extent, belongs to the world of sense, he is an entirely natural being controlled by the laws of nature in that his every perception is caused according to a natural law. But viewed as a rational being, he becomes part of the *intelligible* world which is grounded not in the causal laws of nature, but in reason itself and in reason alone. Once this second view is adopted and the agent recognizes his essential independence as regards nature's causal laws, it becomes conceptually necessary to take *freedom* as (paradoxically) the "cause" of his will: "For now we see that when we conceive ourselves as free we transfer ourselves into the world of understanding as members of it, and recognize the autonomy of the will with its consequence, morality; whereas, if we conceive ourselves as under obligation, we consider ourselves as belonging to the world of sense" (*Metaphysic of Morals*, p. 70).

Note the consistency here between this analysis and the categorical imperative. In the world of sense, we are completely determined by the laws of nature and our actions are regulated by an external principle. Thus, only *hypothetical* imperatives are possible. In the world of reason, however, only reason is determinative. Thus liberated from the laws of sensible nature, we are *free* and therefore able to be moral:

And thus what makes categorical imperatives possible is this— that the idea of freedom makes me a member of an intelligible world, in consequence of which, if I were nothing else, all my actions *would* always conform to the autonomy of the will; but as I at the same time intuit myself as a member of the world of sense, they *ought* so to conform, and this *categorical* "ought" implies a synthetic a priori proposition. (p. 71).

There is a perfect symmetry here between, on the one hand, the "pure intuitions" of time and space as the precondition for experience and, on the other hand, the categorical "ought" as the precondition by which the will is affected by such sensible entities as desire. The pure categories of the understanding, though empirically empty, establish the very form of all empirical knowledge. Without these categories, the natural world—even as a world of appearances—would be incomprehensible. Through the categories, it is possible to frame *a priori* synthetic propositions (e.g., in every causal series, one event precedes the other). Similarly, through the categorical imperative it becomes possible to frame *a priori* synthetic propositions in the moral domain (e.g., in every setting in which the will is impelled by desire, there is a course of action that *ought* to be taken).

Kant was constrained to remind his critics that there is nothing contradictory in ascribing freedom to the will and at the same time speaking of the "laws" of freedom. Indeed, there is nothing contradictory in speaking of the causal determination of appearances and, at the same time, of the essentially undetermined character of those "things in themselves" which we know of only through appearances. Our actions, to the extent that we are located in the purely sensible world, are governed by purely natural laws and these give effect to desire, appetite, emotion, and related instinctive compulsions. As rational beings, however, we are aware of entirely different principles of action, completely independent of feeling or of experience of any kind; dependent only on the determinations of reason. This is the respect in which we (our wills) are *free* and in which we can be said to be autonomous. But to be autonomous is not to be aimless or destitute of purposes. In the intelligible realm, the will's *moral* purpose is governed by the categorical imperative. Only a will liberated from the forces and appearances of the empirical world can be said to be free, and only a will rationally directed by the categorical imperative can be said to be moral.

But what, then, is to be said to those who ask for *proof* of this moral freedom? In the ordinary sense of the term, proof refers to empirical confirmation, but it is precisely because the moral will functions in the purely intelligible world of reason—precisely because as a moral will it is independent of all empirical determinations—that "proof" is impossible. As Kant put it, "where determination according to laws of nature ceases, there all *explanation* ceases also" (*Metaphysic of Morals*, p. 76). Reason, by which the idea of freedom comes into being, cannot *explain* itself precisely because it is not completely determined by the laws of nature.

Post-Kantians, Neo-Kantians, Anti-Kantians

Great philosophical works, apart from their intellectual features, have the suggestive powers of great works of art. They are not only informative but evocative. Kant's critical philosophy attracted disciples and patrons by the score, each finding something in it that others—including Kant—seemed to have missed. It also attracted wary and even hostile appraisers, each of whom was to discover that fatal flaw rendering the entire production an elaborate contradiction. Thus, in the decade following Kant's death (1804), we find any number of agile minds devoted either to "completing" his philosophy, or explaining it better than he did, or burying it completely. It is out of this din of metaphysical excitement that Romantic idealism arose. It is out of this same din that one man's call to order would be heard by the legions we now call "Hegelians" united under the banner of the Absolute Idea. With the possible exception of Spinoza's, Hegel's is the most difficult philosophy to summarize, let alone analyze. Unlike Spinoza, a most solitary thinker largely ignored by and indifferent to the main currents of thought in his own day, Hegel was at the very center of things and self-consciously part of the modern philosophical traditions of the German world. It is useful to pause here to note several of the highlights of that world and to review social and political forces touched on in the first chapter.

Kant's "Was Ist Aufklärung?" was something of a quiet celebration of the spirit of the French and American revolutions. He died before the Napoleonization of Europe but he lived long enough to perceive the radically different possibilities held forth by popular democracies and hereditary monarchies. As with so many German intellectuals in the years following 1789, he tended to overestimate the virtues and look past the vices of the French "experiment." His loyalty to the spirit of Enlightenment surfaces most visibly in this historically uncritical estimation of the consequences of democratic modes of governance; his somewhat naively Rousseauean conviction that the Plain Man's collective genius can prosper only when liberated from the burdens of traditional authority. It is this political outlook that is both justified by and virtually deducible from his moral philosophy. Man's freedom must be posited if there is to be morality in the world. By logical implication, therefore, whatever opposes this freedom necessarily constricts the moral realm.

With the exception of the great Johann Wolfgang von Goethe (1749–1832), all the patrons of German Romanticism either overtly applauded the political upheavals in France and America or at least saw in them the seeds of a better world. At little Weimar and its University of Jena, those twin centers of German high culture, *freedom* was the unifying concept able to draw together poets, metaphysicians, sculptors, theologians, and even a statesman or two. Even Goethe, who could stand aloof from the more mechanical political deductions served up by his friends and disciples, would come to complete his aged Faust as a being now in full possession of a personal, moral will; an utterly free and independent being able to ignore the rude seductions of fame and sensuality. Goethe would live long enough to confront the now (1813) tyrannical Napoleon and would still find in him a defender of culture, a patron of creative genius. What Napoleon found in Goethe is fully captured by the ejaculatory *Voilà un homme!* In some ways, Goethe's own long life (1749–1832) reflects the larger saga of German intellectual development from Kantian rationalism to its culmination in Hegelianism. In his early works, Goethe is found reviving and even mimicking classical themes and literary modes coupled with beautiful but somewhat provincial odes inspired by folklore. Their artisitic merit aside, these earliest efforts reflect the introspective and retreating features of German culture even as Professor Kant was composing his universal philosophy. It is true that works such as *Kleine Blumen, kleine Blätter* may be said to have inaugurated the modern period of German lyric poetry and that his *Die Leiden des Junges Werthers* (1774) brought tears to the eyes of an entire people. But in both it is Goethe's own romantic dilemmas that provide not only the impetus but the explanation. The point is not, of course, that the suicidal young Werther is actually young Goethe whose love for Charlotte Buff was unrequited. It is that Goethe at this point—this period of *Sturm und Drang*—cannot move beyond the boundaries of his own feelings, cannot stand apart from the parade of sentiments and sensations marking the contours of his own life.

But soon we meet the Goethe of *Iphigenie auf Tauris* (1787) and *Torquato Tasso* (1790), the "Renaissance" Goethe who will discover Truth in the classical simplicity of Greek rationalism; a Goethe who looks beyond self and culture if only to comprehend self and culture. And then there is the Goethe of the Italian journeys, returning to a German world he has somehow outgrown or forgotten. It is the Goethe of the final *Faust*, however, who knows himself only through the expressions of his own will and intuition, and who realizes that human life is part of a far grander abstraction concealed by a mind divine. It is in the *Midnight* of part 2, Act 5 that Faust confronts his last test, this time at the hands of four gray ladies: Want, Blame, Need, and

Care. The first three rush off to meet their brother, Death,
leaving Faust alone with Care. He commands her to depart
but before she leaves she casts her breath on Faust and
makes him blind.

> Deeper and deeper night is round me sinking;
> Only within me shines a radiant light.
> I haste to realize, in act, my thinking;
> The master's word, that only giveth might.
> Up, vassals, from your couch! my project bold,
> Grandly completed, now let all behold!
> Seize ye your tools; your spades, your shovels ply;
> The work laid down, accomplish instantly!
> Strict rule, swift diligence—these twain
> The richest recompense obtain.
> Completion of the greatest work demands
> One guiding spirit for a thousand hands.[3]

Goethe's pre-Darwinian hypotheses regarding morphological evolution as well as his studies and theories of color
vision give him a minor but not insignificant place in the
history of science. He served also as an officer of State
and as a patriarchal inspiration to three generations of
artists throughout the European world. Nonetheless, his
place in the history of philosophical and psychological
thought is more contextual than central. To him and to
his friend and collaborator, Schiller, goes much of the
credit for awakening scholars to the problem of *esthetics*
and for infusing German philosophical writing with a
conscientious regard for what is creative and dynamic in
the human psyche. In the Goethean presence, every important philosophical production in the Germany of the
nineteenth century would reserve a special place for art.
Indeed, Romanticism itself is to be understood as the
unique melding of esthetics and metaphysics. In large
measure, it was Goethe who personally and symbolically
represented this development and who stood as "one

guiding spirit for a thousand hands." Faust had offered nothing less than his very soul if Mephistopheles could create in him a happiness that would have him bid time to stand still. In the end, it is only the prospect of "a free people standing on free soil" that excites Faust to stop time in its course. Thus he surrenders his soul to the devil in return for a human liberty which he personally will not live to enjoy.

Accountable only to his own muse, Goethe was not obliged to confront the ageless questions with philosophical formality and logical rigor. The metaphysician who, in his heart, knew that Goethe was "right" still faced that dark and yawning chasm Kant had placed between appearance and reality. To the extent that *freedom* was the central idea of nineteenth-century German philosophy, the problem of freedom was its *quaestio vexata*. If it were no more than one of the trappings of human vanity—a condition sought only for the hedonic pleasures it provides—it can have no moral standing whatever. Similarly, if it is grounded in nothing firmer than the collective opinion of an age, it is properly treated under the heading of fashion, not philosophy. In distinguishing between *laws of nature* and *laws of freedom* Kant had attempted to extricate morals from materialism while preserving those rational foundations necessary if morals were to amount to something more than mere sentimentalism. Disappointment with his solution came from more than one direction. For some, such as Schelling (see below), Kant's two-world view was incompatible with the unity of reality and it became necessary to absorb the person, *das Ich*, into Nature. Others, and especially Fichte (see below) faulted Kant for not accepting the radical Idealism his own philosophy had established. We see, then, that at the most fundamental level the critics who arrayed themselves against Kant's metaphysics were striving to eliminate dualism and to establish a monistic science of man. The basic tension was the old one—the tension between nature and spirit. If Hegel's mission can be summarized in a sentence, we might say that he completely relaxed the tension by imposing a strict *identity-relation* on the two. Nature and Spirit are but two aspects, two manifestations, of the Absolute realizing itself in history. But for the proper introduction to this complex notion, we must turn first to Schelling and Fichte.

Friedrich Wilhelm Joseph von Schelling (1775–1854) is one of those improbable figures who were nonetheless quite at home at Jena and in the Weimar of the 1790s and early 1800s. As a theology student (1790–92) at Tubingen, he could number among his friends and classmates the passionate poet Hölderlin and that future saint of logic, Hegel. By the time he was twenty-three, he was awarded a professorship at Jena, thereby establishing himself as a "prodigy" for the rest of his life.

Jena's resident genius was Johann Gottlieb Fichte (1762–1814). It was Fichte's *Critique of All Revelation*, anonymously published and thought by many to have been written by Kant, that had first won a post at Jena for Fichte.[4] And it was his political and religious lecturing that lost him this same post in 1799, just a year after Schelling had joined the faculty. Of the two, Fichte was the more studiously and officially philosophical and by far the more influential during the first half of the nineteenth century. But as contemporaries, Schelling and Fichte may be said to have divided the world of German thought almost singlehandedly into disciples of Nature and disciples of Spirit.

In his *Critique of All Revelation* (1794) Fichte had given

the religious impulse the same sort of status Kant's meta-physics had reserved for space and time. A "spiritual imperative," arising from man's very moral nature, was taken to be the foundation of the sense of duty. The work anticipated a number of themes which would come to dominate Fichte's later essays, particularly the Berlin lectures of 1806 published as *The Characteristics of the Present Age* and *The Way Towards the Blessed Life; or, The Doctrine of Religion*.[5] It is in the first of these that we learn of the World Plan: "the End of the Life of Mankind on Earth is this—that in this Life they may order all their relations with FREEDOM according to REASON" (*Characteristics*, p. 5).

Unlike Kant, who took the rational and cognitive attributes of mind as the universally distributed "givens" of human nature, Fichte grounded them in the process of historical and cultural evolution. In the earliest stages, the behavior of man was rational but the participants were not conscious of their own rationality. Rather, reason operated as a *natural instinct* to which the actor was more or less subservient. Within such undeveloped communities, however, the rational impulse was especially great among the few who thereupon attempted to regulate the affairs of the many. Only through such impositions by an external authority could the individual person have been awakened to the *idea of freedom*. Thus, from an epoch of instinctual rationality man is driven toward the *epoch of freedom*. But the march from instinctuality to tyranny and thence to freedom leaves man in a "State of completed Sinfulness" (*Characteristics*, p. 9) wherein expressions of personal liberty amount to nothing more than licentiousness. To rein in these libertine excesses, society attempts to establish the connections between freedom and reason through a system of justifications. The fourth epoch is thereby produced. Its defining spirit is constitutionalism and legalism. Yet, the tone of life is set by mere proscriptions whose goal is to protect private interests and prevent public nuisance. Society is once again orderly, rational, and free but the moral side of human life remains incomplete and incompletely expressed. Only in the highest state, *the State of completed Justification and Sanctification,* does *reason as knowledge* give way to *reason as art.* In this epoch, goodness is secured not by laws and punishments but as the fruit of a free and rational people for whom goodness is natural. Where constitutionalism is the spirit of the fourth stage, love identifies the fifth. Selfishness and personalism are superceded by altruism, by an abandonment of one's purely personal identity and by the soul's surrendering itself to the human race as a whole. Fichte observed that

an Age whose whole theory of the world is exhausted in the means of personal existence should value Experience as the only possible source of knowledge, since those very means, which are all that such an Age can or will recognize, are only to be recognized through Experience. . . . [But] in *mere* Experience there is contained nothing but the means of physical preservation. (*Characteristics,* p. 27)

What Fichte opposed to experience is *thought* which he took to be "the substantial form of the True Life" (*Blessed Life,* p. 306). Thought, he said, "creates its own purely spiritual object absolutely from itself, without the aid of outward sense, and without any reference whatever to outward sense" (*Blessed Life,* p. 336). Pure thought, pure abstraction gives rise to cognition (*Wissen*), the essence of absolute being. In its immateriality it is indestructible and in its universalization it is Truth.

So long as man cherishes the desire of being himself something, God comes not to him, for no man can become God. But so soon as he renounces himself sincerely, wholly, and radically, then God alone remains. . . . Man can create no God for himself; but he can renounce himself as the proper negation—and then he is wholly absorbed in God. (*Blessed Life,* p. 438)

It was Fichte who gave currency to that now famous triad, *thesis–antithesis–synthesis.* Note the need, in his evolutionary theory of morals, for an external ruling authority as the antithetical ground upon which the idea (thesis) of freedom becomes recognized. Note, too, how the "state of completed sinfulness" is the logically necessary precursor of a constitutional state: proscriptions are conceptually meaningless unless irrational tendencies are posited. At the most fundamental level, spirit posits itself as Ego but achieves this identity only by positing that non-Ego which the metaphysicians mistakenly take to be an independent and material external world. Fichte eliminates the duality by taking this same (allegedly) external world and recasting it as a logical construction; i.e., as the positing by consciousness of non-Ego. The process is possible, however, only for a being that *feels* and is affected by consciousness. Where the feeling (love) is arrested by sensation, consciousness can rise no higher than sensuality. Where it is commanded by such moral imperatives as those prominent in Kant's system, consciousness rises only to the level of Stoicism and the love of order. It is only when *religious* feeling dominates consciousness that a now free being joyfully acts in the interest of the human race. In this denial of the merely personal Ego, consciousness—Spirit— is loosed from the here and now. The act of negation is the act of creation; the dissolution of self is the only alternative to death.

Fichte's own life, like his philosophy, endured shifting fortunes due in part to ambiguities and seeming contradictions. Viewed in a certain light, his "theology" is Spinozistic pantheism and his politics is, if not socialistic, at least antimonarchial. He could not, then, have expected to please either Church or State through his popular and influential lectures. To this liability he added a morally rigorous and Spartan condemnation of the sorts of lives being lived by most of his students, whose support Fichte also finally lost. And, lest he be fully redeemed by posterity, he saw to it that his oft-quoted and generally misunderstood *Reden an die Deutsche Nation* (1808) would be worded in such a way as to allow him to be cast as a nineteenth-century Nazi! In this "Address to the German Nation" Fichte sought only to steel his countrymen against Napoleon, to summon them to their own traditions, and awaken them to those duties that cannot be defeated. Read in the shadows of a post-Hitler world, the essay has damaged the standing of as un-Hitlerian a scholar as philosophy is wont to produce. He did, indeed, speak of the "greater destiny" of the German people in his *Reden*, but he was quite specific as to what this destiny entailed: "to found an empire of mind and reason—to destroy the domination of rude physical power as the ruler of the world."[6]

It is against this Fichtean background that Schelling's principal ideas are most easily comprehended. They serve as something of an antithesis to Fichte's thesis, and as the prologue to Hegel's synthesis. It is a commonplace, originated by Hegel himself, to emphasize the many twists and turns taken by Schelling's thought during his long life. His earliest work for example, is utterly loyal to his admired colleague, Fichte, whose philosophy he then begins to abandon in his *Ideen zu einer Philosophie der Natur* (1797).[7] Yet, within a decade of having argued for the essential identity of reason and nature—for reason as the absolute principle from which both nature and mind arise—he will turn to the *esthetic impulse* as the ultimate source of creation (*The Philosophy of Art*, 1807).[8] To the academically rigorous Hegel, Schelling's awkward retreats and advances suggested only a naive comprehension of the issues: "Schelling carried on his philosophic education before the public, signalling each fresh stage of his advance with a new treatise."[9] But seen at a greater distance, Schelling appears as the quintessential Romantic of the nineteenth century who will find himself and the meaning of his life only in those universal themes of philosophy, morality, and art— and who will find these themes only by searching passionately within himself. For the Romantic, esthetics and morality are not subjects to be learned or systems to be fabricated. They are different chapters of an autobiography which the author must read if he is to live his own life.

Setting aside the most Fichtean stage of Schelling's thinking, we may say that his originality begins in that part of his *Philosophy of Nature* which rejects Fichte's *subjective idealism* and takes the material world as given. Of course, had he done no more than reassert the existence of matter there would be no reason to sketch out his arguments. What he recognized, and what traditional materialism generally ignores or trivializes, is that the realm of spirit (mind) and the realm of nature (matter), though utterly unlike each other in their predications, quite obviously enter into all sorts of relations. For these to occur, there must be a principle of correlation. Schelling finds this in *force*, the basis of all attractive and repulsive phenomena in nature and, apparently, the basis upon which the internal motions of perception and will take place. Through the concept of force, Schelling sought to establish a purely natural foundation for the Kantian intuitions of time and space. More importantly, it was through this same concept that Schelling argued for a common origin of nature and spirit: attractive force as the principle of the *objective* world and repulsive force as the principle of the *subjective* world. He did not intend this to be taken metaphorically but factually. The objective world of nature arises out of the attractions exerted on each other by nature and spirit, whereas the subjective world arises out of an inner life kept free by repelling externalities. Soon, in his *Erster Entwurf eines Systems der Naturphilosophie* (1797) he will speak of force as *pure activity*, the inexhaustable and creative element of the world of spirit-nature. The Ego, when it regards not objects and their attributes, but the *process of regarding*, is engaged in pure activity. In this way it can know itself as it really is, i.e., *noumenally*. Thus regarded, spirit is limitless in time and space. However, when consciousness brings focus to external things—when sensation takes place—there is the immediate recognition of a limit, a bounded and confined self now making contact with temporally and spatially confined objects. But just as the universe of matter is no less infinite for possessing particulars, so too the universe of spirit is no less infinite for making contact with them. Moreover, sensation is scarcely a passive process governed by the physical laws of efficient causation. Sensation occurs only when the Ego posits non-Ego; when it distinguishes between self and nonself. In this act of self-limitation by the Ego, sensation arises. Properly understood, therefore, sensation is an *act*, not a mere response.

As with Fichte, Schelling understood reality as an unfolding, a process of becoming. The act of perceiving the external world and thus arriving at the concept of self-limitation is an act of *reflection*; and when this same process is turned upon the internal sensations, it is the source of the will. But the emphasis throughout is not on mental "faculties" or sharply bounded categories such as sensation, volition, and intellect. Rather, the emphasis is on *process*— the dynamic interactions between nature and intelligence as both strive to approximate reason, the ultimate source of both. Indeed, as the later Schelling would insist, it is precisely because both originate in reason that they are to be understood as *absolute identities*. It is, however, only in art that the essential identity is apprehended and where freedom and necessity coalesce:

> The fundamental character of every genuine work of art is its unconscious infinity. The artist builds better than he knows, and by a divine instinct expresses that which is but half revealed to himself, and which is not capable of being grasped by the finite understanding. . . . This unity of necessity and freedom is the source of beauty which, as the realization of the infinite in the finite, is the fundamental character of artistic products.[10]

The wedge Kant had placed between the natural realm of causal determinacy and the human realm of moral autonomy was removed in Schelling's Esthetics. In its place a mystic identity was installed which canceled the opposition between freedom and necessity and replaced it with an evolutionary harmony grounded in the Absolute and revealed only in Art. Years later and firmly in Schelling's patrimony, Oscar Wilde would write, "Art finds her own perfection within, and not outside of, herself. . . . Hers are the forms more real than living man, and hers the great archetypes of which things that have no existence are but unfinished copies. Nature has, in her eyes, no law, no uniformity."[11]

Hegel and the Dialectic

In the introduction to his translation of *The Encyclopedia of Philosophy* G. E. Mueller speaks of Hegel as "the world's worst stylist" and cautions readers to remain alert to the nuances, the utterly eccentric meanings routinely assigned by Hegel to otherwise everyday words.[12] Thirty years earlier, in commenting on their translation of Hegel's *Science of Logic*, Johnston and Struthers—who found it necessary to include a glossary with their translation—complain of the author's "notorious 'Himalayan' severity and the strangeness of phraseology."[13] At about the same time, J. B. Baillie would begin his translation of *The Phenomenology of Mind* by noting "a profundity which is often dark as well as deep" in this first of Hegel's truly original works.[14] These are phrases taken from scholars and serious students of Hegelian thought, from those willing and able to dedicate the energy of years to essays that remain in many places inscrutable in any language. To leave the circle of scholarship devoted to Hegel and to venture into more "neutral" territory is to discover those calumnies and condemnations now piled so high as to be a veritable fortress of anti-Hegel literature. On some accounts, the world wars of the present century are to be understood as the conflict between "left" and "right" Hegelians. More than one eminent theologian has had the tenets of Christianity confirmed by Hegel's "system," and more than one celebrated atheist has been similarly fortified by the same. Bertrand Russell would grant that Hegel was "the hardest to understand of all the great philosophers" while in the same breath insisting that "almost all of Hegel's doctrines are false."[15] To the extent that philosophers are ever willing to admit of allegiance to a school, Hegel can probably claim a greater number of adherents than even Aristotle. His philosophy entails religion without requiring it. It can face up to modern science and even absorb it. It can turn the contradictions of Marxism into a metaphysics. It can install freedom as an unqualified good as it simultaneously stands in defense of the State's hegemonous moral authority. Is this all plausible? Is it even possible? Perhaps Hegel was speaking of his own philosophy when he wrote, "To judge philosophy one must participate in it as it progresses and unfolds itself."[16] The progress and unfolding of Hegelian thought are most discernible in his *Encyclopedia* (1817), the outline of his lectures "on the entire scope of philosophy."[17]

Hegel begins his *Encyclopedia* with a distinction between philosophy and all other branches of inquiry, specifically the natural sciences. The latter take for granted the existence of those entities comprising their subject matter and proceed to give them names and classifications. As natural sciences, it is quite understandable that they pay little attention to the great *philosophical* leap that must be taken to get from the objects of inquiry to that conceptual domain in which names and classifications obtain their meaning. But it is precisely the question of conceptual validity with which philosophy must be concerned.

The uniqueness of philosophy does not end here however. The natural sciences deploy more or less settled methods in an attempt to settle matters of fact. In philosophy the method of inquiry is just what stands as the source of continuing controversy. Its mission or practical role is that of mediator: it provides the critical foundation on which the objective subjects of scientific curiosity may be assimilated by the conceptual processes of the knowing observer. At the same time, it is its own subject in that its internal work is devoted to the criticism of each of its tentatively adopted methods of criticism. Taking these two features, Hegel offers a characteristically cryptic summary: "This necessary unity of immediacy and mediation is the *Concept* [*Begriff*] of philosophy" (*Encyclopedia*, sec. 3).

Translating *Begriff* as *idea*, we may paraphrase this to mean the following: At root, the very *idea* of philosophy is the simultaneous interpretation and criticism of all knowledge-claims, including those made by philosophy itself. In this regard, the discipline of philosophy is in much the same position as that occupied by the individual person who, from the facts and impressions of the (immediate) moment, must rise in his comprehension to the level of abstract principles. Here the person *mediates* between what is immediate and what is timeless or *absolute*. Those, like "Newton and the British empiricists," who are content to record and systematically classify their impressions, may develop the natural sciences, but they cannot be said to be philosophical (sec. 3). In reasoning about these merely finite things, such natural scientists ignore the problem of reason itself and must confine their understanding to the narrow realm of transitory happenings. Philosophy, on the other hand, must comprehend (encircle) *the totality of being—being* aware of itself.

This, too, is an extremely complex notion, surely "Himalayan" in its severity. What Hegel seems to be getting at with a phrase such as "Being aware of itself" is the gulf that separates specific things—singular and spatio-temporally limited objects of perception—from that unbounded consciousness that notes them. When he says, then, that "All Being is *Comprehensiveness conscious of itself*" (sec. 5), he is laying the foundation for the claim that *being* and *mind* are synonymous. But is this no more than another form of solipsism or subjective idealism? "It is not an idealism in which the content of knowledge is . . . subjective, imprisoning its products within the subject. . . . The contrast of idealistic and realistic philosophy is of no importance; such expressions as subjectivity and objectivity, reality and ideality, are simply bare abstractions" (sec. 5). The word G. E. Mueller translates as comprehensiveness (*Vernunft*) is, of course, commonly rendered as *reason* but it is not to be thought of as the "pure reason" (*reinen Vernunft*) of Kant's famous *Critique*. If Hegel is to be taken as saying that *all Being is Reason conscious of itself* we must understand *Vernunft* as referring to the historical progress of mind throughout the epochs of speculative discourse. *Vernunft*, then, is not pure reason but the *act of comprehending* which, in historical measure, is the life of thought.

This brings us to Hegel's *dialectic* which is the foundation (the "ground") upon which thought acquires logical truth or reality:

There are three aspects in every thought which is logically real or true: The abstract or rational form, which says what something is; the dialectical negation which says what something is not; the speculative—concrete comprehension: A is also that which it is not, A is non-A. These three aspects . . . belong to every philosophical Concept. Every Concept is rational, is abstractly opposed to another, and is united in comprehension together with its opposites. *This is the definition of dialectic.* (sec. 13)

Here we have a passage that is as dark as it is deep; one that promises to preserve Hegel's place among the world's worst stylists. Still, it can be lightened without being made shallow. It defines every (let us say) valid thought as a composite made up of a thesis (This is an orange), an implicit discrimination (It is not an apple, a pear, etc.), and a very complicated form of *apparent* contradiction that is unavoidable if we are to have conceptions of any kind. To call an object an orange is to identify a particular thing with a universal class—with a universal. The universal derives its meaning from the particular, and the particular can be thought of (as opposed to being merely perceived) only as an instance of the universal. Thus, this *orange* is A (that is, this is ORANGE) but *this* orange is not A. Note, however, that "This does not mean that 'nothing is.' To suppose this is to confuse thoughtlessly the dialectical-ontological negation with a formal-logical self-contradiction" (sec. 16). Indeed, it is just through such a distinction between dialectical and purely formal reasoning that *Vernunft* becomes conscious of itself. In the *abstract* domain of formal logic, A ≠ A is simply unintelligible. But in the *concrete* domain of every thought that is about the real world, just this sort of dialectical-ontological negation is an essential feature of each cognitive event.

Hegel's claim here is not against formal logic, nor is it that the ontologically empty rules of this logic are inapplicable to the real world. That is, he is not asserting that A ≠ A applies only to abstractions which make no contact with reality. Rather, he is advancing a theory of cognition and setting forth what he takes to be the three necessary and sufficient conditions for *thought about reality*. Such thought must be thought about something. But thought about something is necessarily (if only implicitly) thought about non-something: One can only think of X by distinguishing it from non-X. But to think of *this* X is to place a particular in identity-relation with a universal. It is, as it were, to assert an X = X while knowing that the negation is nonetheless true. This third element of thought, which Hegel calls the "speculative comprehension," *unites opposites* and thereby becomes aware of and gives reality to "all essential opposites in the world itself" (sec. 16). In formal logic, reason is equipped with abstract rules but the *form* of reasoning is divorced from the *content*. A = A, no matter what A stands for and even if there is no A in existence; note that A = A implies −A = −A. But dialectical reasoning is reasoning about real existents which become accessible to thought only through the dialectical-ontological negation. There can be no *synthesis* with *antithesis*. Unlike the "pure reason" of rationalism, dialectical reasoning—what Hegel calls dialectical movement—recognizes the artificiality (the utter abstraction) entailed by assertions of singular or one-sided determination. An apple is not an apple independently of all the things it is not. Its ontological status is logically tied to negation. Historically, reason has recognized all this, if only darkly, but has employed it merely in the service of a cranky skepticism that doubts the validity of every thought. Dialectical reasoning, however, in regarding skepticism itself as but a moment in reason's long struggle with itself, moves to a higher plane, the plane of self-awareness. And this, Hegel proposes, is the plane of all being.

We have seen that the Concept (*Begriff*) of philosophy is the unity, the uniting of the mediate and the immediate, and we have also seen that the latter is what constitutes the subject matter of the natural sciences and daily experience. In light of these propositions, we can now make sense of still another of Hegel's "Himalayan" assertions: "As Concept, reality becomes conscious of itself in the thinking mind" (sec. 17). The dialectical ontology requires that real existence be reserved to those entities that are thinkable. All logically true thought is the melding of assertion, negation, and the unification of opposites. Reality, on this construction, just *is* this process by which the Concept becomes aware of itself. This reality is not confined to the thinking mind, however, since mind itself apprehends the *immediate*. In other words, Hegel's "reality" is no less rich or varied or populous than the reality of common sense or ordinary science. Instead, something is added to this reality by philosophy. What is added—and what thereby makes reality *real*—is the Concept. On the purely abstract plane of the logic of rationalism, we discover anticipations of this, but this is a logic without real content. The dialectic, however, provides the actual *concrete universals* of the real world. "On its highest plane philosophy contemplates the Concept of all Concepts, the eternal Absolute—the God who is worshipped in religion. Philosophy then culminates in speculative theology" (sec. 17).

Here we have that nemesis, the Absolute, that was to become Mill's chief target as he set out to dismantle *intuitionism*. Can anything more be said of this Absolute, or must it be treated as one of those ancient Hebrew unutterables against which every attribution stands as a slander? Put another way, is this Absolute simply that old-time religion now made fashionable by some daring metaphysical tailoring? To answer these questions it becomes necessary to distinguish between the sorts of attributions that are proper to *objects* and those that are proper only to *concepts*. More specifically, traditional metaphysics (including and especially that defended by Kant) took the attributional categories of material things as ultimate and, in failing to discover the Absolute through these categories, wrongly and dogmatically concluded that the Absolute was either unknowable or nonexistent.

The logical bedrock of traditional metaphysics is provided by the law of contradiction and the law of the excluded middle. Hegel argues, however, that these principles are valid only for the *finite* and have no relevance to "absolute totalities" (sec. 21). They are logical principles but are not *ontological*. Nor do they acquire validity when supplemented by the tenets of empiricism. The rationalists missed the point when they tried to embrace Absolute reality with the limited equipment of the categories of the finite. The empiricists missed the point when they stripped reality of the *mediate* and left it as a bare and woefully incomplete ensemble of (*immediate*) sensations. Kant was on the right track but did not go far enough. His "critical philosophy" correctly and decisively demonstrated the limits of the rational categories and successfully confined them to the realm of possible experience. Without the data of perception, these categories are simply "there"—contentless and unrequited. But, insists Hegel, Kant should have gone on to examine this very exercise of reason criticizing itself and thus becoming aware of itself. Had he gone this extra distance, he would no doubt have come to see that his vaunted "pure categories of the understanding" are themselves the fruit of dialectic. Not having seen this, Kant was content to partition the universe into *things-in-themselves* (of which we are forever and necessarily ignorant) and subjective *appearances* regulated by the formal categories of the understanding. But,

It is of the uttermost inconsistency to admit that reason is confined to know appearances only, and at the same time to contend that this is the only true knowledge we have. A deficient, incomplete, limited mode of knowledge can only be known in comparison with the really-present Idea of a complete whole. It is sheer unconsciousness not to realize that by this dialectical negation of one side, which thereby is known to be finite and limited, a true knowledge is practiced. It proves the reality and the presence of an unlimited Infinite. (sec. 34)

The temptation, too often unresisted by Hegel's critics, is to dismiss passages such as this as evidence of Hegel's failure to distinguish between knowing *that* and knowing *what*. Thus the critic will argue that Kant's analysis established three epistemological-ontological principles: First, that human knowledge is confined to the sensible as this is regulated by the *a priori* categories of the understanding; second, (and "dialectically") that this implies *that* there is a causally antecedent realm of things-in-themselves of which we know only the appearances; third, that this logical implication in no way furnishes us with a comprehension of *what* the things-in-themselves are or are like. But on Hegel's account, and with the full debt to Kant acknowledged, these very propositions are part of the dialetical-ontological process. To say that there is an X behind every X-caused appearance is, among other considerations, to say that X is nonappearance and that X-appearance is non-X. These, however, are the utterances of Mind as it unites the mediate and the immediate and are, as such, moments in the history of the Concept.

To explore further Hegel's notion of the Absolute it is necessary to differentiate between *pure* thought and *representational* thought. The latter is the common thought about objects which invariably and incorrectly identifies *being* solely in terms of specific attributes. Only through the dialectical negation, however, does it become obvious that being qua being is identical across all possible existents and therefore cannot be the attribute of any specific object (sec. 39). As Hegel says, "The identity of Being in all beings precludes its identity with any or only one of them. The Absolute negates all things that are not absolute. It is their nothing" (sec. 40). And through this analysis Hegel is in a position to deduce several otherwise delphic conclusions; namely, the absolute *freedom* of the Absolute, since to be attributionless is to be utterly *undetermined* and therefore free; the *unity* of Absolute Being, since plurality attaches only to determinate things; the *identity of opposites*—being and nothing—which results in every *Origin*. In all representational thinking, origins are depicted as arising at fixed times and in fixed locations. Pure thought, however, comprehends the true ontological status of origins, which is the unity of being and nothingness. And thus, "The Absolute is simply there in every material or ideal, temporal or non-temporal reality. It is the origin of its presence and of its absence" (sec. 42).

From the very fact that being arises out of a dialectical process, which is to say an active process, it follows that being is essentially *life*. In its purely physical manifestations, life reveals its powers in love and strife or in equivalent forms of attraction and repulsion, self-division and self-integration. To self-conscious life, these paired manifestations, seen in their contradictoriness, produce that very estrangement that guarantees the ontological status of each of the apparent contradictions. This is equally evident in the estrangement of *body* and *soul*; the latter an *internal actuality*, the former its external aspect: "These two sides of life can be abstractly separated into a psycho-physical *dualism* wherein the externally given, the appearing body of life, is nothing but a dead husk; and the internal actuality of life, separated from its objective embodiments, is but irrational subjectivity. Materialism is as one-sided and deficient as psychism" (sec. 89). Again, it is through the dialectic that this seeming duality is discovered to be itself an ontological contradiction. It is by virtue of external materiality that internal actuality is, and vice versa. Life manifests itself to itself in the very (apparent) estrangement of body and soul.

On Hegel's theory, it is only metaphysical dogmatism, such as that displayed by dualists, empiricists, materialists, and natural scientists, that requires sharp boundaries between body and soul, cause and effect, potentiality and real existence. Confining themselves either to the content-less world of logical formalisms or the half-true world of mere appearances, the dogmatists are unable to comprehend real being. The dialectical ontology repairs this by establishing reality on the plane of "the identity of opposites." It is on this plane that every *actuality* alone determines what is really possible: "This *ontological modality of real possibility* is not the "possible" as defined in . . . [the] sciences" (sec. 92), but the very *condition* of possibility itself. What Hegel is getting at is that every existent owes its ontological standing to a process of reciprocal implication and, thus, "only that which becomes actual is really possible" (*ibid.*). He illustrates this (sec. 95) by pairing "Shakespeare" and "the Elizabethan Age." The latter constitutes the *condition* making the former possible, but it is only the actuality of Shakespeare that brings about the (his) unique environment, "the Elizabethan Age." It is this same reciprocation that realizes "cause and effect" and that ultimately establishes the identity of actuality and necessity. What *actually* is, *necessarily* is by virtue of the dialectical foundation of all true Being. And it is this identity of the actual and the necessary that Hegel calls *substance*. Thus, substance is *sufficient Cause* (sec. 100). In its purely subjective manifestation, it appears as freedom, the necessary consequence of its own will. In its objectivized manifestation, it is (necessary) actuality. As Being progresses toward a more complete comprehension of itself, it progressively abandons the merely one-sided determinations of logic and of (empirical) science. Being attains its innermost freedom in the Concept—"this actual subject-object in process of self-realization" (sec. 108). Thus, "The *Concept* is the *essence of personality*" (sec. 109). And when, as it must, it operates with a purpose, when it manipulates the objective world in order to secure its ends—in order to reveal itself in the world—then the Concept is the final cause, the *absolute idea* (secs. 156, 157). As *absolute idea*, it is absolutely free from natural determination; free to become explicitly what it is implicitly.

For Hegel, the individual's "psychology" is a moment in the dialectical movement of the Absolute Idea. The branch of philosophy concerned with moments such as these is what he calls *philosophy of spirit* which examines either the subjective (soul) or objective (mind) manifestations of the infinite in the finite. Only the philosophy of the Absolute, however, transcends this duality and comprehends each in the other.

In its progress toward its Concept, the finite spirit must move through stages and phases of its own creation, limiting itself by erecting one-sided determinations and then freeing itself through dialectical negations of these very determinations. Its chief obstacle is its own *standpoint of reason* (sec. 386) which ties spirit to mere finitudes and the skepticism engendered by them. It is this self-imposed know-nothingism which, unchecked and extreme, is *evil* itself.

Hegel's evolutionary metaphysics marks the stages of the spirit's development. These begin at the level of the *natural soul* and pass successively through *subjective mind, objective mind,* and *absolute spirit.* Natural soul, in its unawakened state, is simply the life of nature. "Nature herself," says Hegel (sec. 308), "begins to overcome its externality" in the forging of animal instincts and cravings. Through the dialectical opposition of the purely vegetative and the nonvegetative, however, the natural soul becomes awakened. Awakened to itself, the soul nonetheless is unconscious of its immersion in the organic world. Where natural soul controls and self-conscious soul obeys, depression and even insanity may result. The primitive, on the contrary, so tied to nature—to "world-soul"—is not torn by the conflict between self-conscious soul and natural soul (sec. 311). In this, the essence of the natural state, the savage is actually so at one with nature as to have a deeper intuitive relationship with it—"presentiments of situations and events and a feeling . . . which to civilized man seem miraculous" (sec. 311). Only in sleep and dreams does the civilized man's self-conscious soul return to the realms of natural soul, the realms of purely natural life—a return that carries the danger of mental illness, the loss of "a free self-conscious personality" (sec. 320). But it is just this fact of self-consciousness that makes evident the "dark region below consciousness" (sec. 330), as light makes evident the fact of darkness. Hegel thus rejects the separation of Ego and non-Ego defended by Fichte and interposes that dialectical unity of opposites whereby the "I am" and the "not I" become ontologically and necessarily coextensive.

It is this subjective mind, rising above the level of natural soul through the process of self-consciousness, that can first begin to struggle with the subject-object tensions of philosophy and life, with the confusing alternation between the mediate and the immediate, the sensuous (thing) and the general (class). Out of consciousness arises self-consciousness. It searches for itself, thereby producing itself. Its earliest manifestation is desire or appetite, which leads to the manipulation, consumption, and destruction of those very things—those merely material entities—of which it might otherwise judge itself to be a part. Note that in desiring anything, one distinguishes oneself from it and one distinguishes the act of desire *in principle* from any and every object of desire (sec. 346).* But the activity

---

* It is in sec. 345 and after that Hegel refers to *intentionality* (*Trieb*) in a manner that will, with modification, be adopted by Brentano and Husserl, thereupon to be incorporated into more current versions of *phenomenology*. The "object" of self-conscious mind is an *intentional* object. To ask, for example, of the status of "the Archangel" in the sentence, "He thought the Archangel was at his side," is to learn that the Archangel is the intentional object of the thought. It is the same with "He desired to live a moral life." The object—a moral life—is the *intentional* object of desire, not an empirical object to be verified through observation, measurement, or public judgments. It is in these respects that the mind may be said to know itself *intentionally*.

of desire, as destructive, simply establishes the mortality of that side of self that is tied to external things. It is then in the negation of the futile that soul rises above the determined world of passable things and announces itself to be free, thus entering upon the path of struggle and doubt. It is, after all, implicit in the dialectical ontology that the selfish imperatives constitute the very condition for the idea of freedom, and that the latter derives itself from the negation of desire. There simply *cannot* be the one without the other for the subjective mind. And it is with the *comprehension* of this interdependence between objective determination and (free) self-determination that subjective mind is *spirit*—that which knows itself through the truth it has comprehended (sec. 362). In its true thoughts it both expresses and discovers the freedom of its will, and in freely choosing to think it both expresses and discovers the truth. It is then a short step to the realization that life's suffering and pain, its frustrations and temptations, its sacrifices and torments are the necessary conditions of moral freedom. Only in a *natural* world thus determined can subjective mind discover in itself that moral *ought* which would have things other than they are. Were the world different, we would not be free to choose that it ought to be.

Collectively, the subjective mind alerted to the imperatives of its own moral freedom shapes the human world into the institutional contours of civilization, replete with laws, property, arbitration, social morality. This is the stage of *objective mind*, of spirit objectifying itself and realizing itself in the durable modes of ordered social life, in the State. Objective mind can rise no higher, and even in its most sublime manifestations it necessarily includes the irrational, selfish, and merely contingent features of individual souls. Accordingly, "A chain of exploded systems marks the fiery path of the absolute spirit" (sec. 453).

At the end of this path are to be found Art, Religion,

and Philosophy, through which the Absolute Idea finds full expression. Only in the sublimity of art's beauty does the soul feel the woeful inadequacy of the senses (sec. 461). The artistic genius is inspired by the divine and his creations liberate man from "mere life" (sec. 462). Through him, nature and spirit become one in the intuition. Perfection is realized and the otherwise opposed realities of the particular and the universal become absorbed into each other. Art may use the medium of nature, but it speaks in the voice of spirit.

In the mythical language and imagery of religion, too, the Absolute presents itself to man as the "substantial power, justice, and wisdom in the universe" (sec. 467). Whereas the purely historical Jesus—the empirical and finite entity known to his contemporaries—cannot sustain the Absolute, the mythical Christ is the depersonalized and eternal image of the Absolute, the God without parts, the God of an invisible church.

And finally it is philosophy, taking religion "as one of its own presuppositions" (sec. 471), and unifying religion and art, that liberates Spirit from each and every form of life: "The three forms of the absolute spirit—art, religion, philosophy—represent the same Absolute. They differ only in the medium of expression. All three are ways of salvation from the oppressive and restricting problems of external nature and finite mind" (sec. 473).

Hegel's *Encyclopedia* (1817, 1827) appeared after his *Phenomenology of Mind* (1806) and his *Science of Logic* (1812), and enjoyed a wide readership if only because of its relatively distilled account of his system. But serious scholars were not to avoid the larger works and it was in these that Hegel more fully developed his criticisms of prevailing psychologies as well as of those on the more distant Anglo-American horizon. He was, for example, utterly scornful of those "faculty psychologies" that had arisen out of the confusions of empirical philosophy and that tried to retain the unity of consciousness amid the chaotic diversity of mental processes. He insisted, in *Phenomenology of Mind*, that psychological individuality can be found only "in the universal element of Mind" (p. 333) and that the approach of empirical psychology was therefore "much more uninteresting than even to reckon up the species of insects, mosses, and so on" (*ibid.*). Not only does such a psychology artificially set up its own boundaries within mind and convert its subject to a mere spectator, but it cuts this same subject off from that very sphere of *action* in which the individual spirit reveals itself. And to the extent that the person himself adopts this mode of self-knowledge, he can arrive only at skepticism and at a kind of self-division. For now here he is, a screen on which some (unknowable) reality plays, but at the same time still another person who somehow contributes to the picture. Thus does an erroneous philosophy breed that "*Unhappy Consciousness*, the Alienated Self which is the consciousness of self as a divided nature, a doubled and merely contradictory being" (p. 251).

On the whole, the tendencies of the age to which Hegel opposed his own system were those of materialism and skepticism; more generally, metaphysical dogmatism of every sort. He was alert to and troubled by the political storms, the revolutionary zeal, the cultural and religious doubts of his time, and convinced that much of this was either the result of a defective philosophy or at least was the business of a genuine philosophy to correct. The central place his works give to *alienation, self-estrangement* and the like would, of course, become fixtures in the Marxist lexicon, just as his analysis of the unconscious would fuel the theoretical engines of the psychoanalytic movement. How Hegel might have assessed this is, to be sure, open to debate, but there would seem to be good reasons for thinking that he would have judged these succeeding activities as just more of the problem.

Marx and his disciples would come to flatter themselves into believing that they had "stood Hegel on his head," but their actual record displays convenient ignorances of the dialectical ontology. When Hegel speaks of *alienation*, for example, his focus is not confined to transactions between persons and governments or persons and their own labor. The alienation, instead, is of the most fundamental epistemological sort: It is the sudden recognition by mind that it exists apart from the only world in which its own existence becomes possible; a world that is somehow different from the known world in which mind actually is. The Marxist version of this dilemma generally proceeds from such maxims as "Consciousness is the creation of society," and similar contradictions, which can find metaphysical support only in one or another form of psychophysical materialism; i.e., for "society" to fashion individual consciousness, it has only the medium of "brain" to serve it. Further, it must take mind to be that passive receptacle of empiricism that becomes filled with what is really "out there." But of course the very question at issue is what is really "out there" and it is scarcely settled by announcing that representational realism is beyond dispute. Moreover, "society" is not a stimulus in the sense that a blue light or a pure tone is, but a construction which cannot be *empirically* analyzed without being annihilated in the process. Similarly, in preserving the notion of "the unity of opposites," the Marxist of today traduces the Hegelian version by permitting that notion to defend *formal* contradictions. Note that Hegel never questioned the validity of formal logic. Rather he distinguished between logical and ontological domains and argued that ontological evolution (the historical progress of spirit) was powered by extra-logical principles. It takes more to "stand Hegel on his head" than reading his *Encyclopedia* upside down!

The psychoanalytic movement, being less "philosophical" than Marxism, lends itself less to a comparison with

Hegelian thought, although the points of contact are numerous and significant. It would not do to say that Hegel put the unconscious on the map of nineteenth-century concerns, for in this he was anticipated both at home and abroad. But in connecting the unconscious to evolutionary history—in presenting it as the *natural* substrate of all ultimately self-conscious mind—he clearly established a pattern of understanding that would be followed by later psychoanalytic theorists, and especially by those nominally indebted to Darwin.

In the year preceding the opening of Wundt's Leipzig "laboratory," G. Stanley Hall would offer this estimate of Hegel's standing in the new and scientific psychology:

As a mental discipline, then, as a wholesome stimulant of every motive of philosophical culture, and as the best embodiment of the legitimate aspiration of the philosophical sentiment, we have gradually come to regard Hegel's system an unrivaled and unapproached; yet, at the same time, as fatal as a finality, almost valueless as a method.[18]

Alas, for the "method" the new experimental psychology was to choose, this Hegelianism could be only the least promising of candidates. As an *ism* it did not tell science what to do or how to do it, nor did it hold out hope for discovering new laws or even new facts. Such entities as this fresh experimental psychology were, themselves, but "moments" in the history of the Concept, and not especially momentous even in this small way. Nonetheless, the problems underscored by Hegel—the problems of life, mind, and society—would seldom retreat completely from the affairs of psychology. In the applied fields such as educational psychology, men such as John Dewey would come to punctuate their "pedagogic creeds" with Hegelian principles.[20] And, as we shall see in the next chapter, Wundt himself, once he moved beyond the narrow channels of sensation and into the larger context of Social Man, would be at least unconsciously Hegelian to the core.

The legacy of Hegel's philosophy is diffusely present in modern psychology and in the social sciences at large. His *Reason in History* made clear once and for all that the social, cultural, and political sides of human life cannot be reduced to a chain of merely causal happenings but must be understood in the uniquely human language of purposes and plans.[20] His *Phenomenology of Mind*, through the winding paths later cut by Brentano and Husserl, not only gave primacy to *experience* in the arena of psychological concerns but required this subject to be understood in its own terms and not simply according to the methods of psychophysics or the canons of empiricism. This same work, and the *Encyclopedia*, installed the problems of ethics as well as the productions of art and the mysteries of religion firmly within the provinces of psychological inquiry, daring the inhabitants to discover a method worthy of such subjects. To date, they have not.

As the full sweep of modern psychological writing and research is scanned, there appear to be two empires alarmingly hostile to each other or, perhaps worse, alarmingly unconscious of each other. In one we find the disciples of Mill; in the other the children of Hegel. The first of these empires is productive and busy, but ever more weary and concerned that it has found nothing *absolute*. The laborers in the second empire began with what is absolute, but are now chastised for having found nothing *concrete*. Thus is Psychology divided into the immediate and the mediate, with no sign of integration at this *moment*.

As for Hegel's pronouncements on natural science and the scientific community's reaction to them, enough has been said and written, at least since the time that Helmholtz would imply that the Hegelians were "crazy."[21] Certainly the portions of his *Science of Logic* and *Phenomenology of*

Mind addressed to what would now be taken as natural science are the least satisfying. In the former, his long chapter 2, "Quantum," contains many discrediting references to Newton's methods and insists upon relationships between quantity and quality that the scientific mind is apt to find useless, if not incredible. In the second volume of the same work, "Mechanism" too is absorbed into the larger Hegelian metaphysics where one discovers, for example, that "Only Free Mechanism has a Law" which finally is revealed in the "free necessity" of its individuality.[22] Read in the shadows of a busy laboratory, such phrases are not likely to summon the allegiance of experimenters! And all too often Hegel's more devoted followers tended to direct such grand abstractions critically at the day-to-day theories and findings of science, thus encouraging men like Helmholtz to purify science of every trace of metaphysics. This, as was noted in the previous chapter, was Mill's chief aim as well. And it was just this sometimes passionate antimetaphysical bias that imparted to the emerging experimental psychology an assortment of virtues and vices that remain to be disentangled. There is, after all, no such thing as a suppositionless science—the very phrase is an oxymoron. All science, then, is to this degree "metaphysical."

Hegel led his century to what seemed to be the ultimate implication of this fact. Thus led, the intellectual members of the age proceeded to run in different directions; some toward a higher religion, some toward the promised truths of art, some into the murkier reaches of the unconscious natural soul, and some into the active world of politics and social ethics, eager to aid the Absolute Idea on its journey toward self-realization. Science watched, and then happily turned away. Psychology, then as now caught between science and metaphysics, divided its house.

4. WILHELM WUNDT

The contemporary intellectual community is far less familiar with the works of Wundt than with those of Mill and Hegel. He was, however, a more prolific writer than either and, for several decades, at least as influential among those who took psychology as their principal interest. He is also a more recent figure whose long life (1832–1920) bracketed the most fertile productions of the nineteenth century and the twentieth century's growing suspicion toward these very productions. His scholarship was as inexhaustible as it was far ranging—logic, philosophy, physiology, psychology, linguistics, and cultural anthropology each receiving specific and original attention in his books and essays.. As E. G. Boring notes, Wundt's literary career (1853–1920) yielded more than 50,000 pages, "about one word every two minutes, day and night, for the entire sixty-eight years."[1] But he did not only write; he also read and was on intimate terms with both the technical and the theoretical sides of nineteenth-century science. His academic training included study with Johannes Müller and du Bois-Reymond at Berlin and with Helmholtz at Heidelberg. But neither his degree in medicine nor his apprenticeships and appointments in physiology anticipated the essentially philosophical approach he would bring to bear upon psychological issues. If, as is often averred, he was responsible for psychology's first experimental laboratory—if we was himself an experimenter at heart—then he was surely the first *philosophical psychologist* spawned by experimental science.

Over the past few years there has been a spate of Wundt scholarship, much of it inspired by centennial celebrations of his founding of the Leipzig laboratory in 1879. Although the actual laboratory seems to have been a very modest affair, and although history has yet to settle on the significance of this undertaking, recent studies have done much to clarify and correct the received picture of Wundt.[2] Less successful, however, have been those attempts to locate him within the general scientific and philosophical context of nineteenth-century German thought; to understand his works through the problems they were designed to solve; ultimately, to disclose his sense of and aims for psychology. To the extent that these aspects of Wundtian psychology remain obscure it is not possible to judge twentieth-century departures from it or the twentieth century's debt to it. And with respect to the current but already fading excitement over Wundt—*centennial fever*— it remains the case that the best-known Wundt is the one bequeathed by E. G. Boring. But this Wundt is part invention, part impression; a man dragged out of his own milieu and presented to modern psychologists as if he had had them in mind all along. There was surely this Wundt, the man who would strive to define the discipline for posterity and who lived long enough to worry about the turns it was already taking in the present century. But through it all, the actual Wundt was a nineteenth-century person toiling in the thick groves of German *Geisteswissenschaft* and *Naturwissenschaft*. Admittedly precocious and productive, he was nonetheless a child of his century and his culture, and to fail to know this Wundt is to fail to know Wundt entirely.

Scientific Psychology—Doubts and Possibilities

As has been discussed in the preceding chapters, the arguments for and against a "scientific" psychology were among the more passionately contended of the nineteenth century's many scholarly disputes. Wundt could not have been better positioned either temporally or geographically to make an important, even a unique contribution to this discourse. His scientific training in physiology and medicine was without rival and took place at a time when the tensions between science and metaphysics centered on problems of psychology. Kant's chair at Königsberg had passed to J. F. Herbart (1776–1841) early in the century, and Herbart was perhaps the most psychological philosopher of the entire epoch. His *Lehrbuch der Psychologie* (1816) argued strongly for a scientific psychology against each of Kant's specific objections.[3] It was Herbart's aim to demonstrate that a rigorously deductive and mathematical psychology was not any more elusive in principle than a developed astronomy. But like Kant, if for somewhat different reasons, Herbart rejected the possibility of a valid and complete *experimental* psychology. As he put it in his *Lehrbuch*:

Psychology cannot experiment with men, and there is no apparatus for this purpose. So much the more carefully must we make use of mathematics. . . . All mental life, as we observe it in ourselves and others, is shown to be an occurrence in time, a constant change, a manifold of unlike conditions combined in one, finally a consciousness of the Ego and the non-Ego, all of which belongs to the form of experience and are unthinkable. (pp. 4–6)

Here, still very much in the patrimony of Kant, Herbart was underscoring the alleged impossibility of mind reflecting objectively on itself without changing itself in the process. But at the level of sensation and of the simpler concepts, Herbart's psychological hypotheses were fashioned out of common observations and (even) experimental manipulations. In fact, so skillful was Herbart in his mathematical and deductive psychology that Gustav Fech-

ner (1801–1887), the father of *psychophysics*, would note
in his *Elemente der Psychophysik*:

> The question of whether and to what extent it is possible to
> measure sensation itself . . . still remains open. . . . [T]he measure
> has been doubted or denied, until very recently, as possible at
> all. Even Herbart's attempt at a mathematical psychology was
> unable to cope with this problem . . . in spite of the fact that
> Herbart had this measure practically within his grasp.[4]

Without examining the detailed history of sensory measurement, it is enough to recognize that between Herbart's
Lehrbuch of 1816 and Fechner's pioneering text of 1860,
incontrovertible evidence had emerged in support of the
claim that at least some form of experimental psychology
was possible. What remained as an open question was
whether such a psychology could move beyond simple
sensations and could meaningfully address the larger
aspects of mind as such. Tied to this were any number of
related questions arising from the rapid advances in physiology and physics, the appearance of Darwin's monumen-
tal treatise (1859), the quick progress of anthropological
and linguistic studies across cultures, and, of course, the
ever intensifying conflicts between science and philosophy,
science and religion.

No one who had benefited from the sort of biological
and experimental instruction Wundt had received in the
course of his premedical and medical education could
have failed to appreciate the extent to which psychological
and physiological processes were related. Even as Wundt
concluded his training, Helmholtz was completing his
physiological theories of basic visual and auditory functions; Georg Prochaska and Marshall Hall had already
worked out the gross anatomy of reflex-response systems;
a veritable army of surgeons and physiologists had documented the relationship between brain centers and a wide

variety of cognitive and affective states; clinicians in Germany, France, and England had already pretty much decided, on the basis of evidence, that mental illness went hand-in-glove with cerebral dysfunction; Herbert Spencer and Alexander Bain in England had just "biologized" psychology to the point where the burden was now squarely on those who still doubted.

But on the other side of all this was the heavy philosophical scholarship of Leibniz, Kant, Fichte, Hegel—those captains of German thought who had so relentlessly challenged psychological materialism and all other "one-sided" attempts to comprehend the human spirit. And note that this scholarship was as much a part of Wundt's time, as thoroughly ingrained in the thinking of the instructed classes, as anything he might have learned from Müller or Helmholtz at Berlin. This is a point worth extending, for the influence of German metaphysics is apparent and sometimes even dominant in nearly all of Wundt's major publications. Indeed, it is as evident in his coy assurances that he will not traffic in "metaphysics" as it is in those works that are unblushingly metaphysical.

In an attempt to review this significant feature of Wundt's psychology, it becomes necessary to make comparisons that may appear less than generous. On the one hand we can study such influential texts as Bain's *The Senses and the Intellect* (1855) and *The Emotions and the Will* (1859), or Spencer's *First Principles* (1862), and recognize the confident labor of men who know wherein truth resides; men who have already and finally made peace with naturalism and mechanism and who now need only translate the problems of psychology into forms accessible to the scientific point of view. On the other hand, we can then thumb through the pages and pages of Wundt only to find qualifying and diffident strains, tentativeness, awkwardness of argument. In none of this is "style" a way of understanding the differences. The ungenerous but defensible comparison is between Wundt's philosophical competence and sensibilities and the somewhat less refined sensibilities of his less equivocal contemporaries. Put less harshly, the case may be made this way: England by midcentury was in the philosophical clutches of J. S. Mill, at least to the extent that its science made any contact with philosophy at all. At the same time, German intellectuals— whether scientists or not—had learned the Kantian and Hegelian lessons of "one-sidedness"; at least they learned to pause before making inductive leaps into regions in which induction may have no place. Wundt, therefore, was no less committed to inductive science than was Mill, and he surely knew more directly about research and theory in the natural sciences than did Mill, Spencer, and Bain combined! Wundt was not simply an experienced re-searcher but a distinguished one. Perhaps because of this he was less optimistic about the prospects of the laboratory replacing "metaphysics" in the task of explaining the human condition. And so we find him throughout his long and productive career standing as the champion of an experimental psychology of individual consciousness, and as something of a reluctant Hegelian in his treatments of the human will, human society, and human history. The one Wundt gives us a physiological, naturalistic, and experimental discipline indistinguishable in principle from the biological sciences; the other gives us a rational and metaphysical psychology indistinguishable from that genre of historical studies minted in the mind of Hegel. Each of these Wundt's is apparent in his approach to the conceptual foundations of psychology. Of these, the most instructive are (a) the nature of psychological explanation, (b) the possible relationships between psychology and biology, and (c) the connections between individual and social psychology.

Psychological Explanation

Wundt's Heidelberg lectures of 1861 appeared later in book form under the title *Lectures on Human and Animal Psychology.*[5] He begins the penultimate chapter's third section thus:

An attempt to construct the history of a nation or of mankind at large in terms of the laws of natural causation would not only be vain in practice; it would be wrong in principle. If the individual can say that, in place of acting as he did in some particular case, he might have acted otherwise, we must also be able to say of every event in history that it might have happened differently. In both cases the *necessity* of natural causation is wanting. For historical events and for the voluntary actions of an individual we can only adduce determining *motives*; we cannot prove constraining *reasons*. (p. 428)

Here is a passage authored decades before Wundt's *Völkerpsychologie* but establishing the extent to which he had already begun to dissociate natural and social phenomena. It is a passage comfortably grounded in the "reasons-causes" distinction powerfully developed by Leibniz and central to Hegel's philosophy of history. The distinction, of course, was carefully drawn by Aristotle and, in the modern period, by Thomas Reid in his critique of Hume's theory of causation. What it separates is the world of colliding billiard balls and the world of human history. One is the world of mere matter, the other the world of *idea*.

Only when this metaphysical dualism—a dualism regarding not only the language of explanation but also the actual constituents of the universe—is recognized can one comprehend Wundt's approach to the Mind/Body problem and his *voluntaristic* theory of human action. Wundt invariably shied away from both materialism and "spiritism" in his discussions of the relationship between psychology and physiology. To the extent that he took a firm position on the issue at all, he generally recommended a form of *psychophysical parallelism*, itself another of Leibniz's bequests to nineteenth-century German thought. A quick review of parallelism will repay the effort.

Historical "solutions" to the Mind/Body problem can be placed in a small number of categories. Radical materialism settles the dispute by denying that there is mind and by asserting that all the things attributed to "mind" are, in fact, properties of matter (brain) waiting to be discovered by the neural sciences. More moderate forms of materialism accept the existence of mental states and events, but attribute them uniquely to processes occurring in the brain. This position, known as *epiphenomenalism*, is a form of *dualism* (in that it takes both mental and material events to be real and distinguishable) but it retains its materialistic credentials by declaring all psychological outcomes to be causally determined by physiological antecedents. On yet another construction—the one made famous by Descartes—the mind (soul) is able to influence the course of bodily events but is itself independent of such purely material influences. According to this *Cartesian* dualism, all interactions between mind and body are one way, with the mental realm standing as cause and the physical as effect. It might be thought of as an epiphenomenalism with mind and body undergoing a reversal of roles. In the extreme form, this line of reasoning leads to varieties of *immaterialism* (such as George Berkeley espoused) which restrict the realm of real existence to *ideas* only.

Each of these attempted solutions carries its own unique burdens. The extreme positions have enjoyed small but vocal followings over the centuries, although the vast majority of philosophers and scientists may be said to have resisted them. Most persons, regardless of professional affiliations, remain stubbornly convinced that they have minds and that there is matter. Indeed, were either of the extreme positions officially adopted, quite literally *nothing* would change. Whether everything now called "physical" is actually no more than a construction out of thought, or everything now called "mental" is but a peculiar manifestation of purely physical interactions, we still must address the external world *as if* it were real and do so *as if* our thoughts, perceptions, feelings, and beliefs really did exist. Accordingly, disputes have most commonly centered on the moderate positions, on varieties of dualism.

Yet, as with so many compromises, dualism finally satisfies no one. If we define the major terms in any of the usually accepted ways we begin to see what so many have found wanting in it. Granting that by "mind" we mean a nonmaterial entity ("substance")—an entity located in no space and displaying no "parts"—we have simply removed every conceivable means by which it might come to affect or be affected by "matter." Thus, even though the modern citizen is likely to choose epiphenomenalism when presented with all the alternative solutions to the Mind/Body problem, this same citizen will find it extremely difficult to specify how, for example, an idea can move a muscle; how a gland can create a thought.

Intellectual frustration is the mother of philosophical novelty. The sensed implausibility of monistic materialism, monistic idealism, and cheeful dualism is what finally drove Leibniz to propose a very odd but at least noncontradictory alternative: *psychophysical parallelism.* It takes the existence of mind and matter for granted, but treats the ineliminable differences between them as proof that interactions are impossible. In his *Monadology*, Leibniz stated the case this way:

And supposing there were a machine, so constructed as to think, feel, and have perception; it might be conceived to increase in size . . . so that one might go into it as into a mill. That being so, we should, on examining its interior, find only parts which work one upon another, and never anything by which to explain a perception.[6]

In other words, a machine that thinks or perceives presents as difficult a case to the materialist as does a thinking or perceiving person. Nothing in the machine's moving parts will be anything like a thought or percept. And because of this Leibniz concluded that there could be no *causal* relationship between the two classes of events. Rather, the two must conform to their own respective laws and principles, and unfold according to the prescriptions of their own independent realms. They are, said Leibniz, related by a *preestablished harmony*, as are two synchronously set clocks designed to tell the same time. They run their respective courses in parallel, displaying perfect correspondence but without ever interacting. Stated yet another way, this time in connection with the difference between causes and reasons, Leibniz' argument is that "Souls act in accordance with the laws of final causes. . . . Bodies act in accordance with the laws of efficient causes or of motion. The two realms . . . are in harmony, each with the other."[7]

Wundt, as we know, had chosen Leibniz for a book-length treatment so there is no question about his intimate knowledge of Leibnizian philosophy. The same depth of understanding of Hegel's formidable critique of materialism may also be taken for granted. In light of this, Wundt's support of *parallelism* is quite understandable. To avoid the errors of materialism while keeping the new psychology safely within the province of natural science, he must remain aloof to tempting but tangled theories. We find him, then, in the last chapter of his *Lectures*, insisting that "mental phenomena could not be referred to bodily as effect to cause" since, "Nothing can ever be derived from motion except another motion." Then he summarizes his position:

Psychical can only be adequately explained from psychical, just as motion can only be derived from motion, and never from a mental process, of whatever kind. At the same time . . . mental processes are connected with definite physical processes within the body, and especially in the brain. . . . How are we to conceive of this connection? . . . The connection can only be regarded as a *parallelism* of two causal series existing side by side, but never directly interfering with each other in virtue of the incomparability of their terms. (p. 442)

Wundt's credentials as a proponent of physiological psychology begin with the fact that he was among the first to popularize the term and wrote one of the specialty's most influential texts. Thus, his adoption of parallelism did not proceed from any mystical conviction. It arose from the simple desire for theoretical and conceptual coherence. He did not deny that mental states were reducible, but he argued that they could be reduced only to other mental states.

We recognize, then, a nearly mechanical consistency between Wundt's position on the Mind/Body issue and his advocacy of noncausal explanations of social and historical phenomena. In neither case is it profitable to think of his position as just another version of that fashionable "double-aspect" theory embraced by so many nineteenth-century scientists. The double-aspect theorist asserts that mind and brain are simply two *aspects* of what is finally the same (monistic) reality, a reality which the same theorist generally does not define. The double-aspect theorist, however, cannot consistently hold his ground on the Mind/Body problem while acknowledging valid distinctions between reasons and causes in our attempts to explain historical and social events. Note that what is at issue here is not the question of *reductionism*. It is true, but only trivially so, that Wundt rejected reductive materialism, but so does the double-aspect theorist. The more fundamental matter is Wundt's position on the very nature of explanation—his epistemology—and not his derivative position on description. Wundt did not simply contend that historical and social events must be *described* in psychological terms, but that they can only be understood and explained that way; that attempts to explain them in the language of natural causation are not only vain in practice but *wrong in principle.*

The position one takes on the nature of explanation virtually dictates the methods one will adopt in the investigation of phenomena. And both of these proceed from the source of all speculation, the question of *ontology*, the question of what there really *is* in the universe. Wundt is best known to psychologists for the Leipzig laboratory and the early studies of the "contents of consciousness." He is also but incorrectly known for something called "introspectionism," although this only fits Wundt's program if the term is taken to refer to Fechner's psychophysical methods. What is clear, however, from the very direction taken by the Leipzig laboratory, is that the *fact* of consciousness was taken for granted. It is in this most basic ontological respect that Wundt appreciated the impossibility of reconciling psychology to radical materialism. To contend that psychological phenomena either are or are invariably caused by physiological processes—that once the physiology is understood, there is no psychological residual—is to contend that a science of psychology can never aspire to more than provisional status. On a certain construal, it is to contend that psychological research is actually beside the point. However, the entire weight of German philosophical thought came down against such a view, as did that background *empiricism* that had been more or less official in scientific circles at least since the eighteenth century.

In relation to this latter point, it is important to recall that feature of Kant's achievement that is properly regarded as the triumphant completion of empiricism, his *phenomenalism.* In this, such diverse writers as Locke, Berkeley, Hume, Kant, and Herbart were largely of a single mind and had provided all the arguments Wundt might need to retain psychology's independence. They had securely tied all that was knowable to the conscious mind and had at least implicitly installed some sort of psychology as the final arbiter of every epistemological claim. This is the informing respect in which Wundt is to be understood as an "empiricist," and the respect in which we need not be surprised by the anti-associationistic tone of some of his major works.

Associationism is a doctrine pertaining to the laws governing the formation of complex ideas. As such, it neither requires nor supports empiricism, for the latter is an epistemological doctrine regarding what is directly knowable. Thus, both Kant and Mill were empiricists in this sense, although Kant was not a traditional associationist. Wundt, then, was an empiricist in that he took the facts of direct experience as the subject matter of every science. What distinguished psychology from other sciences was its attention to the actual *process* of experience rather than its products. But in thereby opening the subject to the full array of mental processes, he necessarily accepted those social and historical creations that are unimaginable in the absence of human purposes, and inexplicable in any but their own language. Just as mind in principle cannot be understood exclusively through the causal laws of matter, so also society cannot be understood through these laws. Human culture and history arise out of mind, and the latter is simply not part of the unbroken chain of causal necessities.

Wundt's "Voluntarism" and the Problem of Self

Space was reserved in chapter 2 for an examination of Hume's radically empiricistic theory of "self," and for the critique of such theories assembled by Thomas Reid. Of the several striking compatibilities between the psychologies of J. S. Mill and Wundt—except of course on the matter of associationism—their respective approaches to the problem of self are particularly instructive. Recall that Locke's account did not survive Reid's attack, and that Hume's "bundle of perceptions" thesis seemed to hold up only slightly better. It was Hume's contention not that self was the gift of personal memories but that it arose out of the causal connections that tie our ideas together. Mill's position was cut from the same bolt. Now let us look at Wundt's phrasing of what is finally the Humean position:

It is in this way that the concept of the self ("I") arises: a concept which, taken of itself, is completely contentless, but which, as a matter of fact, never comes into the field of introspection without the special determinations which give a content to it. Psychologically regarded, therefore, the self is not an idea among other ideas; it is not even a secondary characteristic, common to all or to the great majority of ideas; it is simply and solely the perception of the interconnection of internal experience which accompanies that experience itself. (*Lectures*, Lecture xvi, sec. 6.)

We see in this passage that for Wundt, as for Hume, the *self* is nothing more than our awareness of the interconnections among our own experiences. The *I* is simply the common term in every report of experience; the *condition* attending the very process of experience. Like Hume and Mill, it was through this sort of analysis that Wundt sought to rid psychology of "the tendency to hypostatise mental events" (*ibid.*), to remove every trace of those medieval "substances" and to replace them with phenomena that could actually be addressed experimentally.

So far so good. But it is precisely because this theory is perfectly consistent with the balance of Hume's and Mill's psychology that it could not be consistent with Wundt's larger metaphysical commitments. The Humean *self* is part of the Humean natural order and is completely blanketed by Hume's regularity theory of causation. But Wundt, as we have seen, had already removed human history and culture from just this natural order. The problem Wundt did not recognize is grounded in the difference between the concept of self and that of "self-identity," and so he fell into the same trap that had caught Locke, Hume, and Mill. This was all discussed in chapter 2 and the criticisms offered there apply to Wundt's position, chapter and verse.

What is more important here, however, is the problem he did recognize. Let us take Wundt's dilemma this way: He has advocated a dualistic theory of explanation, justified by the separation of human history and society from the purely causal order of the kingdom of things. He has taken the human *will* to be primary in the determination of significant human actions. But for there to be a *will*, there must be a willing agent—a *self*. Thus, the question arises, if *self* is no more than the perception of the processes of internal experience, is the *will* no more than the effect of these same processes? It was also in Lecture xvi that Wundt had developed his theory of self by describing self as "the subject which we supply for the apperceptive quality." *Apperception*, however, in the received (Kantian, Hegelian) sense, refers to our knowing *that* we know and not merely to *what* we know. Yet, understood this way, apperception does not need a subject, it entails one!

What makes all of this a dilemma for Wundt, though not for the Humean, is Wundt's dualistic ontology. Had Wundt not found it necessary to adopt the (Leibniz-Hegel) distinction between reasons and causes, had he not been moved to exempt human culture from that same causal nexus in which the material affairs of the universe are imbedded, he could have grounded volition in apperception, and apperception in sensation. This, as we have seen, is not the course he followed. As a *social* theorist he framed his explanations according to the developed models of

Kant, Fichte, and Hegel; models proceeding from that most fundamental term, *das Ich*. But this invited the possibility of "hypostatizing" mental terms, the possibility of a return to the murky metaphysics of "substances." Then, as a *psychological* theorist attempting to explain the individual mind, he framed his explanations in the argot of empiricism, thereby confining the psychology of the individual to the nonhistorical, nonsocial arena of purely natural phenomena. The core problem stated briefly is, how is Wundt to get from here to there without setting foot into the territory of the Absolute and without surrendering the entire enterprise to the materialists?

We discover at this juncture Wundt's concept of *character* as his chosen *via media*; the concept that Mill also employed to get over the rough spots; the one that stood at the center of Hegel's theory of human history. Hegel had invoked it in this fashion:

The whole energy of will and character is devoted to the attainment of one aim. . . . This particular objective is so bound up with the person's will that it alone and entirely determines its direction. . . . It is that which makes the person what he is. For a person is a specific existence. He is not man in general—such a thing does not exist—but a particular human being. The term 'character' . . . expresses this uniqueness of will and intelligence.[8]

In Lecture XXIX, section 4, Wundt makes nearly the identical point: "The motives which determine the will are parts of the universal chain of natural causation. Nevertheless, the personal character, which alone can constitute volition, cannot be assigned a place in this causal nexus" (p. 434). And to those who might insist that character is itself the consequence of culture or environmental shaping, Wundt replies: "The assertion is undemonstrable. Character itself helps to determine education and destiny; the hypothesis makes an effect of what is to some extent also a cause" (*ibid.*).

Here, too, however, it is not Wundt's aim to uproot "character" from the observable world and move it into the domain of the Absolute. Wundt, that is, is not mimicking Hegel on this point. Rather, the part taken by character in Wundt's system is psychological, not metaphysical, and for this reason it is treated in part as "an original possession" and in part as a social phenomenon. But even this is not significantly at variance with Hegel's understanding, as Wundt seems to realize when he admits: "Every cause that stands behind the existence of the individual is itself the outgrowth of a still more remote chain of causation, and to follow this link by link to the end would be to trace out the causality of the universe" (p. 436). Such an endeavor is not the proper business of psychology, for psychology must begin with the fact of character, not its ultimate origins. In attempting to understand human actions the matter of origins is essentially irrelevant in any case; this because:

The more complete the determination of character by personal experience, the greater is the confidence of our prediction that it will act so or so in a particular case. So it happens that the more the will matures, the farther it travels from its original inherent determination, the more certain does its direction become, and the closer the approximation of its external manifestations to a mental series necessarily and causally related. (p. 436)

We see in these passages Wundt's understandable desire to have it both ways, as it were, and the satisfaction of this desire achieved through the gambit of disciplined inconsistency. What Wundt is trying to argue is that the original direction of character is not imparted by externals, and that character itself does much in time to determine its own conditions. However, experience soon begins to work on it; the person becomes "socialized" and our predictions of his conduct become more accurate. In time, what presents itself as character to the outside world is chiefly the expression of an internal "mental series" which is now and necessarily its cause. It was character that Wundt took to be "the ultimate cause of the will," but he was still able to retain his *voluntarism* by leaving character itself not only incompletely determined but also self-determining. The issue that is skirted in all of this, however, is just the issue of individual differences in character, the issue of the extent to which in its own self-determination the individual personality, far from being caused by a mental series, determines just what the series will be. This issue can only be skirted once a theorist has become committed to an even quasi-Humean interpretation of self. The great advantage of older "substance" theories is that they merely took self for granted, arguing that if the will was caused by anything it was caused by the self doing the willing! This was not an especially deep notion and surely not satisfying to a later era immersed in the excitements of skepticism. But it satisfied the requirements of common sense, it fit well into the reported experiences and sensibilities of the ages, and it served as a way out for those like Wundt who could not conceive of a psychology dubious about the reality of human volition.

Wundt, however, did not arrive at his voluntarism by way of common sense; either the sort advocated by Reid or the more familiar variety so soundly condemned by Kant. It was Kant's own "laws of freedom," discussed in the preceding chapter, not to mention Romanticism's daily exultations in the name of freedom, that may be said to have conditioned the German intellect of the nineteenth century to voluntaristic conceptions of man. That Wundt should give more space to "character" than to freedom per se is to be understood partly as evidence of his more deliberately psychological mission and partly as but another sign of his eagerness to avoid even the appearance of metaphysical speculation. But if freedom can be found in few of his written lines, it is nevertheless often present between the lines, nearly always in a tangle of terms. This is especially apparent in Lecture xv (sec. 3), "Simple and Complex Voluntary Acts." Here is the place where Wundt attempts to analyze the concept of volition most precisely and to relate it to such processes as ideation, feeling, motivation, and choice. In the section just preceding, Wundt makes the interesting claim that voluntary behavior is not unfailingly the evolved form of primitive reflexes, but that reflexes may often be the bequest of ancestral purposes made automatic over the seasons of evolution. He adds to this an equally telling criticism against that other traditional view according to which volition arises exclusively from intellectual processes, Wundt arguing here that "Introspection invariably points to *feeling* as the antecedent of will" (emphasis added).

What, then, is the cause of volition? Wundt begins his answer by subtracting all the conscious constituents introspection yields as we examine consciousness in a volitional state; he subtracts the motor elements, perception, even ideas, noting that these "do not exhaust the psychological analysis of will. . . . What must be added to all this . . . is the reference to an active subject. . . . But what is this 'active subject'? The most obvious answer appears to be: the willing subject is our own self. But that answer does not in any way assist our psychological analysis. For what, again, is this 'self'?" (pp. 230–31). As we have seen, Wundt's "self" theory has foreclosed the obvious answer, so he must consult consciousness again for an alternative. What he finds to be the *causes of volition* is a motive, but, "Now what is a motive?" And he answers his own question with a now famous Wundtian definition: "every motive is a *particular idea with an affective tone attaching to it*" (p. 231).

Recognizing that this definition becomes a tautology as soon as "affective tone" turns out to be motive-like—as soon as it "solicits the will"—Wundt must add to his analysis of volition thus: "The chief motive for actual volition is . . . not some particular sense-impression . . . but the entire trend of consciousness as determined by its previous experiences." (p. 232). However, this "entire trend of consciousness" is just that decision or disposition to act that we ordinarily call volition; and the determinations of "previous experiences" in this connection can only refer to whatever it is that allows our choices to be informed, discriminating, intended, and deliberate. The point here is that Wundt's "psychological analysis" of the will has left its object in precisely the same state as it was since the time of the ancients. That Wundt's account is more compelling than reflex theories or ultraintellectual theories of volition would be redeeming had either of these alternatives much of a following. As Wundt presents them, however, they are really straw men. It is true that Aristotle, for example, had gone to some lengths to establish that actions committed in ignorance are involuntary, by which he attempted to reveal the conceptual relationship between intellect and choice, knowledge and freedom. But it was surely not Aristotle's position that the concept of volition was exhausted by intellectual attributes or processes. Similarly, those who, like Holbach, argued that complex human volitions or purposive actions arose out of the more primitive and unreflecting instincts of the lower orders never claimed further that these volitions were now to be understood as reflexes or instincts. What is interesting, therefore, about Wundt's analysis is not that it is so original but that it is so prosaic. What gives it the appearance of complexity is its roundabout nature, its pyramid-like construction. Excising this we discover that he would be quite comfortable with an explanation of volition grounded in the notion of "a willing self," if it were not for the fact that such a notion does not further the "psychological analysis." But what we never discover is the advantage such an analysis possesses over so abiding

a verity as a willing self. Like J. S. Mill, he defended the
scientific method for individual psychology but, unlike
Mill, he admitted its fatal limitations when applied to social
and cultural history. What he could not do, apparently, is
come to grips with the implication of this, namely, that
perhaps the very same limitations would forever bar this
method from unearthing the nature of individual consciousness as well.

Consciousness: The Origin and the Effect of Culture

As we turn to an examination of Wundt's *Völkerpsychologie*
it is important to keep in mind that we are not looking at
another of his interests but at the very same interest—
human consciousness and the laws of its development and
function. Although the interest is the same, however, the
method and perspective must be altered, and this primarily
for two reasons. There is first the inapplicability of introspective forms of inquiry to the problems of sociocul-
tural psychology.* He makes this clear in a passage that
might well have been written by J. S. Mill:

[Cultural psychology's] problem relates to those mental products

---

* The expression "folk psychology" is not an apt translation of
Völkerpsychologie. As Wundt presents the subject, it entails a study of
custom, ritual, institutions; patterns of interpersonal, family, and tribal
affiliation. In effect, then, it is cultural anthropology as the method by
which to study the determinative role of such factors in the forging of
individual consciousness; or put more economically, the social determinants of thought. For brevity's sake, the subject will be referred to in
these few pages as *cultural psychology* so that it will not be confused with
what now presents itself as social psychology and sociology. Wundt's
cultural psychology is closer to the latter than to the former but is
significantly different from both. Unlike most of contemporary social
psychology, his interests were seldom confined to dyadic interactions.
Unlike much of contemporary sociology, his primary objective remained
the individual mind and the manner in which it is led by larger cultural
forces and ageless cultural habits.

which are created by a community of human life and are, therefore, inexplicable in terms of merely individual conscious- ness, since they presuppose the reciprocal action of many. . . . It is true that the attempt has frequently been made to investigate the complex functions of thought on the basis of mere intro- spection. These attempts, however, have always been unsuccessful. Individual consciousness is wholly incapable of giving us a history of the development of human thought, for it is conditioned by an earlier history concerning which it cannot itself give us any knowledge.[9]

Recall that Mill's objection to reliance on introspection was that the powerfully formative effects of our earliest experiences and the durable effects of the earliest associ- ations were entirely inaccessible to adult consciousness. Wundt here makes a similar point. The manner in which we *now* think has been shaped by our unique histories which we simply bring along with our observations but unconsciously. Since we have no recollection of the earliest influences on the processes of our thought, we are at once still in the grip of the past but without being able to discern even the type of grip it is.

Nevertheless, the actual subject matter of cultural psy- chology and the principles by which it is to be understood "never refer to . . . origins that are by nature inaccessible to experiential knowledge." Rather, they are to be found in the language and customs of a group; its written and graphic records, its beliefs and superstitions, its formal and informal practices, laws, and guiding maxims. Collec- tively, these data describe the *group consciousness* which, through the process of "reciprocal action" comes to define and be reinforced by the consciousness of each individual member. In the circumstance, the only reliable method of investigation is the historical method, akin to what natu- ralists had come to call the "natural-history" method.

The subtitle of Wundt's *Elements of Folk Psychology* is "Outlines of a Psychological History of the Development of Mankind." What he means by a *psychological* history is just what Condorcet meant in his *Sketch* of the historical development of the human mind.[10] Wundt, we see, is another nineteenth-century scientist laboring in fields first cultivated by the Enlightenment. The guiding if invisible hand is, of course, the Idea of Progress. The background assumption is that of evolutionism, here applied to the diversity of human cultural forms and fashions. But enfolding the entire enterprise are those Fichtean and Hegelian "moments"; those positing and counter-positing forces that bring forth the new by negating the old. Wundt never speaks of anything as brooding as the journey of the Absolute, but his *Völkerpsychologie* might easily be interpreted as a kind of applied Hegelian psychology.

It was through *Völkerpsychologie* that Wundt hoped to complete psychology. The subject held out the promise of filling in just those gaps remaining once experimental and introspective methods had been fully exploited. Experimentation is limited by its very nature, and when directed at something as dynamic and plastic as the human mind it is uniquely limited. All that experimental introspection can yield are the transient properties of an already developed mind; not a statement of how this development occurred or how this individual mind actually functions in culturally significant settings. But the limitations of experimental science raised no general doubts about the observational rigors of naturalistic science. The world is still populated by a wide variety of cultures which, taken collectively, offer a living record of the development of the race. As Wundt put it, the primitive origins of mind are to be sought not "*under* the earth, but *on* the earth" (*Völkerpsychologie*, p. 17).

The importance of this study, however, is not confined to its value to psychology. It was Wundt's enduring conviction that the ageless problems of ethics, philosophy, political science, and science itself were bound up with confusions and errors regarding the psychological makeup of humanity. He thought of psychology as something of the ultimate grounding upon which these other subjects rested and the general context within which they must be understood. Wundt's position here must not, however, be construed as the sort of *sociologistic* perspective now enjoying such enthusiastic (and uncritical) support. It was not his contention that physics or logic or moral science arises out of nothing firmer than the vagaries of individual psychology or the shifting habits of tribes and nations. This, in fact, was precisely the perspective that Wundt rejected and that much of his work was designed to challenge. His loyalty to the proposition that there are "universal human characteristics" (p. 21) did not waver, nor did his judgment that the principles of science are objectively valid independently of any psychological or social basis upon which they might be accepted or rejected or unknown. In treating psychology as the *ground* for all other intellectual and artistic activities, Wundt was taking psychology in a sense both broader and deeper than it has come to be taken in our more technical era. In keeping with Hegel's analysis, Wundt's conception of psychology was of an historical unfolding of human potential, a process based upon universal human characteristics but directed by extra-personal forces; forces that can only be understood at the level of *culture* and that can only be identified through the study of language and custom. Thus, it was not to be psychology's mission to establish the truth or falsity of the claims of other sciences, less those of philosophy. Instead, it is through a developed psychology that we come to understand and explain the stages reached by these other disciplines in the various epochs, and the factors governing their evolution within definable human aggregates. This is what Wundt means by a "psychological history" as distinct from, for example, a political or military or religious history. With respect to the latter, it is the psychological reality that must first be uncovered if laws, wars, and beliefs are to be even intelligible. Systems of government, principles of social organization, attitudes toward the unseen, concepts of justice all reflect what actual persons take to be true. They are the embodiments of consciousness at a particular stage of its development. To understand an age, then, it becomes necessary to understand the consciousness of the age, its psychology. Lacking this, we are forced to judge every manifestation of science, value, and faith according to our own standards, without having the benefit of recognizing the origins of these very standards.

If primitive man is, indeed, on the earth and not under it, Wundt must have a means of recognizing him. "We shall . . . call that man primitive in the relative sense of the term . . . whose culture approximates most nearly the lowest mental achievements conceivable within the limits of universal human characteristics" (p. 21). To study him is to study *mind* at a point closer to its origins. This Darwinian outlook had already become dominant in psychological circles decades before Wundt's volumes appeared and found expression in a variety of psychological contexts. Alfred Binet, for example, had undertaken research on the mentally retarded not out of a clinical interest in the causes and nature of retardation, but because such persons were fixed at a stage of mental development and thereby allowed psychology to study the stage for an indefinite time. There are grave difficulties associated with this perspective, some of them recognized by a Wundt or a Binet, but some generally and confidently overlooked by Victorian social science. The severely retarded human adult is not simply someone who remains five years old indefinitely, nor is he in any significant respect a normal five year old. Similarly, "primitive" man is not someone now early on a course that culminates in admission to one of London's more esteemed gentleman's clubs. It is worth repeating that the evolutionism so vivid in Wundt's psychology and in the psychology of his entire era was firmly established in the Enlightenment. Its implications were understood very differently by a Darwin and a Hegel, but the essential point would have been readily adopted in the nineteenth century had Darwin and Hegel never appeared. That is, without the apparent support provided by the theory of evolution, the intellectual leaders of the nineteenth century would (as they *did* in the decades just preceding Darwin's publications) endorse the principles of social and moral evolution.

What these principles asserted is that the human condition is not fixed; that progress is the normal course and is retarded only by the imposition of external constraints; that a favoring environment leads inexorably toward an ever more developed capacity for refined thought; that the durability of any culture depends upon the proximity of a stronger and more aggressive one; that the currently dominant forms of language, affiliation, and belief came into being by successful competition with alternatives. In these respects, we might note that the Victorian world view was not especially judgmental; rather, it was taken to be objectively descriptive of the way things are and how they got that way. Thus, when the nineteenth century took note of "savages" and "primitives," it was not for the purpose of ridicule or condemnation, but for the purpose of study. Such specimens were regarded as the living fossils of human social history; regarded as "noble" by those in the Romantic patrimony of Rousseau and as "the white man's burden" by those of a missionary turn of mind. To the scientist, however, they were simply *there*, to be investigated for what they might tell us about the evolution of language, myth, society. The thesis, sometimes expressed and sometimes only implicit, was that such specimens are what we were and would have remained had not certain external conditions impelled us to a higher level of achievement.

Given the thesis, it was possible to discover which of the developed forms of civilized life were in fact natural and basic to human life and which were the somewhat artificial accretions supplied by the accidents of history.

It is also useful to recognize that this perspective was as compatible with radical forms of environmentalism as it was with radical forms of hereditarianism. The former was content to dismiss variety as the nearly mechanical consequence of available natural resources, the number and nature of natural competitors, the relative isolation of a given community from more-or-less advanced neighbors. But the hereditarian too was quick to acknowledge the deleterious effects of prolonged inbreeding, and ready to predict the salutary effects that would arise from the introduction of "better stock."

But whatever complacency this widely held perspective might have inspired was offset by the conflicts it produced. It infected all moral and esthetic discourse with a relativism that was not compatible with the deepest values of the age. Even Thomas Henry Huxley would come to speak of ethics, for example, as something we created to *oppose* natural selection. Simply stated, the nineteenth century's leaders of thought could not accept the proposition that the mud huts of aboriginal man and the Gothic cathedrals of Europe equally depicted nothing more than the "selection pressures" faced by the respective architects; or that the only basis upon Western justice and the law of the jungle can be validly compared is the extent to which each favors the survival of those living under it; or that Newton and the Bushman are two creations of what is finally the same principle of means-ends adaptation.

Wundt was not a relativist in his science or his ethics. Accordingly, his *Völkerpsychologie* presents an often distracting admixture of Kantian-Hegelian categorical judgments and Darwinian *situationism*. His investigations of primitive family structure lead him to the conclusion that monogamy is the basic type of organization, and that promiscuity, polygamy, and "agamy" are curruptions elicited by unusual conditions (pp. 44 ff.). He observes that even in polygamous cultures, there is always a "chief wife," a fact permitting the inference that the current polygamy arose out of monogamous bonds. "Whenever the social organization of primitive man has remained uninfluenced by peoples of higher culture, it consists in a firmly established monogamy of the form of *single marriage*—a mode of existence that was probably carried over from a pre-human stage resembling that of the present-day anthropoids" (pp. 51-52). The same reasoning directs his comments on primitive languages and related phenomena of mind. Thus "when the well-known principle of the struggle for existence is applied to the field of mental phenomena," we will invariably find, among other facts, that, "The stronger race crowded out the most important mental creation of the weaker, its language" (p. 55).

Of course, as anyone who now charts the progress of spoken English over the past half-century will recognize, the "crowding out" is not a one-way affair. Clearly, the influences of a lower or less defined culture are not unfelt by the more developed one. But Wundt is not addressing the effects within a culture caused by the intermingling of classes and castes. Rather, he is positing a theory of cultural evolution based on the consequences of the struggle between separate and different tribes.

Consistent with the Darwinian outlook, Wundt further identifies primitive language with emotion rather than thought. What the primitive communicates with his gestures, facial expressions, modes of dress, and music is his underlying feelings. It is by extension from such gestural-emotive languages that the mythology and the art of the primitive arise: "This world of imagination, projected from man's own emotional life into external phenomena, is what we mean by *mythological* thinking. The things and processes given to perception are supplemented by other realities that are of a non-perceptible nature and therefore belong to an invisible realm" (pp. 74–75).

When the functions of such artistic productions are studied, we learn that the entirety of primitive art can be explained in terms of magic, decoration, and memory. There is little evidence of *ars gratia artis*. The primitive mind must do battle daily, hourly, with the harsh realities of primitive life. As such, it is a mind that seldom rises higher in its aspirations than the desire to be saved from death or disease. Its sense of its own past is crudely recorded in the form of marks and pictures. Its aesthetic productions are often so surprising to itself that it takes the results to be proof of occult forces. Regarding the moral tone of primitive thought, Wundt speaks of the savage thus: "His morality is dependent upon the environment in which he lives. Where he lives a life of freedom, one might almost call his state ideal, there being few motives to immoral conduct in our sense of the word. On the other hand, whenever primitive man is hunted down and hard pressed, he possesses no moral principles whatsoever" (p. 115).

Primitive life reveals the lowest level of attainment reached by those who otherwise possess the "universal" human characteristics. The next higher level of human culture is what Wundt refers to as the culture of the *Totemic Age* in which "the relation of animal to man is the reverse of what obtains in present-day culture" (p. 9). What Wundt means by this is that the totemic culture is organized in herd-like fashion, further divided into clans each of which locates its origins in the life of an animal-ancestor; hence the ubiquity of animal-symbols at the head of the totem. The genuine tribes of totem cultures are distinguishable from primitive aggregates in any number of ways; e.g., primitive weapons are invariably of the long-distance variety, whereas totem weapons are designed for hand-to-hand (intertribal) combat. The totemic tribes are

more settled. Some sort of law governs their practices.
Incest is replaced by *exogamy* as the brute is replaced by
the *chief*: "At some time totemic culture everywhere paved
the way for a more advanced civilization and, thus, . . .
represents a transitional stage between the age of primitive
man and the era of heroes and gods" (p. 139).

In inexorably evolutionary fashion, the tribal chieftan
of the Totem Age later emerges as the head of state in the
Age of Heroes and Gods. The totemic animal ancestor
evolves into a manlike god, combining the virtues of the
actual hero with the powers of the mythic demons. The
Totemic *Märchen*—in which sun and moon and planets
play out the adventure of a mysterious journey—will
appear as the saga and the epic in the Age of Heroes and
Gods. Thus, "Instead of the boy who sets forth upon
magical adventures, we find the youth who has matured
into manhood and whose mighty deeds fill the world with
his fame" (p. 280). For the first time the idea of a unique
personality becomes ensconced in man's conception of himself and his peers. Now it is the sword that is dominant!
And with the notion of deserts comes a form of meritocracy
whose reliable correlates are the idea of personal rights
and that of a ruling class. With the god as hero and the
hero as a kind of deity, the age further distinguishes itself
by its theocratic modes of governance and concepts of
justice. We now find gods dwelling in specific places and
having recognizable personalities. As heroes, they are
historical beings, like ourselves though much older. As
demons they are immortal and utterly unlike ourselves.
Their saga in an essentially theocratic state is the religious
legend in which they figure as the archetypical *saints*. But
herein lies the antithesis, for it is the very saga of the gods
that draws an indelible line between the hero's world of
conflict and death and that other-wordly realm of deathless
joy.

The *idea of redemption*, born of the longing to exchange this world, with its suffering and wants, for a world of happiness in the beyond, took possession of the age. It is the negation of the heroic age, of the heroes which it prized, and of the gods which it revered. Along with this world, these cults of the beyond repudiate also the previously existent values of this world. The ideals of power and property fade. Succeeding the hero ideal, as its abrogation and at the same time its consummation, is the ideal of humanity. (p. 410)

Thus arises the Humanistic Age, out of the ashes of warfare and trial, promising the end of factionalism and the realization of that vision historically revealed in the tenets of Christianity and Buddhism (p. 497).

Here then is Wundt's four-stage theory of cultural psychology, explaining the passage from *primitive* to *totemic* to *heroic-deistic* and finally to *humanistic* ideals in a manner as consistent with Fichte and Hegel as it is with Darwin. Herbart's thesis that each idea gains supremacy by successfully competing against what now occupies consciousness is taken for granted. Fichte's idealistic anthropology, which charts the march of freedom through epochs of thesis-antithesis-synthesis, is adopted with few exceptions and few citations. The Hegelian world view jumps off the pages, most strikingly in Wundt's final chapter, "The Development to Humanity." Wundt faults his philosophical predecessors for their want of method, their reliance on "rationalism," but he does not pause to examine how such a defective method produced results so consistent with his own. In fact, however, the older philosophical anthropology was as attentive to the evidence as is Wundt's psychological anthropology; as attentive but less explicit, less laborious. They knew before Wundt did that the several epochs of cultural activity differed according to the specific ideas or concepts animating each; that from even the grossest levels of observation one could easily detect the core ideas giving character and uniqueness to an age. Wundt supplied not only a far greater mass of data than they, but a systematic argument in defense of empirical methods as the only reliable way of understanding such ages. He did not thereby invent "social psychology"—he specifically noted the difference between it and his *Völkerpsychologie*—or, for that matter, any existing specialty within contemporary psychology. Stating the case fairly, we are more correct to label him a narrator in these regards than a pioneer. Nevertheless, his name carried great and earned weight in the emerging social sciences, and his volumes conveniently summarized and critically examined an immense wealth of information that had been accumulating for decades. If a science is to flourish it must have teachers and Wundt was, to say the least, a master teacher both in person and in print.

The science J. S. Mill would have brought into being under the title "ethology" was very similar to Wundt's *Völkerpsychologie*. In this regard, Wundt should be positioned between the nearly complacent inductivism of Mill and the always confident idealism of Hegel. Wundt would surely have identified his methods as those of the empirical sciences and his general laws as the sorts of empirical generalizations Mill had expected for his science of Ethology. But Wundt's overall theory is Hegelian from start to finish. It is Hegelian in its veiled and protesting teleology; in its focus on the progress of ideas; in its selection of freedom as humanity's *raison d'etre*; in its adoption of negation as the engine of development; in its implicit assertion of one-sidedness as a correlate of incomplete evolution; in its proclamation that human history can only be comprehended by an analysis of human *ideals*, human goals and reasons.

As it is Hegelian, it is also and in a way even more directly Herbartian. Herbart, after all, had sought to construct a consistently empirical and quantitative psy-

chology and had given impetus to the thoughts of no less
a figure in the history of experimental psychology than
Fechner. Thus, Herbart's own doubts about experimental
psychology were more than offset, and his treatment by
later commentators in the scientific traditions of psychology was consistently positive. It was Herbart who had
written:

Psychology will remain one-sided so long as it considers man as
standing alone. For, in the first place, he lives in society and not
merely for this world; secondly, these two facts give rise to
various attempts to sketch ideals whose attractiveness elevates
them . . . to an actual mental power. . . . In every social whole the
individual persons are related to one another in almost the same
way as the concepts in the soul of the individual. . . . Conflicting
interests take the place of the opposition among concepts. . . .
The direct results of the psychological mechanism which here
makes itself felt on a large scale are, that the many are depressed
by the few so much as to lose social significance. . . . [But] the
laws of movement controlling the psychical mechanism do not
suffer complete stagnation. . . . If observations of this kind were
completely elaborated, they would furnish a science of politics . . .
similar to . . . empirical psychology.[11]

Herbart's evolutionary thesis is evident in this excerpt as,
in the balance of the chapter in which it appears, is his
conviction that the oppressed masses ultimately collect and
combine their forces to regain "social significance." This
sentimental side of socialism appears in nearly all influential German sources to which Wundt would have turned
throughout his education and early career. It was the
Weltanschauung of the German intellectuals in the half-
century bracketed by Kant and Marx and it punctuates
the great bulk of sociological and political writing of the
period. It is as evident in the nationalistic *Reden an die
Deutsche Nation* of Fichte as it is in the universalistic ethics
of Hegel.

Wundt was not a political man, but a scholar. He was not given to polemic in his books or lectures. Yet, behind the often drab objectivity of his pronouncements we will discover the excitement of the reformer, the enthusiasms of one who senses a change in the air, a coming age in which the traditional obstacles to freedom are set aside by an enlightened humanity impelled not by fear but by ideals. "Mankind must prepare the way for human nature" (*Völkerpsychologie*, p. 475).

Völkerpsychologie and *Physiologische Psychologie*— A Resumé

What we are left pondering after a review of Wundt's cultural psychology is whether it was psychology at all, or was ever intended as such. As the word is used in all of Wundt's noncultural works, *psychology* is synonymous with both "experimental psychology" and "physiological psychology." The latter is used in two different but overlapping respects. There is first the general meaning of *physiologische* as a systematic and law-governed explanation of mental phenomena; and there is the narrower meaning that seeks to describe the contents and methods of what we would now call "neuropsychology" or "psychobiology." Wundt's *Völkerpsychologie* clearly was never intended to be *physiologische* in the second sense, although it could be argued that it was thought of this way in the first sense. But it is equally clear that Wundt always thought of *Völkerpsychologie* as a subject obtaining its methods and perspectives from nonlaboratory disciplines; those of history, linguistics, anthropology.

The relationship as he understood it between *Völkerpsychologie* and the "other" psychology—the one variously called psychology, experimental psychology, physiological psychology—was one of methodological independence and empirical interdependence. Social and cultural influences furnish the individual mind with habits, inclinations, archetypes, and stereotypical modes of perception and cognition. But these influences from without must work on those internal principles and laws of thought that comprise "the universal characteristics of humanity." And so a degree of interdependence is obvious. It may be illustrated thus: The experimental psychologist sets out to study, say, perception, cross-culturally. He may discover that certain classes of stimuli reliably evince different judgments from members of different cultures. Unalerted to the methods and data of *Völkerpsychologie*, he risks confusing differences that are imposed on individual consciousness from without with inherent differences of *mind* as such.

This much can be said for the cultural psychology's necessary reliance on the findings from experimental psychology. Is there reliance in the other direction? To answer this, we must remind ourselves of what Wundt took to be the limits of experimental science even within the province of individual psychology. As he says in the first of his *Lectures on Human and Animal Psychology*:

We cannot experiment upon mind itself, but only upon its outworks, the organs of sense and movement which are functionally related to mental processes. So that every psychological experiment is at the same time physiological, just as there are physical processes corresponding to the mental processes of sensation, idea, and will. (pp. 10–11)

Wundt's thesis is that all psychological observations in an experimental context are necessarily indirect, permitting only inferences about the actual mental processes standing behind the observed phenomena. From the facts of sensory and motor functions, one is able not only to ascertain the mental substrates but also the physiological substrates.

This is what Wundt means in claiming that the psychological experiment is simultaneously an experiment in physiology.

As mind cannot be directly examined in the laboratory, so too can the laboratory only supply those conditions of stimulation readily accessible to the organs of sense. Limited to these, the psychologist cannot construct explanations beyond the rudimentary processes of perception, cognition, memory, and volition; processes confined to relatively transient events delivered to a mind whose general processes have already been largely determined. Such settings are incapable of addressing the *evolution* of mental functions and are therefore insufficient to host a general science of mind. This can be remedied in part by incorporating lower organisms into laboratory studies of perception and sensory and motor physiology; i.e., it can be remedied in part by what we now call *comparative* psychology. But here too there are ineliminable gaps in our knowledge because of the relatively incomplete development of mind among the lower orders of life. It is in just these respects, as noted earlier in the chapter, that Wundt's *Völkerpsychologie* was intended to complete psychology proper. Through it the psychologist is able to follow the genetic course of mental processes from the level of primitive cognition to that of developed nation-states.

The Manifold of Consciousness

The revival of interest in Wundt during the centennial ceremonies of 1978 and 1979 has, one might hope, put aside several of the traditional confusions surrounding discussions of his work.[12] In some respects, the corrections tend toward the other interpretive extreme, perhaps the inevitable consequence of dealing with such a prolific and long-lived author.* Amid this wave of reinterpretation, it would seem to be prudent to stay quite close to the actual texts, wary of the "Titchenerian" Wundt emerging from the translations provided earlier in the present century.

Wundt's principal works on experimental and physiological psychology routinely employ words such as *Elemente* and *Verbindungen*, thus allowing the construals of "elements" and "compounds" as central to Wundt's theory of mind. But *Verbindungen* is at least as aptly rendered as "combinations," particularly in light of Wundt's debts to Herbart's notion of the blendings and fusions of concepts. Moreover, as we have seen, Wundt was especially opposed to radically reductionistic models of psychology and would not have attempted to ground the discipline in anything as mechanical as the addition and subtraction of sensory or ideational "elements." As understood by Wundt, such terms as consciousness, mind, memory, perception, and the like refer not to objects but to *processes.* His psychology is everywhere a dynamic one which takes for granted that *change* is the ubiquitous law of mental life. He carries this so far as to exclude even the possibility of the unaltered survival of a single idea:

The circumstance that new processes exhibit relations and similarity to others previously existing, can no more prove the continued existence of the idea as such, than it can be inferred from the similarity of the movement of the pen in writing a definite word now to that involved on a former occasion, that this movement has continued to exist in an invisible form from the time it was first made. (*Lectures*, pp. 236–37)

On the same grounds he opposes the "faculty" psychology of the preceding century. To say, for example, that every

---

* There are those, for example, who are so eager to refute the allegation that Wundt's individual psychology is "elementaristic" that they finally make him over into something of a *Gestalt* psychologist.

act of consciousness involves discrimination is to say only that consciousness is *activity*, and that part of this is the activity of discrimination—not some separate faculty of mind.

Understood in this way, Wundt's psychology may be thought of as elementaristic only with respect to the processes, not the contents of consciousness. To say that we are conscious, then, is to say only that we are aware of ideas, of feelings, and of certain volitional impulses. These are the most general headings covering the contents of thought. Under *ideas* are also to be found memories, images, and sense perceptions. A psychology of ideation must be addressed to these several contents, the laws governing their formation and interaction. That there are such laws, Wundt declares, is already established by the psychophysical experiments of Weber and Fechner and the laws arising out of them. It is also clear that only a *psychological* interpretation of these laws is plausible (*Lectures*, pp. 59–63). Neither a materialistic reduction nor a parallelist position speaks to the facts and laws of perception. Wundt recurs to this point in several of his books and in a later chapter of the *Lectures* in connection with what he calls the "General Law of Relativity":

Wherever there occurs a quantitative apprehension of sensations, whether as regards intensity or degree of quality, the individual sensation is estimated by the relation in which it stands to other sensations of the same sense-modality.... The most obvious interpretation of the law is this: that we never apprehend the intensity of a mental state as if it stood alone; but measurement implies a direct comparison of one conscious state with another. And so ... the law of relativity is not restricted to the sphere of sensation, but is applicable in every case where the intensity of a mental process is quantitatively apprehended and compared with that of others. (p. 119)

The subject matter of psychology, we learn, is what is *given* in consciousness, and the goal of psychology is the discovery of the laws by which these *givens* grow out of the basic processes of thought, feeling, and volition. This is the empiricistic side of Wundt's system, and the side that survives the curious interpretations of his translators, disciples, and critics.

Wundt's dissatisfaction with the associationistic theory of ideas has already been mentioned and now remains to be discussed. Part of it has to do with the history of the theory which Wundt took to be too philosophical, too innocent with respect to the actual complexities of thought. Nonetheless, he was prepared to accept the broad features of associationism once these were extended to include what he called *simultaneous* association, and once the doctrine was refined to distinguish between *similarity* associations and *contiguity* associations. We see, then, that Wundt's theory of cognition was to these extents associationistic, but more in the Herbartian than in the Humean tradition. But there is an entire side of cognition which Wundt exempted from processes of this sort—the side pertaining to *logical thought*, to what Wundt called "concept-ideas." He makes the distinction this way in noting the difference between recognition and cognition on the one hand and conceptual thought on the other. But

if cognition, recognition, and concept are so far alike it is just at this point that we are able also to lay our finger upon the essential difference between the first two processes and the third. The temporal series is always a similarity- or contiguity-association, in which (as the name implies) each idea persists as an independent unity. For objects which resemble one another, or which are contiguous in space and time, may certainly be combined to form more complex ideas; but every part of the resulting compound process is still independent, so that if it becomes dissociated from its companions, it continues unimpaired in consciousness. But with concept-ideas, as with all conscious content which belongs to a logically coherent thought-process, the case is very different. The significance of the individual is now entirely dependent upon the whole of which it forms a part. . . . Thus the concept "man," when we think of it without reference to any context of judgment, can only have this significance: that it may be subject or predicate of a large number of judgments. Only as such an indefinite element of a logical thought is it a "concept" at all. (pp. 310–11)

On the basis of this distinction, Wundt's cognitive psychology thereupon moves quickly away from the associationistic tradition. We soon discover that associative processes are now to be contrasted with *intellectual* processes, the latter marked by *activity*; by the *apperceptive connections of ideas*; by the fact that genuinely intellectual processes fall "under the concept of internal voluntary action" (p. 312). It is now the *self*, taken as "the general tendency of all our conscious content at any given time," that must be posited as the *cause* of every truly intellectual event or concept-idea.

We now begin to recognize that in moving away from traditional associationism, Wundt was further obliged to move away from that "spectator" theory of knowledge which had been the backbone of empiricistic psychologies since the seventeenth century. In place of the older theory's reliance on the formation of mental pictures or copies of the external world, Wundt substituted *process*. In place of the percipient as a passive screen upon which the world of fact projected itself, Wundt installed an active, inwardly directed mind whose entire history participated in each of its acts; a mind so constituted as to impose logical coherence on all its intellectual operations and furnished by associations only in its nonconceptual operations.

This process is best seen in the acts of logical thought . . . expressed in language. These are completely different, even in outward form, from the associative series. In the latter one idea joins on to another indeterminately; but logical thought is governed by a . . . law, admitting of no exception. . . . The clearest expression of this law is to be found in the grammatical distinction of the parts of the sentence. (p. 314)

What Wundt is getting at here—and in a manner anticipated by Descartes and Leibniz and productively pursued in the twentieth century by Noam Chomsky—is that an associationistic theory of language simply fails to describe, let alone explain, language in its most defining respects. The parts of a sentence are not strung together by anything resembling either contiguity associations or similarity associations. These may figure in the actual contents of language but they figure not at all in the basic structure of language. The latter is rule-governed and proceeds from thought processes that can only be described in terms of their *logical* coherence. Indeed, it is precisely in the differences between associatiative and intellectual processes that we may locate the psychological differences between man and beast: "The step from association to intelligence proper is undoubtedly the longest ever taken in the course of mental evolution" (p. 365).

Taken together, Wundt's principles of activity, process, apperception, and intellection, when understood against the background feelings and desires of the person, constitute that *manifold of consciousness* to which a scientific psychology must be addressed. Far from elementarizing the mind, Wundt often wrote of these processes in a manner suggestive of contemporary "feedback" models. This is particularly the case in his discussions of the interdependence of thought and feeling and of the cognitive aspects of human emotion. Feelings alter the train of ideas and, thus altered, the latter transform the feelings. As always in Wundtian psychology, the process is dynamic and, although often initiated from without, is generally sustained by the inner principles of mind.

Wundt's influence on the immediate future of experimental psychology has been noted often, but we also discover in his program at least the seeds of a *phenomenology* soon to be espoused (but not so-called) by William James and then to be rendered explicit by Edmund Husserl. Wundt's science, after all, is the science of mind as this reveals itself in its contents and operations. It is a science that does not disregard the external sources of experience, but acknowledges the difference between source and substance, between a causal sequence and a dynamic process.

But if Wundt anticipated one major development in psychology, he came close to legislating against an even more august one—psychoanalytic theory. To the extent that he wrote about the "unconscious" at all, Wundt generally confined his remarks to what Leibniz had called the *petite perception* and to the "negative sensations" implied by the psychophysical law. Thus, he surely had no Freudian sense of unconscious motivations. And on the matter of dreams, hypnotism, and hynotic induction, he had the gravest reservations. His own approach to the problem of mental illness was guided by the volitional and associative principles of his general psychology. Thus we find him speaking of mental disturbances as the result of "increasingly restricted . . . and stable ideas, which repeat themselves over and over again" and taking these "fixed ideas" as the hallmark of a mind disintegrating[11] (*Lectures on Human and Animal Psychology*, p. 322). Up to this point, the agreement between Wundt and such emerging giants of medical psychology as Pierre Janet is very close. But it was Janet and his French colleagues who had placed great emphasis upon hypnotism as an experimental instrument and who had thought of the unconscious as the *via regia* to an understanding of the diseased mind, and these were precisely the notions rejected by Wundt. What Wundt demanded of an experimental psychology was an investigation of conscious processes as these are displayed by a trained, properly motivated, and apperceptive observer. Hypnotism, accordingly, could not be worse suited to the needs of such science. In light of this attitude, we are not surprised when one of Janet's famous contemporaries, Alfred Binet, writes: "With relatively few exceptions, the psychologists of my country have left the investigations of psychophysics to the Germans."[13] For on this very topic, Wundt had declared, "It is wholly unnecessary to assume the existence of a mysterious mental double, the 'other self' or secondary personality, or to set up any other of the fanciful hypotheses so plentiful in this field" (*Lectures*, p. 331).

Wundt was confident that an analysis of the associative and intellective processes would provide at least the first terms of a scientific theory of mental illness, and that the phenomena of somnambulism, hypnosis, and autosuggestion were grounded in the processes of attention and volition. Hypnotism works, he argued, because of the subject's surrender of his will, his belief in the powers of the "magnetizer." Here as elsewhere it was Wundt's aim to base psychology on the publicly observable facts of consciousness, and to explain psychological outcomes through laws admitting of experimental verification. Recourse to observers who are untrained or semiconscious, to methods that bear no resemblance to experimental procedure, and to explanations having no kin in the balance of scientific psychology was just the sort of habit that had denied psychology its scientific status throughout the ages.

These same considerations were at work in Wundt's somewhat wary review of the literature on animal psychology. His comments on George Romanes' influential *Animal Intelligence* briefly set forth some of the criticisms that C. Lloyd Morgan would later direct at *anthropomorphism* as he laid the foundations for a behavioristic comparative psychology.[14] But Wundt's disinclinations regarding anthropomorphism were balanced by a confident appraisal of the facts of human mental life. His position may be summarized this way: He was properly concerned that we not take superficial similarities in the actions of man and lower organisms as proof of similarities in the underlying psychological processes. But he was just as concerned that

we not trivialize human intellectual processes by noting
how well animals do some of the things we do. What
animals actually do may often appear to be manlike and,
indeed, some human activity is not significantly removed
from the psychological processes common to all the advanced species. But even in such unelevated spheres of
conduct as that of play, the differences become obvious:

The impossibility of transcending a certain circle of ready-made
associations characterises the play of animals (even of the most
highly developed), as it characterises their mental life in general.
Over against the countless varieties of the play of children,
reflecting all conceivable relations of life, stands the single form
of mock fighting among the animals. (*Lectures*, pp. 357–58)

The animal is tied to a narrow circle of ready-made
associations, and does only that which instinct and memory
allow. It lacks that defining intellectual feature of mind
which makes human thought *sui generis*. It is in this analysis
that Wundt would seem to have established the limits of
a Darwinian psychology or what is now fashionably called
"sociobiology."

The Wundtian Legacy: Recapitulation

As noted at the beginning of this chapter, there has
been so much written on Wundt—he looms so large in
psychology's most recent century—that he often appears
devoid of an intellectual context. To casual students of the
history of psychology, he just happened! We see, however,
that Wundt's context was the recently divided world of
German thought; a world in which science and philosophy
were seeking opposite poles of discourse and in which
each claimed exclusive proprietorship of psychology's enduring issues. What places Wundt apart from so many of

his contemporaries is not that he spoke decisively for either camp, but that he maintained an objective detachment in the face of the pretensions of both. He took what was least cluttered and arguable in the systems of Kant, Fichte, Herbart, and Hegel and with these he fashioned a modest but compelling critique of psychological materialism. In this way he preserved the independence of psychology and forestalled indefinitely its absorption by physiology. But in another part of Herbart's work and in every part of the psychological works of Helmholtz, Weber, and Fechner he discovered the methods and measurements that made an experimental psychology possible. One of his major accomplishments, therefore, was the creation of an experimental perspective not tied to materialism.

Another side of this accomplishment is evident in his critique of associationism and defense of voluntarism. Wundt was thoroughly familiar with the range of any psychology grounded in the traditional maxims of empiricistic and associationistic philosophy. These maxims had artificially set limits on the willingness of their patrons to accept what was already known to be true about the mind. Wundt's devotion to fact was exceptionless, even when the fact made a comforting theory implausible. The *fact* of mental life is its activity, not passivity; its direction by the will, not its subservience to external objects; its conceptual and not merely perceptual character. Wundt was content to render unto associationism the things that were associative, but to conceptualism the things that were not. To restrict mind to the former was effectively to ignore just those processes that separate human thought from animal "intelligence."

At the level of human culture, Wundt was equally willing to require psychology to face the fact of human history; a history that could not *in principle* be understood according to the causal chains that exhaust the subject of natural science. Just as apperception describes the volitional component of experience, and just as the interplay of intellect and emotion can only be understood in terms of the aims and intentions of thinking man, so also can the forms of culture only be addressed in the language of *reasons*. The domain of history entails the conscious strivings of reflective beings, as the domain of the individual mind entails processes of a self-initiated and goal-directed nature. The latter can be studied experimentally, but not explained biologically. The former cannot even be studied experimentally and so cannot be absorbed by the natural sciences.

If it can be said that Mill attempted to provide a single inductive science of psychology and failed, and that Hegel attempted to provide a single transcendental psychology but finally offered no psychology at all, then we might add that Wundt succeeded only by aborting the mission. He developed *two* psychologies, neither of which could be easily fit into the accepted templates of nineteenth-century monistic metaphysics. His individual psychology was far too objective and experimental to satisfy the Hegelian; far too "psychological" to satisfy the materialists. His cultural psychology, on the other hand, was not experimental at all and could not figure in any intelligible way in the plans of the emerging community of "scientific" psychologists. To the extent that it was vaguely Hegelian, it was too dilute for one camp and too pungent for the other.

Thus, what the official psychology of the early twentieth century took from Wundt was the psychophysical methodology; the usefulness of comparative studies; the broader empiricistic perspective and its laboratory rigors; the topics of perception and what is now called "information processing" as fit subjects for measurement and curve fitting. What it abandoned, however, was nothing less than what Wundt had sought to establish: An experimental science of consciousness devoted to the principles governing the interaction of thought, emotion, and volition. But modern psychology abandoned all this for the soundest of reasons: It couldn't discover a way of doing it.[15]

5. WILLIAM JAMES

Genius reveals itself in varied modes, attracting the largest following through the mode of invention but shaping the consciousness of an age chiefly through the modes of analysis and synthesis. Neither Mill nor Hegel nor Wundt may be said to have invented or discovered some great scientific principle permitting the world to achieve a specific goal more quickly or effectively. The same is true of William James. He founded no school, unearthed no verity, solved no problem. But like Mill and Hegel, and to a greater extent than Wundt, he traced out the boundaries of thought and supplied the terms with which an entire generation would discuss and understand Psychology. On some accounts, he might be credited with founding a laboratory for experimental psychology at Harvard even before Wundt's at Leipzig, but it is surely not on this basis that his significance depends.[1] He is also and less equivocally credited with initiating courses in physiological psychology, again at Harvard, in the 1870s, but as we shall see he is scarcely to be remembered as one who would have tied mental science to biology. If we are to discover the nature of James' influence on his contemporaries and immediate successors, we must look past those of his activities which seemed to have anticipated our own interests and toward those that spoke to the dominant interests of his time.

Since many articles and more than one doctoral dissertation have labored to establish priority in the matter of

Psychology's first laboratory, it may be proper to explain briefly why the entire issue is really beside the point. Questions of the sort, "When was the first experiment in psychology conducted?" are not answerable by exclusively historical methods because the terms are too indefinite. The plausible answers to such a question will all depend on how one defines "experiment," "psychology," and even "conducted." On a loose construal, psychological experimentation took place at least as far back as Aristotle's observation of the illusion of *twoness* when a stylus is moved back and forth between the crossed fingers of one hand. When experimentation is defined more strictly to include the use of repeated measurement and the scaling of relevant independent and dependent variables, we must look to the nineteenth century for founders. But Weber and Fechner both predate Wundt and James in this regard, even if Weber and Fechner did not take the administrative step of naming the rooms in which they made their observations.

There is, however, an even more compelling reason for not taking such questions too seriously. They are not actually *historical* questions, but *chronological* ones, in the same sense that "When did Bob sell his sports car?" is not a historical question. To frame such questions in historical terms, we must concern ourselves with historical rather than merely biographical occurrences. This point can be made clearer with an illustration. Suppose archeologists digging in Central America uncovered a small room, dating from at least the third millennium, and containing calibrated brass weights, pendulums, vernier calipers, and other devices for measuring the accuracy of perceptual judgments. Suppose, further, that clay tablets were found in the same room and displayed etchings of graphs depicting what we now take to be Fechner's psychophysical law. Would we say, equipped with these findings, that the history of *psychophysics* begins in Central America, circa 3000 B.C.? Would it not be more correct to applaud the cleverness of the nameless savant, but to continue to take Fechner as the founder of psychophysics? It was Fechner whose work altered the manner in which the issue of quantifying experience was understood by all those who devoted themselves to this issue and who passed it on to succeeding generations of scholars and scientists. That is, psychophysics as a *historical* phenomenon begins with Fechner, even if as a purely biographical "happening" something like it may have occurred five thousand years ago. It is in just this respect that choosing between Wundt and James vis-à-vis psychology's first university laboratory does not involve a choice between two answers to a historical question. The *historical* question is essentially an impersonal one: What factors and forces were operating toward the middle of the nineteenth century such that psychological questions were increasingly brought under the methodological aegis of laboratory investigation? Put in these terms, the question admits of historical analysis and still permits us to give proper credit to Weber, Fechner, Wundt, James, and a handful of others.

It is also important not to be distracted by such facts as James' early courses in "psychophysiology." By the time James began his academic duties at Harvard there was a veritable tradition of discussing psychological issues within a biological and neurophysiological framework. The influence of Gall's phrenological works, which began to appear in the first decade of the nineteenth century, and the rebuttals and loyalties these works inspired, had placed the nervous system at the very center of what the eighteenth century rather innocently called "mental science." Both within universities and at their margins, the "cerebral theory" was either taken for granted or was taken as plausible in the psychological writings of Bell, Flourens,

Magendie, Spencer, Bain, Griesinger, Müller, Helm-holtz—a legion of famous men coming years and decades earlier than James.

It is not, then, the title of a Harvard course or the date his students trundled into a laboratory that earns James the attention of today's historian. His *historical* achievement, accomplished primarily through his published texts, was that of imposing a character on academic psychology which it has never completely shed nor fully recognized. There is no contemporary Jamesian school of psychology, as there is no Darwinian or Helmholtzian or Wundtian school. Nonetheless, to the extent that there is and has been a force in the world of thought called American psychology, James's legacy has been honored. There is little in the twentieth-century history of Psychology in America that has not been colored and shaped by his works; little in the failures and frustrations of this same psychology that he did not anticipate.

The Principles of Psychology was published in two volumes in 1890, a dozen years after James had undertaken the work and about ten years after his publisher expected it.[2] As early as 1867, writing from Berlin, he is found telling his father of his plans to go to Heidelberg: "There are two professors there, Helmholtz and Wundt, who are strong on the physiology of the senses. . . . As a central point of study I imagine that the border ground of physiology and psychology, overlapping both, would be as fruitful as any, and I am now working on to it."[3]

We see, then, that by age twenty-five he had already begun to chart his course, moving away from a medical career which he had never really seriously considered and also away from strict physiology whose laboratory demands exceeded his often diminished physical powers. On this latter point, however, we are not obliged to take too seriously his occasional excuse for abandoning the life of the research scientist. It is true that James' early years were plagued by a variety of physical maladies and that he avoided undertakings likely to require physical endurance. But the entire drift of his thought, from early adulthood, was in the direction of systematic and critical scholarship— scholarship writ large. Matters of health may have abbreviated his time in the laboratory but it was his intellectual personality that numbered such days from the outset.

In a manner uncommon to the genre, *The Principles of Psychology* instructed professors even more than students, although by 1890 there was no shortage of texts in the new "science." Spencer and Bain had each contributed two-volume works some forty years earlier and Wundt and his students had added any number of introductory works. The influence of the *Principles* is not to be explained on the basis of priority, therefore, but in terms of the intrinsic merits of the work and the growing authority of its author within the most elevated circles of thought. James' own friends included nationally and internationally recognized figures in science, the arts, and politics. He travelled and lectured widely and often, maintained an active correspondence for many decades, saw to it that his most able students received important academic appointments, and made effective use of a broad range of literary and scientific forums. His penetrating intelligence summoned the attention of the best minds of his age, and his style and method of argument kept him accessible to a large and appreciative public audience. As we shall see, his genius was not of the sort that concludes an important debate, but that gets it going and keeps it going on a productive track. He and his *Principles* did not found American psychology in the sense of inventing a new method or uncovering a basic law. Rather, his works and ways saved academic psychology from sinking to the mere busy-work of the laboratory or rising so high toward metaphysics as to abandon its proper subject. He was never won over by the calming assurances of this or that "school," this or that unbridled generalization. Where science could offer nothing better, James remained loyal to common sense. He opposed factionalism but never resisted the evidence adduced by the parties in conflict. He promoted his own empiricism and "pragmatism," but never at the price of blindness to their limitations. *He let the show go on.*

Fire and Clay

After a brief chapter outlining the scope of Psychology, James' *Principles* proceeds immediately to "The Functions of the Brain." By 1890 this organization had become something of a formula—one adopted by Spencer, Bain, Maudsley, Wundt, and many others. But with James there is more than adherence to a formula; there is the decisive commitment to provide the reader with an unambiguous and entirely forthcoming account of the degree to which the subject matter of psychology can be comprehended by the brain sciences; the degree, that is, to which the "fire" of mind can be reduced to the "clay" of body. He devotes the chapter to a systematic review of the methods and general findings of these sciences, pausing to offer instructive criticisms not only of Gall and the school of phrenology but also of those who have failed to appreciate the subteties of the "localization of function" issue. On the whole, however, the chapter lends support to the claim presented by James in his opening pages: "the brain is the one immediate bodily condition of the mental operations" (*Principles*, 1:4) and, therefore, "a certain amount of brain-physiology must be presupposed or included in Psychology" (p. 5).

The question, then, has to do with the nature of such presuppositions or inclusions, for it is these that will determine the sort of psychology we have. One set of suppositions leads to what James calls the "automaton theory" which appears either in the form of a radical materialism that utterly denies *mind* or an *epiphenomenalism* that dismisses mental states as the mechanical consequences of brain function. What the theory in all its forms specifically rejects is that two-way interactionism by which mental life is able to guide or influence the physiological processes of the brain. According to the "automatists" the neural side of the equation is the causal; the mental, the effect. Consciousness cannot be efficacious in the workings of the brain and (by implication) need not be studied at all, since to know the brain's functions is to know determinatively what the mental processes must be. Regarding consciousness, "One may bow her out politely, allow her to remain as a 'concomitant,' but one insists that matter shall hold all the power" (p. 135).

The arguments for the automaton theory were as common in James' time as in our own. They proceed from one or another form of "unity of science" notion, taking for granted that, as chemistry is absorbed by the laws of physics, so also is biology absorbed by the laws of chemistry and psychology by those of biology. The physical world is directly accessible to the senses whose products equip us with all we need to fashion those causal principles by which this world operates. But the "mental" world, if such there is, cannot play a causative part in any of this for, as Mercier put it in 1888, "Try to imagine the idea of a beefsteak binding two molecules together." Science, whose business it is to construct that text of causation by which the material world becomes intelligible, need not worry about a *mind* throwing matter into disarray. Instead, it will take mind as simply one more consequence of molecular bonding; one more result of matter in motion. "The soul," wrote Huxley, "stands related to the body as the bell of a clock to the works, and consciousness answers to the sound which the bell gives out when it is struck".[4]

This view, which James took to be an unwarrantable

impertinence (*Principles*, p. 138) had been rejected by Wundt, as we noted in the previous chapter, but had begun to win the adherence of many of the more accomplished scientists in England and America. Critics were not scarce, but were drawn primarily from the ranks of "spiritualists" and those in the Hegelian tradition. The scientists who voiced objections tended not to ground their counterclaims in the facts of mental and biological life. James, however, approached the thesis as he would any scientific claim; within the context of what was known of or safely implied by the facts of science itself. He observed, for example, the that cerebral functions were notoriously unstable in that they were specifically designed to register the widest range of environmental occurrences and changes. It is just this instability that permits the nervous centers to be responsive to the data conveyed by the senses. The very developed brain, the "high brain,"

> may do many things, and may do each of them at a very slight hint. But its hair-trigger organization makes of it a happy-go-lucky, hit-or-miss affair. It is as likely to do the crazy as the sane thing at any given moment. ... The performances of a high brain are like dice thrown forever on a table. Unless they be loaded, what chance is there that the highest number will turn up oftener than the lowest? ... *Can consciousness increase its efficiency by loading its dice?* (p. 140)

What James is getting at here is the directive and selective functions of consciousness; functions that *must* be performed if the "hair-trigger" responses of the central nervous system are not to reduce the organism to a capricious and aimlessly reactive mirror of environmental impingements. Ever the *functionalist*, James insists that the creature described by the automaton-theory, if it exists anywhere, can be little more than a reflex device which survives by virtue of a fortuitously prewired set of reflexes. But where there is consciousness at all, it must have a function, and the most plausible function is that of selecting significant features of the environment and directing the appropriate cerebral processes. "Loading its dice would mean bringing a more or less constant pressure to bear in favor of *those* of its performances which make for the most permanent interests of the brain's owner; it would mean a constant inhibition of the tendencies to stray aside" (p. 140). "The brain" says James, "is an instrument of possibilities, but of no certainties." If it is to serve the interests of its owner, it must be made to conform to the ends of life, and it is the mission of consciousness to impose this conformity on an otherwise "hit-or-miss affair."

In this same connection, James was careful to recognize how consciousness at least implicitly must be included in any careful Darwinian account of the behavior of men and animals. To remove it from the arenas in which the advanced species function is to render the Darwinian account incoherent:

we treat survival as if it were an absolute end, existing as such in the physical world, a sort of actual *should-be*, presiding over the animal and judging his reactions, quite apart from the presence of any commenting intelligence outside. We forget that in the absence of some such superadded commenting intelligence (whether it be that of the animal itself, or only ours or Mr. Darwin's), the reactions cannot be properly talked of as "useful" or "hurtful" at all. Considered merely physically, all that can be said of them is that *if* they occur in a certain way survival will as a matter of fact prove to be their incidental consequence. The organs themselves, and all the rest of the physical world, will, however, all the time be quite indifferent to this consequence, and would quite as cheefully, the circumstances changed, compass the animal's destruction. In a word, survival can enter into a purely physiological discussion only as an *hypothesis made by an onlooker* about the future. But the moment you bring a consciousness into the midst, survival ceases to be a mere hypothesis. No longer is it, "*if* survival is to occur, then so and so must brain and other organs work." It has now become an imperative decree:

"Survival *shall* occur, and therefore organs must so work!" *Real* ends appear for the first time now upon the world's stage. (p. 141)

The conscious animal is not hypothetical in its relation to survival. It is oriented toward the goal of survival and its conduct is organized around the *conscious* awareness of means and ends. Where there is consciousness, this is its function, and to serve this function it must be efficacious— which means among other considerations that it must be able to affect the brain. The pure automaton requires no such consciousness. We, however, do and, more to the point, we know that we do. It must not be part of the mission of science to deny what every man knows to be true; thus, a science can have only the shortest of histories if grounded in denials of this sort. Accepting consciousness (for it must) the task of science is that of understanding its functions and their laws. Psychology, like physics,

must be *naive*; and if she finds that in her very peculiar field of study ideas *seem* to be causes, she had better continue to talk of them as such. She gains absolutely nothing by a breach with common-sense in this matter, and she loses, to say the least, all naturalness of speech. (p. 137)

But if (consciousness) is useful, it must be so through its causal efficaciousness, and the automaton-theory must succumb to the theory of common-sense. I, at any rate . . . shall have no hesitation in using the language of common-sense throughout. (p. 144)

Thomas Reid had not said it better, for he had said the same. Where science and common sense collide, science must be in possession of undoubted facts or must proceed from a metaphysical foundation provably more complete and firm than that which common sense can claim. It is perilous even for a developed science to cast itself as the adversary of common sense, and fatal to one that is both young and specifically charged with the task of understanding the human understanding! The automaton theory was too "metaphysical" in the usual sense and not metaphysical enough in the sense in which James preferred to use the term: "Metaphysics means nothing but an unusually obstinate effort to think clearly" (p. 145). By this same standard, James must also reject the *Mind-Stuff theory* (*Principles*, ch. 6) and the associationistic psychology arising out of it. Stated tersely, this is the theory according to which mental states are *compounds* of more elementary units. It was the favorite theory of such evolutionists as Spencer because it seemed to support the view that mind, far from being an exception to the (evolutionary) laws of continuous development, was actually the result of a gradual addition of elementary (molecular) configurations. Taking the physical world as containing some sort of "mind dust," the Spencerian was content to absorb all mental phenomena into that process of continuing development alleged to explain the purely morphological evolution of species. Accordingly, *mind* constituted no sudden break, no dawn of the new, no mysterious entity. The simplest organisms were thus taken as possessing less "mind dust." Yet, as James said,

that is a verbal quibble. The fact is that discontinuity comes in if a new nature comes in at all. The *quantity* of the latter is quite immaterial. The girl in "Midshipman Easy" could not excuse the illegitimacy of her child by saying, "it was a very small one." And Consciousness, however small, is an illegitimate birth in any philosophy that starts without it, and yet professes to explain all facts by continuous evolution. (pp. 148–49)

A like confusion has been inspired by associationistic psychologies, at least where these have been deployed in support of monistic metaphysics. At base, these psychologies either assume or refuse to oppose the chief tenets of materialism. And even when their aim is not the rejection of consciousness, their net effect on psychological reasoning is. What traditional associationism fosters is the view that sense impressions constitute the rudimentary elements of mind and that all the complexity of the latter is to be understood as nothing more than combinations and accretions of the former. These elements—these particles of "mind dust"—are then conceived as obedient to laws similar to those regulating purely material interactions; e.g., gravitational laws as used by Hartley in his associationistic theory. The obvious advantage of the theory is that it eliminates the need to speak of consciousness or of the mind's active powers. It removes the *self* from such transactions and readies mental science for the sort of refinements so successfully wrought upon the subject of classical mechanics. It *depersonalizes* psychology by permitting the voyage of mental life to proceed without a single and namable steersman. All that is required is an ensemble of associative elements or units combining according to (Humean) laws, compounding themselves into ever more complex assemblies, and always at the mercy of events in the external world. Mind or consciousness is thus only this process of compounding. The process begins with elements too slight to weigh on consciousness but, by summation and integration, culminates in the (*suprathreshold*) conscious event. To take a trivial example, the experience of *yellow* now becomes understood as the consequence of a compounding of the separate elements of *red* and *green*.

As Thomas Reid had insisted that, for there to be treason, there must be a traitor, so too does James insist that: "*All the 'combinations' which we actually know are* EFFECTS, *wrought by the units said to be 'combined,'* UPON SOME ENTITY OTHER THAN THEMSELVES" (p. 158). Elements do not simply add to themselves, thereby becoming something other than what they were. "Each remains, in the sum, what it always was; and the sum itself exists only for a bystander"

(p. 158). To give each of a dozen men a single word but to have none of them know the words given to the others will never allow a sentence to come from the group, no matter how the men are arranged. In this and in all cases whatever coherence may be extracted from the constituents can only be extracted by some external party, some bystander.

> This argument . . . against the associationists has never been answered. . . . It holds good against any talk about self-compounding amongst feelings, against any "blending," or "complication," or "mental chemistry," or "psychic synthesis," which supposes a resultant consciousness to float off from the constituents *per se*, in the absence of a supernumerary principle of consciousness which they may affect. The mind-stuff theory, in short, is unintelligible. (p. 161)

Now, as we shall see, James finally came down against the real existence of consciousness, at least as the word is taken to refer to something different from or transcending experience. The first of his *Essays in Radical Empiricism* is addressed to the question, "Does 'Consciousness' Exist?" which James answers in the negative, except where consciousness is taken to stand for a *function* rather than an entity.[5] James's ontology begins and ends with *real experience*; experience as it is had, as it is given, as it is immediately and reflectively known. His opposition to the automaton theory, the Mind-Stuff theory, and associationism is grounded in precisely the facts of had, given, and known experience. What these facts report is the continuity of thought, the *stream of consciousness* as a whole. In parallel with this real succession of thoughts and percepts—this succession of experiences—there is a succession of states of brain. And as mind must be taken in the fullness and continuity of process, so too must the physiological processes of brain *in toto* be taken as the necessary condition.

The spiritualistic reader may nevertheless believe in the soul if he will; whilst the positivistic one who wishes to give a tinge of mystery to the expression of his positivism can continue to say that nature in her unfathomable designs has mixed us of clay and flame, of brain and mind, that the two things hang indubitably together and determine each other's being, but how or why, no mortal may ever know. (p. 182)

Taking consciousness to be a function as contrasted with a substance or some other sort of "thing," the psychologist is able to avoid the traps toward which Kant, Hegel, Comte, and even Mill so often wandered. James defended the introspective method as one *"we have to rely on first and foremost and always"* (p. 185), but as one that was also passing away and being replaced by experimentation. "The simple and open method of attack having done what it can," says James, "the method of patience, starving out, and harrassing to death is tried" (p. 192). And to the experimental method is added the *comparative method*, that form of naturalistic observation made famous by Darwin and fashioned into comparative psychology by Spalding, Romanes, and others; a method which seeks to determine the functions of human psychology by examining lower organisms, savages, children, and the insane:

So it has come to pass that instincts of animals are ransacked to throw light on our own; and that the reasoning faculties of bees and ants, the minds of savages and infants, madmen, idiots, the deaf and the blind, criminals, and eccentrics, are all invoked in support of this or that special theory. . . . The interpretation of the "psychoses" of animals, savages, and infants is necessarily wild work, in which the personal equation of the investigator has things very much its own way. (p. 194)

That experimental and comparative data, in large enough numbers, would one day "combine" into something theoretically cogent was a possibility James generously allowed.

But when all is said and done, it is again (and always) to introspection that psychology must turn, for only it can directly produce that living and actual mind that functions in the real world. It is a method, however, that lends itself to abuse—to varieties of the "psychologist's fallacy" by which the investigator comes to think of thought as identical to the mental fact as the psychologist studies it. It is this fallacy that nourishes and is nourished by the Mind-Stuff theory, for when it is committed it produces those utterly artifical *elements* of thought of which no actual thought is composed.

The introspective method recommended by James is one that takes the *stream* of thought as its basic datum. The method is fallible and difficult. It must be constantly supplemented by the less systematic but more general knowledge we have of ourselves and the world; the knowledge that cannot be recaptured by the new "prism, pendulum, and chronograph-philosophers" (p. 193). But there is no gain in adopting a method that reliably and accurately misses the point! The point of psychology is, in the end, that constellation of laws and principles capable of explaining the course and facts of mental life. If this point is not to be missed, the phenomena of mental life must be taken as they come; not stripped of their dynamic properties, of their *wholeness*, of their immediacy. As they do not occur in packages of mechanically combined associations, any theory that imposes such a character on them is simply vacuuous. And when the same theory obliges the brain to operate in a similarly mechanical bang-bang fashion, as if the physiology of the brain were just so many moving parts, we then come to possess a psychology that libels the mind and invents a brain to support the libel. From the standpoint of psychology, the mind and the brain—the fire and the clay—must be taken as in fact they reveal themselves; as processes ideally suited to the achievement of significant ends, regulated continuously by selective and

directive functions and interacting in a such a manner as
to minimize chaos. At the most general introspective level
of observation, thought displays five indubitable attributes:
(a) it is *owned* in the sense that the thinker *has* it; (b) it
constantly changes in vividness or content; (c) it is known
so to change by its owner; (d) it is taken by its owner as
something independent of its object; (e) it *chooses* its object
from an array of possibilities (*Principles* ch. 9). No two
ideas are ever identical and no thought, once lost, ever
returns as *itself*: "Experience is remoulding us every moment, and our mental reaction on every given thing is
really a resultant of our experience of the whole world
up to that date" (*Principles*, 1:234).

We often think of complex objects—objects that can
only be understood in the abstract as ensembles of parts.
But the thought itself is an undivided state of consciousness,
not a congeries of such parts. Again, psychology must
resist the temptation to impute to *thought* as it occurs the
attributes of the things thought about. To succumb to this
temptation is to forge an innocent associationism destined
to be ridiculed in the court of common sense; an innocent
neurophysiology destined to be banished from the temples
of science.

It is not at all clear whether James put the Mind/Body
problem on a new and surer footing or whether he merely
juggled it. Similar to Wundt, he recognized the issues of
psychology to be *sui generis* and not measurably affected
by advances in our knowledge of physiology. His emphasis
upon the brain-as-a-whole originated in a combination of
scientific and metaphysical reasoning which, though ar-
guably sound, could not contribute to research in the brain
sciences, since none of the available methods permits us
to examine the "brain-as-a-whole." In like manner, it is
not easy to assess James' two-way interactionism *contra*
Cartesianism, epiphenomenalism, and monistic materialism. At the level of common sense, the level at which

James was often most comfortable, it does seem clear that our thoughts count for something; that we do *choose* to attend to this and ignore that. To the extent this is so, and to the further extent that processes such as thought and attention have the brain as their necessary substrate and condition, it would seem to follow that mind influences brain.

Nonetheless, there is no obvious way of demonstrating this in a convincing experimental fashion, nor is it clear how the metaphysical issues arising from the Mind/Body problem would become less vexed if this kind of interaction were documented. James, as we have seen, was opposed to the hypostasization of consciousness, taking the latter to refer only to the actual stream of thought. He rejected "substance" theories spun by the spiritualists as confidently as he dismissed epiphenomenalism and Mind-Stuff theories. Ultimately he adopted that "radical empiricism," whose ontology was completely exhausted by experiences and possible experiences. He thought he could carry out this adoption without claiming either Berkeley or solipsism as one of the natural parents, but in this he underestimated Berkeley's subtlety and the solipsist's persistence. On the whole, therefore, James' contribution to the Mind/Body issue was constructively negative rather than inventive. While not declaring it to be a pseudoproblem or a mere terminological debate, he framed it in an appeasing, naturalistic way that gave both the spiritualists and the scientists their respective turfs. The science of psychology could stand firm in its loyalty to brain physiology as the *conditio sine qua non* as it proceeded to examine directly that subject matter growing out of the centuries of metaphysical (introspective-philosophical) inquiry. But consciousness, even as nothing more than the stream of thought, still entailed a subject—a SELF—and James' approach to the Mind/Body problem made this deeper implication even more insistent.

The Consciousness of Self

It is characteristic of James' thinking to rule out nothing that experience regularly affirms, even if the price is a less than economical thesis. This is at once the power and the problem of Jamesian psychology and that feature of it that turned away so many of the systematizers who came soon after him. It is also what separates his work from the more influential psychological productions just preceding his own. All this becomes apparent when we examine his lengthy treatment of the concepts of *self* and *personal identity*.

We have explored the approaches to these concepts taken by Reid, Mill, Hegel, Wundt, and several others. James was thoroughly familiar with the received opinions on the subject and anxiously aware of their deficiencies. Without repeating the analyses set forth in the previous chapters, it is enough to recall their general terms. The traditional position of those James dubbed "spiritualists" is that all experience logically entails a subject—a self— that is irreducible. The argument for irreducibility or, what is the same thing, for a *unified self* is grounded in the continuity of experiences and memories. As James himself recognized, the challenges to Descartes' contention that mind always thinks—challenges drawing support from such phenomena as sleep, hypnotism, somnambulism, and more recently hysteria—are less than convincing. At most, they only establish that the thinking mind is not always subsequently aware of its thoughts and that it may often fail to take note of certain of its operations as it proceeds to perform others. More to the point, however, is the "spiritualist's" claim that when there is thought there must be a thinking subject, a self, that can only be comprehended as a unified, irreducible, immaterial substance; in a word, a *soul*.

In its winding and halting history, this *substantialist*

theory of self would claim the allegiance of a wide assortment of philosophers, including some who would agree on very little else. The most powerful school subscribing to this thesis as James wrote was that of the neo-Hegelians proudly carrying the banner of the *pure ego* on their march toward the Absolute. James' opposition to this school was relentless, and on the point at issue he made his antagonism clear:

Transcendentalism is only Substantialism grown shame-faced, and the Ego only a "cheap and nasty" edition of the soul. . . . The Ego is simply *nothing*: as ineffectual and windy an abortion as Philosophy can show. . . . Kant deemed it of next to no importance at all. It was reserved for his Fichtean and Hegelian successors to call it the first Principle of Philosophy, to spell its name in capitals and pronounce it with adoration, to act, in short, as if they were going up in a balloon, whenever the notion of it crossed their mind. (p. 365)

But although he will have nothing to do with the transcendentalist's concept of Ego, he knows that the older substantialism was not without metaphysical force. At least at the level of common sense and ordinary introspection, nothing could be clearer than that every thought is *someone's* thought. James' problem, then, is to honor this fact while not succumbing to the "Hegelisms" some have drawn from it.

At the other pole of metaphysical speculation there is of course materialism and the ironworks varieties of associationism. This tradition, speaking through Hume, exhausts the concept of *self* by reducing it to a "bundle of perceptions" and making it the consequence of the associative laws of contiguity, resemblance, and cause and effect. Here, too, the advocates are not without evidence and plausibility. For every "self" there is a body. In any case, there is no empirical fact indicating selves without bodies. It is also the case, again at the level of common sense, that we habitually identify ourselves according to our thoughts, feelings, and memories, not to mention the long list of biographical details uniquely assignable to each person. James' problem here is one of respecting all this without succumbing to that radical materialism and innocent associationism which he has already rejected.

Tracking the middle course, James begins his analysis of the concept by partitioning "self" into two broad categories that might be called the public and the private. To the public self he assigns a material self and a social self; to the private category, a spiritual self and the pure Ego (pp. 292 ff.). By the *material self* James means not only each person's actual body but his physical possessions and familial (hereditary) ties, toward both of which he is impelled by instinctive inclinations. Regarding the *social self*, James contends that "*a man has as many social selves as there are individuals who recognize him* and carry an image of him in their mind" (p. 294). This social self is close in meaning to what should be called one's *personal identity* in contrast with one's *self-identity*. Turning to the private versions of self, James offers first that spiritual self which is the gift of introspection; the "empirical me" by which we are able to *think of ourselves as thinkers*. It originates in a certain class of *feelings* which are introspectively located in the head. His own introspections lead James then to this conclusion: "In a sense, then, it may be truly said that, in one person at least, *the 'Self of selves,' when carefully examined, is found to consist mainly of the collection of these peculiar motions in the head or between the head and the throat*" (p. 301). There may be more to it than this, but James can find nothing else in his own reflections. The "empirical me" is the entity discovered by feelings of a certain kind, located if only ambiguously "between the head and throat."

All that remains for James to address is the pure self or the *Inner Principle of Personal Unity*. His analysis begins not so much with a denial of the soul as with the claim that none of the subjective phenomena of mind require the concept of a soul for an explanation. The "empirical me" has been shown to arise from a constellation of feelings; feelings in and about the body; feelings especially tied to the health and integrity of this body and governed by what must be at least minimally evolutionary considerations. Just as no soul need by invoked to account for the nonpersonal phenomena of experience, none is required for these personal feelings or feelings of self. The aim, here, is not to rid all discourse of soul-talk, but to establish that a scientific psychology can proceed with its mission utterly aloof from such matters. What it must provide is an account that is superior to the traditional ones, if only because it is a scientific account and relatively assumption-less in its underlying metaphysics. Indeed, "as *psychologists*, we need not be metaphysical at all. The phenomena are enough, the passing Thought itself is the only verifiable thinker, and its empirical connection with the brain-process is the ultimate known law" (p. 346). In the same place, and underscoring his "radical empiricism," James rejects substantialism thus: "To say that phenomena inhere in a Substance is at bottom only to record one's protest against the notion that the bare existence of the phenomena is that total truth."

In attempting to define "the passing present Thought," which he also calls "the judging Thought" as precisely as what has always been meant by the self, James at once evades what is most suspect in both the associationistic (Hume, Mill, Bain) and the transcendentalistic (neo-Kantian) accounts. He traces *"the definitive bankruptcy of the associationist description* of the consciousness of self" (p. 359). to Hume's failure to take the connectedness of thought as a fact of experience. The associationists "cut up" the stream of consciousness and were then forced to account for mental processes in terms of laws (contiguity, resemblance, cause and effect) which simply could not succeed in their mission. Turning Mill's philosophy of science on Mill himself, James says:

Mill, speaking of what may rightly be demanded of a theorist, says: "He is not entitled to frame a theory from one class of phenomena, extend it to another class which it does not fit, and excuse himself by saying that if we cannot make it fit, it is because the ultimate facts are inexplicable." The class of phenomena which the associationist school takes to frame its theory of the Ego are feelings unaware of each other. The class of phenomena the Ego presents are feelings of which the later ones are intensely aware of those that went before. The two classes do not "fit" and no exercise of ingenuity can ever make them fit. No *shuffling* of unaware feelings can make them aware. To get the awareness we must openly beg it by postulating a new feeling which has it. This new feeling is no "theory" of the phenomena, but a simple statement of them (p. 359, fn.)

If an *awareness* of satiety did not attach to my recollections of a previous meal, there is no way that the mere coupling of eating plus satiety could lead to such an awareness. The awareness is as much given in the phenomenal record as are the facts of eating and satiation. Subtantialism can be rejected because it is not necessary in accounting for the record, and associationism can be rejected because the record is impossible on its theory. *"There need never have been a quarrel between associationism and its rivals if the former had admitted to indecomposable unity of every pulse of thought, and the latter been willing to allow that 'perishing' pulses of thought might recollect and know"* (p. 371).

It is still necessary, with all this behind us, to ask whether James did justice to his topic. His treatment, like that he gave the Mind/Body problem, is more effective as criticism than an invention, more conducive to conciliation than to progress. He chides Mill* for so qualifying the association-istic account of self as to threaten to restore substantialism, but James' own "passing Thought" becomes more sub-stance-like the more work James calls on it to do. What he seems to want to accomplish is a solution to the problem of self by making an amalgam of the empirical self and the present, passing thought. The way this is supposed to work is as follows: The thoughts by which awareness of body and of both personal and familial possessions comes about are coextensive with the public social self. Moreover, there is no entity that ever enters a convincing claim on either to possessory elements of the empirical self or the recognitions registered by others toward the social self. Given the awareness and its contents, and in light of there being no plausible counterclaimant, thought arrives as *consciousness of self*. Particularly important in all this are those awarenesses tied to events occurring "between the head and the throat."

Had an account of this sort been offered by Hume or Hartley or even James Mill or his son, it could be taken as a primarily metaphysical claim designed to install mechan-istic principles in the place of substance principles. We could then ask whether the substitution was conformable with the facts and whether it constituted a more satisfying set of hypotheses than its competitors. But the *radical* empiricism of William James obeys a stricter set of laws. It mandates unblinking obedience before the facts of

---

* "Mr. Mill's habitual method of philosophizing was to affirm boldly some general doctrine derived from his father, and then make so many concessions of detail to its enemies as practically to abandon it altogether. In this place the concessions amount, so far as they are intelligible, to the admission of something very like the Soul" (Principles, 1:357–58). The object of this criticism is Mill's reference to that "inexplicable tie" that unites present and past sensations. It is the adjective that bothers James. He judges Mill's defense of it as constituting a tacit endorsement of some form of substantialism.

experience. Further, it declares common sense the victor in any conflict in which a competing perspective can do no better than a draw. To this extent, James' radical empiricism is closer to the Common Sense philosophy of Thomas Reid than it is to Hume's or to that of either Mill. Accordingly, James' account is to be judged—his overall philosophical position *demands* that it be judged—under the light of empirically verifiable data; that is to say, under the light of experience, as this experience is immunized against "the psychologist's fallacy." Is it the case, then, that one's consciousness of self is identical to an assortment of private sensations and public endorsements? Is it the case that one's feelings of "motions" taking place "between the head and the throat" are the primary data of self-consciousness?

Since James arrives at this view introspectively, his critic would seem to be licensed to do likewise. And one critic, at least, must judge the entire proposition to be a tissue of myths. The *I* that enters into every relation of which there is awareness is, first of all, entirely indifferent to the doubts or the corroborations of the crowd. It takes their doubts as absurd and their corroborations as gratuitous. Even the diseased or disordered *I*, an *I* that can assign no name to itself and cannot ascribe to itself any significant (auto-) biographical detail—the utterly amnesic *I*—is as certain of *itself* as the introspecting psychologist is of himself. Without quibbling over James' distinction between the empirical and the spiritual self, it is enough to note that neither requires the other and that both are secure in the face of a doubting public. At bottom, then, what James is trying to accomplish is the replacement of the *pure ego* by the *judging thought* without the loss of any of the empirical properties of the former. But let us suppose him to be successful in this, such that his argument amounts to the proof of a formal identity: *pure ego = judging thought*. What is gained? To the extent that the former may be taken as a plausible defense of substantialism, the latter must be taken *identically*, or the formal identity fails. To the extent that the latter is solely empirical, containing nothing that is not tied to an ensemble of feelings, it loses the one great advantage (perhaps the only advantage) substantialism has had over its critics: The advantage of supplying the privately but universally recognized *subject* of every feeling. What new metaphysical possibility is announced by locutions such as "feelings feeling themselves" or "thoughts thinking themselves." The latter is so close to the Hegelian notion of the Absolute realizing itself in human history as to be a charter member of the corporate "Hegelism." Empirically, *I* have no evidence whatever of a thought thinking itself; only of *myself thinking*. Nor can I admit even to the more modest claim of sensing "motions between my head and throat" on every occasion of reflection, wonder, or belief. It is true, at least autobiographically, that there seems to be a head-end activity connected to thought and feeling in a way that there is not a foot-end or hand-end or chest-end activity, but it is the *I* and not the feeling that notes this difference.

What James found so wanting in traditional associationism was the failure to appreciate the *connectedness* of the stream of thought and the functional significance of the actual manner in which thoughts merge into one another. Traditional associationism was too mechanical, too statistical, too wed to the idea of a haphazard mental world in which all the order was created by impersonal laws of contiguity and resemblance. His own modified associationism was to repair these defects through the inclusion of evolutionary forces and self-directing cognitive processes. Thus,

In no revival of a past experience are all the items of our thought equally operative in determining what the next thought shall be. Always some ingredient is prepotent over the rest. . . . In subjective terms we say

that *the prepotent items are those which appeal most to our* INTEREST.
. . . Expressed in brain-terms, the law of interest will be: *some one brain-process is always prepotent above its concomitants in arousing action elsewhere.* (pp. 571–72)

If it can be said that traditional associationism was a Newtonian psychology, James' version is a Darwinian psychology. There is no need to pause to criticize such auxiliary notions as *"the portion of the nerve tract supporting the going thought"* by which James hoped to explain the several forms of associational learning (p. 581), or his assurances that, "We trust to the laws of cerebral nature to present us spontaneously with the appropriate idea" (p. 589). This is all the neuropsychology of 1890 speaking, and it is no less dated because it still commands a following. Historically, these utterances shaped the thinking of the age in those parts of the reflective world that had resisted or were ready to disown "Hegelism." The James who would reproach Mill for lapsing into the scholastic idiom of "inexplicable ties" is the same James whose own approach to the inexplicable is by way of a theoretical nervous system. The approach did not, of course, explicate anything. It was and was intended to be a promissory note which contemporary psychology is still trying to cash in but with indefinite success.

Perception

Chapter 20 of the *Principles* run to nearly 150 pages and is the longest by far in the two volumes. Its subject is space perception, the treatment of which discloses, more than any other topic, James' position on psychological matters and the source of his extraordinary influence. The length of the chapter alone alerts us to the importance attached to the subject by the author, an importance that extends far beyond the physiological and perceptual details of the sensations of space and depth.

Since the time of Kant, the categories of space and time had nourished nativistic theories of mind and had fortified a great diversity of antiempiricistic philosophers. The very phenomenon of "space" erected so durable a barrier against *radical* empiricism that Mill, Bain, Helmholtz, and Wundt—these otherwise legendary empiricists—quailed before it. Helmholtz could explain space perception only by invoking the delphic process of "unconscious inference" and, in a similar vein, Wundt had to rely on something called "synthesis." The details of their respective accounts are less important than their theoretical justifications: Since space is not *given* by any property of a stimulus, it must be *constructed* (inferred; synthesized) by the nonsensory (intellectual-cognitive) processes of the percipient. What this requires of Spencer and the Mills, "intoxicated with the principle of association" (*Principles*, 2:270), is the impossible task of accounting for the sensation of *space* through a compounding of totally nonspatial sensations. They, with Wundt and Helmholtz, may be lumped as "psychic stimulists," ensnared by the very Kantian principles they so eagerly disown.

I call this view mythological, because I am conscious of no such Kantian machine-shop in my mind, and feel no call to disparage the powers of poor sensation in this merciless way. . . . The essence of the Kantian contention is that there are not *spaces*, but *Space*—one infinite continuous *Unit*—and that our knowledge of *this* cannot be a piecemeal sensational affair, produced by summation and abstraction. To which the obvious reply is that, if any known thing bears on its front the *appearance* of piecemeal construction and abstraction, it is this very notion of the infinite unitary space of the world. It is a *notion*, if ever there was one; and no intuition. (*Principles*, 2:275)

James' criticism of Helmholtz' "empiristic" theory is relentless, especially on the Helmholtzian point that *touch* might be the primary source of visual perceptions of space:

Of course the eye-man has a right to fall back on the skin-man for help at a pinch. But doesn't this mean that he is a mere eye-man and not a complete psychologist? In other words, Helmholtz's Optics and the "empiristic theory" there professed are not to be understood as attempts at answering the *general* question of how space-consciousness enters the mind. They simply deny that it enters with the first optical sensations. Our own account has affirmed stoutly that it enters *then*; but no more than Helmholtz have we pretended to show *why*. Who calls a thing a first sensation admits he has no theory of its production. (pp. 279–80)

Before examining James' alternative formulation, it is important to appreciate his effectiveness as a critic in these pages he devotes to space perception. As with all of the topics treated, this one too is submitted to a thorough review of the extant findings and methods and a critical appraisal of their bearing on the most general questions of psychology. To those, for example, in the patrimony of Thomas Brown, who would explain space perception as originating in the sensations produced by movement of the limbs, James examines the recent research of Goldscheider on *passive* movement. What these studies strongly suggested (and what we now know to be the case) is a separate sensory pathway originating in the joint sacs, activated by displacement and delivering information independently of other modalities of stimulation. All this occurs in the absence of any *muscular* contractions, meaning that we are able to process spatial information without the benefit of muscular cues, whether these arise from voluntary or involuntary (passive) activity.

Then, too, there is James' own originality as he attempts to lay the foundation for his radically empiricistic theory of space perception. The theory, stated baldly, is that *space* is given in the original sensation and that it need not be "constructed," "synthesized," or "inferred" by some higher mental process. Take the example of a stick presented to view in the horizontal plane. Since "the peripheral parts of the retina are equated with the central by receiving the image of the same object" (p. 214), the object is in fact *spatially given*. The case of three-dimensional perception is only slightly more complicated. The example offered by James (p. 215) is that of a stick anchored at one end, the end closest to the eye, and rotated in a circle. In the horizontal plane of view, the stick's full breadth is perceived. As the rotation begins and continues, the far end of the stick appears to approach the near end, apparently becoming shorter all the while until, in the vertical plane, it is completely occluded by the near end. Thus is depth conveyed.

But how much depth? What shall measure its amount? Why, at the moment the far end is ready to be eclipsed, the difference of its distance from the near end's distance must be judged equal to the stick's whole length. . . . *Thus we find that given amounts of visual depth-feeling become signs of fixed amounts of visual breadth-feeling.* (p. 215)

This is all very well and good, and with a few modifications supplied by the last century of research on visual perception may even be said to be true. The problem, however, is that it begs the question completely. Recall that what James set out to do was dethrone the "psychic stimulists"; to rid Psychology of the lingering vestiges of *innate ideas*; to break what was left of the tie between a hopeful *science* of the mind and all "Hegelisms" spawned by the Kantian system. Mill had attempted as much but, as we have seen and as James saw, he failed to the extent that his brand of associationism could not keep pace with the facts of mental life. Helmholtz, too, had made the same attempt but, on the rocks of space perception, his sturdy empiristic craft listed in the direction of quasi-Kantian "unconscious inferences." And Wundt's "psychic synthesis" was, on James' reckoning, just so much soul-talk. Whereupon James enters the fray, radical empiricism etched into his shield, and announces—what? That *space* was in the stimulus configuration all along!

Of course, in an ironic, even a perverse way, he is right. But when he tries to defend the claim he finds he must employ such phrases as, "The peripheral parts of the retina are equated with the central by receiving the image of the same object." Now, what can "peripheral," "central," and "same object" mean unless the concept of *space* be granted a priori? I gaze at the nearby Oxford English Dictionary whose length extends beyond my fovea. As its margins trail off into the periphery of my visual field, I take it to be the *same object* because it is located without interruption *in space*. There has never been a quibble, by Kant or anyone else, over the external and internal sensory cues we come to master in the process of ordering the world's objects spatially. Some have emphasized muscular cues; others the sense of touch; still others the data from the joint sacs, the semicircular canals, the heavings of our own chests during respiration, the convergence and divergence of the eyes, the spread of excitation over the retinal mosaic, the movement of objects along the surfaces of the skin, the diminished loudness of retreating objects— the list is very long. But the bare and verifiable *empirical* fact is the displacement of an object, and there can be no displacement except *in space*, which is itself not an object. James was closer to the mark when he confessed that, "Who calls a thing a first sensation admits he has no theory of its production," but in this confession he necessarily included his own statements with those of the Mills, Wundt, and Helmholtz. Kant's position remained unscathed and even untouched, since Kant never treated space as a "sensation." He took it to be an *intuition* a priori that must be postulated for there to be spatial sensations of any kind.

It is again appropriate, however, to distinguish between James' philosophical-scientific achievement and the very different matter of his historical influence. It goes without saying that he did not "solve" the problem of space perception either in its metaphysical or its purely psychological installments. When all the pendulums and chronographs are put away for the night and all the charts and numbers are dutifully filed, we are still forced back to the Kantian thesis: That the ordering of our perceptions in space and time proceeds from an endemic disposition of mind not reducible to the physical collisions in the external world. Kant would have no difficulty with James' innocent insistence that space and time are "there" all along. He would only oblige James to point to *himself* and not to the external world in designating what he must mean by "there."

Historically, however, James' analysis of perception was a breath of fresh air. His empiricistic arguments outstripped those of Helmholtz and joined with those of Mach in preparing the way for a completely antiseptic experimental psychology of perception.[6] He inspired the scientific psychologists with the reassurance that the facts of experience were the only facts; that all seemingly transcendent ones *could* be interpreted experientially; that the facts of a *first* sensation need not be interpreted at all. Consistently with this perspective, he absorbed nothing less vexatious than human emotion into the same matrix. The famous James-Lange theory of emotion is given in a sentence: *"The bodily changes follow directly the perception of the exciting fact, and . . . our feeling of the same changes as they occur* IS *the emotion"* (p. 449). Too often those who criticize or ridicule this thesis fail to recognize its attachment to the balance of James' program and mission. Just as the topic of space perception had left psychology's door open to "psychic stimulists" and their unintended "Hegelisms," so also had the subject of emotion been detached from body and brain. On the traditional construction, we see a bear and this perception, bypassing the rest of us, leads directly to a frightful but reasoned decision to show that animal a clean pair of heels. James' alternative was intended to put the balance of ourselves into this equation. The bear reaches us as a *percept* and in that form works on our *bodies*. The completed work is that of exciting a variety of physiological changes and it is these that initiate the lifesaving motor responses. The *emotion* is nothing more than the feelings of these physiological changes. It is not something added to them. "*If we fancy some strong emotion, and then try to abstract from our consciousness of it all the feelings of its bodily symptoms, we find we have nothing left behind,* no 'mind-stuff' out of which the emotion can be constituted, and that a cold and neutral state of intellectual perception is all that remains" (p. 451).

The Will

James' theory of emotion is rich in Darwinian flavors and fits comfortably into his broad *functional* psychology. In their uncomplicated state, the emotions begin as instinctual and reflex mechanisms, triggered by external events of biological consequence, and known to the actor by the physiologically induced feelings (visceral sensations) that accompany them. Can this sort of account embrace something which, on the surface, seems so different; namely, the will?

The problem faced by James here is a version of the one presented by the phenomena of self-consciousness and depth perception. The extreme metaphysical positions on such matters are those of idealism and materialism, neither of which can support a budding science. Common sense legislates that psychology must take the fact of volition as just that, a *fact*. No matter how trendy monistic materialism may be in metaphysical circles, a discipline promising to explain the psychological realities of human life cannot expect to keep its audience having first announced that there is no such thing as volition! What James hopes for psychology is the ability to offer a scientifically acceptable account of everything universally confirmed by the experiences of the Plain Man. What he hopes to avoid are those metaphysical sophistries which solve a problem of explanation by denying the facts for which the explanation is sought. These are motives nobly born but, it must be said, unquenched in the execution.

The theory of volition most closely associated with James' *Principles* is the *ideo-motor* theory. It is based on the hypothesis that all original stimulus-response sequences are involuntary, grounded in the instinctive and reflexive machinery of neonatal life. Though these sequences are not accompanied by volition, however, their performance is registered in the brain. Thus, *"A supply of ideas of the various movements that are possible left in the memory by experience of their involuntary performance is . . . the first prerequisite of the voluntary life"* (p. 488). The infant reflexively withdraws its little hand from the flame, intending nothing, but now inescapably storing the memory that connects the action to the reduction of noxious sensations. Against Wundt, Bain, and others, James rejects the "innervation theory" which would give us a direct sensation of the motor events, insisting instead that all our feelings are tied to sensory processes. James was right in this, but the issue is no longer lively and his own theory did not depend on its outcome to the extent he believed.

Thus far, James' hypothesis is that all volitional actions must originate in the pool of initially unintended reflex chains, residing in memory as ideas of possible actions. What must be added to this pool if there is to be bona fide volitional behavior is the combination of *attention* and *effort*: "We see that attention with effort is all that any case of volition implies. *The essential achievement of the will, in short, when it is most 'voluntary,' is to* ATTEND *to a difficult object and hold it fast before the mind*" (p. 561).

To make sense of this passage, we must recur to volume 1 of the *Principles* (pp. 447–54) where James, after due regard for Occam's razor and due disregard of material-ism, places himself among "the believers in a spiritual force." He admits this in his chapter, "Attention," which nearly unravels the fabric of his radical empiricism. It is here that attention is given to the status of a "star per-former" in the drama whose cast has been dominated by the laws of stimulation and association. This star performer appears to be that rarest of species in the Jamesian collection—an original psychic force. "Nature *may*, I say, indulge in these complications; and the conception that she has done so in this case is, I think, just as clear (if not as 'parsimonious' logically) as the conception that she has not" (*Principles*, 1:453).

Putting this star performer into the ideo-motor theory, however, makes of James' account of volition not an explanation but a restatement of the common man's belief. Apparently, one is able to act voluntarily by *choosing* (through an original psychic force) from among the pos-sibilities for action recorded in memory. The original force which nature *may* indulge can be called attention, but for all theoretical purposes James might just as well have called it the will itself. I am at least as conscious of my will as I am of my attendings, and just as certain that the two are not the same. As James was so insistent in pointing out that something cannot come from nothing, he could not possibly succeed on his own terms in evolving volition out of anything that did not contain it. Accordingly, he deposited in "Attention" an "original psychic force," and openly registered himself among the patrons of *spirit*.

To the ideo-motor theory itself, there can be more than one objection. Conceptually, the theory would seem to confine all volitional aspects of consciousness to the realm of possible behaviors, although there are many volitions to which no action could possibly attach; e.g., the believer's will that the will of God prevail. In anticipating contemporary dispositional theories, James also courted their liabilities. James would probably answer that this is not really a manifestation of will but of motive or desire, but his theory of motivation is also tied directly to possible actions. An additional burden of the ideo-motor theory is that it seems to require that every genuinely voluntary action either be composed of previously stored elements of possible action or be original in a merely statistical sense. This interpretation is strengthened by his treatment of "Great Men and Their Environment" who are to be understood as the outcome of Darwin's natural variations and (social) selection.[7] Whether the range of human inventiveness, great and small included, is credibly attributable to the operations of natural variation, environmental selection, and personal choices from the recorded memories of past actions I leave to the reader's judgment. In his "Great Men" essay, James rebukes Spencer for placing so low a premium on what has always been taken to be evidence of human *initiative*,[8] but the strength of this criticism is at the price of that "parsimony" which a truly radical empiricism must promise.[9] James saw in human history a "lasting justification of hero-worship . . . and the pooh-poohing of it by 'sociologists' is the everlasting excuse for popular indifference to their general laws and averages."[10] But with all this said, he could not go the full Wundtian route, taking human character to be the cause of the will, but this character itself to be beyond the grasp of natural science's causal accounts. Here, too, James purified the study of genius for a psychology that would either tie itself to the naturalistic perspective or abandon its dream of scientific status.

Pragmatism, Pluralism, and the Will to Believe

Nearly all of James' writings after the publication of the *Principles* were devoted to philosophy. As he concerned himself more and more with the ethical and epistemological foundations of that subject, and as he faced the criticisms directly aroused by sections of the *Principles* he moved steadily away from the dualistic (subject-object) ontology of the *Principles* and toward the monistic ontology of his radical empiricism. Everything was now to be understood in the language of *experience* and judged according to its real if shifting lights. The more articulate this drift of his thought became, the closer James came to what would become the school of Phenomenology.[11] But the more durable tie and the one that James himself would have acknowledged was to Realism; if not in its engagingly Reidian form, then at least in its down-to-earth late-Victorian manifestation. Charles A. Strong, a defender of this position, is noted for his influence by Perry:

James owed much to Strong, especially in the development of pragmatism. It was largely owing to Strong's insistent realism that James refused to be drawn by his left-wing associates into the pitfalls of subjectivism, and repeatedly affirmed that human knowledge and practice must accommodate themselves to an external environment not of their own making.[12]

The ties between the Common Sense school of the late eighteenth century and the pragmatism of the twentieth are perhaps less historical than conceptual, although the founders of the latter (James and C. S. Peirce) were thoroughly conversant with the works of Thomas Reid and his disciples. Peirce explicitly acknowledges the connection in his *Issues of Pragmatism*. He notes that when the pragmatistic point of view first began to claim his allegiance, he wondered whether "indubitable propositions" actually changed with the seasons or whether, in fact, the notions that now seemed so invincible to him had commanded respect before:

During the last two years ... I have completed a provisional inquiry which shows me that the changes are so slight from generation to generation, though not imperceptible even in that short period, that I thought to own my adhesion ... to the opinion of that subtle but well-balanced intellect, Thomas Reid, in the matter of Common Sense (as well as in regard to immediate perception) along with Kant.[13]

This passage is interesting in more than one way, for it shows that Peirce was among the first and the few to appreciate the compatibilities between the Kantian and the Reidian approaches. Nearly all of Peirce's many citations of Reid are approving. It would, in fact, do no injustice to James or Peirce to suggest that both the letter and the spirit of Pragmatism and Pragmaticism* are to be found either in the lines or between the lines of Reid's major essays. The point here is surely not one of historical priority nor a thinly veiled method of resurrecting Reid's celebrity (if not his influence). Rather, it is to show the consistent psychology that *must* arise when the careful scholar sets out to avoid the traps set by skepticism, materialism, and idealism. Reid knew that, for all his vaunted doubts, Hume not only did not but *could* not deny his own experiences. Thus, Reid's entire assault on skepticism is constructed out of the facts of experience, the approach Reid traced to Locke and Newton. A metaphys-

---

* The latter term was minted by Peirce to make his own version distinguishable from James', with whom he disagreed on a number of important points.

ical proposition clearly at variance with the universal perceptions of mankind carries an immense burden which it can support successfully only by turning up indubitable facts to the contrary—and these facts then become in principle at least part of these same universal perceptions.

Recall from earlier chapters that it was also Reid who sought to ground the legitimate claims of philosophy in the commonest fact of nature; the fact of *survival*. The official skeptic must abandon his metaphysics in the marketplace, and the hungry caterpillar is never tempted by it at all. With appropriate bridges, this is the perspective that finally yields pragmatism's most famous and economical definition, framed by Peirce thus: "Consider what effects, that might conceivably have practical bearings, we conceive the object of our conception to have. Then, our conception of these effects is the whole of our conception of the object."[14]

Here is a maxim that can be seen as animating much of James' psychological work—especially his ideo-motor theory of volition—and one that would even aid in the creation of behavioristic explanations of cognition. At root, however, it is a Reidian form of common sensism. It was Reid's constant reminder that words stand for something, and that the social commerce language permits is impossible unless such meanings are shared meanings. To discover how a word or phrase is *understood* by the world (or the tribe or the person), one must witness the effect of that word or phrase on the ordinary conduct of life. Note Reid's regular complaint that philosophers have "corrupted language" by using common words in uncommon ways, in ways that are not conformable to practice or conducive to useful ends. It was also Reid's constant reminder that certain facts cannot be analyzed beyond a certain point and must simply be taken as facts. The common errors of philosophy are often the result of a penchant for doubting any fact that cannot be reduced to some simpler one. As we saw, Reid took the self to be just such an irreducible entity. James sought to go further (with mixed results), but James too was at one with Reid in taking the elementary facts of experience to be the irreducible data of any possible mental science. If a good argument can be given to support the claim that James was at heart a *phenomenologist*, the same argument would embrace Reid.

Pragmatism is a word that has suffered more from attempts than from refusals to define it sharply. Peirce's maxim conveys the essential point but does so in a way that would admit more into his own philosophy than he would want. Some have taken it to be an early form of operationism and others as the core-concept of various forms of positivism.[15] For James, the word had a special if not precise meaning, one that is perhaps better conveyed in *The Will to Believe* than in his later and self-consciously pragmatic period: "Unfortunately, neutrality is not only inwardly difficult, it is also outwardly unrealizable, where our relations to an alternative are practical and vital. This is because, as the psychologists tell us, belief and doubt are living attitudes, and involve conduct on our part" (p. 50). Comparing James with himself after a half-century of studying both, Peirce would conclude that James "was even greater in practice than in theory of psychology," a description that accords well with James' official Pragmatism.[16] The latter, like his *functionalism* in psychology, grew out of the recognition that life is *lived*, that action is the means by which we enter the world, that all our perceptions and cogitations are for this end. The Philosophy of the textbooks can only give us pause and doubt, impelling our intellectual powers toward a neutrality that life will simply not permit. Seeking to escape the circle of doubt, we arrive at last at the indubitability of our experience which, over the course of its history, has equipped us with a range of possibilities for action. This is the history that bridges our needs and our world and, though often clouded over and wobbly, it is the only bridge we have. *The function of thought is action.* Accordingly, the meaning of its objects is to be found, in Peirce's words, in the practical effects we conceive these objects to have.

This, of course, is precisely the point at which James' pragmatism merges with his pluralism, and where both divorce themselves from the comforts of scientific positivism.

> Our science is a drop, our ignorance the sea. Whatever else be certain, this at least is certain—that the world of our present natural knowledge *is* enveloped in a larger world of *some* sort of whose residual properties we at present can frame no positive idea.
>
> Agnostic positivism, of course, admits this principle theoretically in the most cordial terms, but insists that we must not turn it to any practical use. We have no right, this doctrine tells us, to dream dreams, or suppose anything about the unseen part of the universe, merely because to do so may be for what we are pleased to call our highest interests. (*The Will to Believe*, p. 50)

Neutrality, however, is not our proper or even possible attitude. Thus, we do and we must dream dreams, and we do and we must suppose all sorts of things about the unseen part of the universe. James would qualify the "will to believe" as a "right to believe" in his later discussions of these essays, but on either account he recognizes the *fact of belief* as the major instrument available to a fallible and vulnerable creature in an unsteady and often opaque universe.

Pluralism is the grudging metaphysics that our actual experiences sanction. It is opposed to every form of monism, idealism, universalism, whether these are drafted by scientists, philosophers, or theologians. It is the concession that we must grant on the basis of the surest knowledge we have, no matter how opposed to it some pet theory may be. At the banquet of reality, our experiences take their share and no more, cognizant that "something else is self-governed and absent and unreduced to unity":

> Monism, on the other hand, insists that when you come down to reality as such, to the reality of realities, everything is present to *everything* else in one vast instantaneous coimplicated completeness—nothing can in *any* sense, functional or substantial, be really absent. . . .
>
> For pluralism, all that we are required to admit as the constitution of reality is what we ourselves find empirically realized in every minimum of finite life. Briefly, it is this, that nothing real is absolutely simple . . . that each relation is one aspect, character, or function, way of its being taken, or way of its taking something else.[17]

Whatever the standing of pluralism and pragmatism is or may come to be in philosophy, they were *isms* that had the same liberating effect on American psychology as that engendered by James' *Principles*. Through his defense of the pluralistic world view James provided at least a tacit justification for a science whose parts did not fit, whose methods seemed so often to be ad hoc, whose theoretical integrations in one area seemed to belie those developed in another. His own kinship with psychics and defense of psychic research were taken as mere eccentricities by the stolidly scientific spokesmen for the new American psychology, but the kinship and defense were not really quirks. They are as much a part of pragmatism and pluralism as is any other part of James' psychological enterprise. If telepathy or clairvoyance are candidates for possible experience, they are possible candidates for psychological science. If psychic research and its findings do real work in the world, if they hold out the potential for new and successful actions directed toward reality, then they carry their own justification with them and are not to be legislated against by what is no more than a metaphysical prejudice.

James affected academic psychology directly, not only though his *Principles* but through his contacts with others; with G. S. Hall who studied with him, with John Dewey at Chicago, with James Rowland Angell, James Mark Baldwin, and scores of lesser lights in the emerging galaxy of a distinctly American approach to the subject. Some of the luminaries, Dewey for example, had first begun to glimmer in Hegelian colors, only to be pulled toward pragmatism by the weight and the way of James' words. Others remained more narrowly committed to the laboratory, now satisfied that a natural science of the mind was no contradiction in terms. John B. Watson would complain years later that he saw no difference between the structuralists and the functionalists (perhaps because his contact with Dewey was direct and with James remote), and then proceeded to fashion a behavioristic psychology defended with arguments and principles that were Jamesian from first to last. Many psychologists as the present century unwound would celebrate the achievement of Darwin and place their discipline within the evolutionary context, often not pausing to acknowledge how James had made this inevitable. The *instrumentalism* of the Chicago school was as much the child of pragmatism as it was the father of behaviorism, but James was often ignored by the genealogists because of his willingness to recognize that purely hedonic motives are insufficient to account for the full range of human ethical actions. Besides, it was easier to work with rewards and punishments in the laboratory— psychology now having settled on cats and dogs—than to attempt to define and manipulate nonhedonic conditions of motivation. Here it was James' realism, his constructively "radical" empiricism that denied him the honor of founding a "school." (Can there be a "school" of pluralists?) To the burdens of realism he added his selection of the *stream of thought* as the cornerstone of a scientific psychology and this, as is now well known, could not live in peace with behaviorism. Alas, it lives no more placidly with Darwinism.

As I have attempted to show in this essay, it is always necessary to keep clear the distinction between a scholar's historical influence and his scientific or philosophical successes. The case James makes out for a radical empiricism is not one that will cause idealists, materialists, skeptics, or modest phenomenalists to abandon their respective metaphysical positions. The problem of Self is not settled by substituting a "passing present thought," and the gap between the external world and our perception of it is not filled by reminding us that we only have direct knowledge of the latter. Nor will the theoretical mathematician, now puzzling over some nuance of imaginary or transcendental numbers, some geometer toying with the peculiarities of Riemannian space, know what to make of the claim that the meaning of such conceptions is no more than the possible effects they might have practically on the world. Less will the religionist find comfort in the notion that he has both a will and a right to believe, on the purely negative ground that we do not know everything. The materialist is not disarmed by a theory of mind that moves in the direction of *panpsychism* and the theologian is not comforted by a polytheism according to which none of the gods is omnipotent! But as James moved to and around such notions, he touched others. If he came down finally against anything, it was finality itself. He chased the Absolute from Harvard, then from Chicago. What had nearly become a durable American Hegelianism lost its roots in psychology. The latter could now get down to the practical business of science, confident that even if it was not to accomplish everything, it would at least be able to do something.

6. THE NINETEENTH CENTURY REVISITED
A Postscript

The attention paid to J. S. Mill, Hegel, Wundt, and James in the preceding pages should not obscure the veritable legion of writers who devoted themselves to psychology in the last century. Herbert Spencer and Alexander Bain in England, Taine and Ribot in France, are but four of the great systematizers of the period. Between 1850 and 1900, and in the more specialized compartments of the discipline, we can add the names of Maudsley, Charcot, Binet, Janet, Lipps, Ebbinghaus—we could go on into the dozens and still omit persons of consequence. It was in that century that David Ferrier's *The Functions of the Brain* put experimental surgery on a nearly contemporary footing and set forth the methods and the problems with which the emerging neuropsychology would begin its mission. C. Lloyd Morgan's *Introduction to Comparative Psychology* (1894) and E. L. Thorndike's *Animal Intelligence* (1898) are the older members of a contemporary literature, not the culmination of a now outmoded tradition. Henry Maudsley's *Physiology and Pathology of the Mind* (1867) could pass for a modern text in medical psychology, were the author not so rhetorical in his defense of the "medical model." If, as Whitehead said somewhere, the nineteenth century "invented the method of invention," it invented psychology as a discipline able to produce its own subject matter;

produce it in the laboratory, in the clinic, in the question-
naire, and the psychometric tests.

Today's psychologist who looks to the past for the
sources of today's specific endeavors is likely to look past
Mill, Hegel, Wundt, and James. None of the four can
claim a school of psychology now; none could claim one
in his own time. Hegelianism, of course, scarcely exists
as a unified "school" of philosophy, even though certain
issues lend theselves more or less to the Hegelian point of
view. These four men provided an intellectual context
within which disciplines could be refined. Hegel, it is true,
served up a complete philosophy, but in the same sense he
and the others served up complete psychologies; complete
not in method or data or laws but in language and topics
and expectations. The very notion of *completion* is antithetical to the Hegelian metaphysics, but it is also antithetical to the equally evolutionary metaphysics of Mill,
Wundt, and James. Evolution emerges from Hegelianism
formally; from Mill, Wundt, and James functionally and
empirically.

But there is another reason why today's psychologist
thinks less of these four than, for example, of a Fechner,
a Freud, a Thorndike, a Binet. The latter recommend
themselves because they did the sorts of things we do. The
compass of their efforts does not exceed our ability to
connect them to some current field of psychological inquiry
or practice. They are closer to being colleagues than
"fathers." And when we learn that the grand systematizers
of the nineteenth century—those who lived and wrote
long enough to know of the works of these older colleagues
of ours—paid them only the slightest attention, we are
tempted to suspect ignorance or bigotry. James, for example, lived long enough to read now-famous works by
Thorndike, Freud, and Binet. James' English friend, James
Ward, published a massive text as late as 1920, when these

same three enjoyed a wide following.* James, in a few later pieces, made some gracious comments on the psychoanalytic school, but in his *Principles* it is clear—from the construction he places on the findings reported by Janet— that he would not have thought much of a psychology that devoted itself to what was *not* in consciousness. On the matter of psychological testing, we have only this fragment from James with which to gauge his estimations: "Mssrs. Darwin and Galton have set the example of circulars of questions sent out by the hundred to those supposed to be able to reply. The custom has spread, and it will be well for us in the next generation if such circulars be not ranked among the common pests of life" (*Principles*, 1:194).

The heart of this criticism is the Jamesian commitment to realism; a commitment matched by Mill, by Wundt and, alas, even if not especially by Hegel. But it is important to appreciate the enlarged sense in which this word is used. By realism I do not refer to a specific epistemological thesis or school of philosophy. The four men whose works have been the subject of this book *saw* the world, its persons and problem, its possibilities and conflicts, its scientific facts and its moral ambiguities, and proceeded to devise a means by which to improve it. They were all for action and the active life. And as odd as it may sound when applied to Hegel, it may be said that they were all pragmatists, though not all Pragmatists.

By the standards of laboratory science, none of them succeeded, for none of them (with the possible but really minor exception of Wundt) provided a data-base upon which further and fruitful experimentation was con-

---

* I refer to his *Psychological Principles*, the second edition of which appeared in 1920, five years before Ward died. It runs to 470 pages. Freud and Binet are not cited at all. Thorndike's work is mentioned, but Ward thinks it would have been better to put the fish inside the cage and leave the cat outside! (p. 186 n.)

structed. Mill's celebrated "methods" were primarily a shorthand summary of what experimental science had adopted at least since the time of Galileo. James was notoriously ill-suited to the laboratory life and Hegel was contemptuous of its one-sidedness. The differences among the four were great, with Mill and James explicitly opposed to Hegelian thought and Wundt rising no higher than the level of peace-keeper. But it was in these very tensions and criticisms that psychology's possibilities were framed.

This is particularly clear when we compare the systems of Mill and James. Both men were empiricists, both were defenders of the scientific approach, both attempted to construct a psychology without taking recourse to idealisms of any kind. Mill thought the task could be completed by associationism and that the entire range of mental complexities could be *reduced* to the sort of atomic structure discovered by science in the material world. James, getting to work on the same task several decades later, quickly saw the artificiality of this system as an account of what we actually do experience. He could, at that point, have simply jettisoned empiricism as so many of his contemporaries did, but he pushed on to a more radical empiricism which took the facts of the world exactly as they are experienced. In the process, he made an experimental psychology of *cognition* necessary, one that could not be reduced to the elements of sensation and one that would have to employ what we now call ecologically meaningful arrays of stimulation. As he rid American psychology of Hegelianism, so also did he expunge that reassuring Humean psychology that threatened to make experimentation nugatory. In the final passages of his *Principles* the older tradition is swept away, even if today's perspective is not fully developed:

The so-called Experience-philosophy has failed to prove its point. No more if we take ancestral experiences into account than if we limit ourselves to those of the individual after birth, can we believe that the couplings of terms within the mind are simple copies of corresponding couplings impressed upon it by the environment. . . . It is hard to understand how such shallow and vague accounts . . . as Mill's and Spencer's could ever have been given by thinking men. (*Principles*, 2:688)

As Mill's historical achievement had been the rescuing of mental science from Absolute Idealism, James' was the preservation of empirical psychology by the surgical removal of its older and lethal elementarism.

The four in their different ways also did much to externalize the ethical and moral dimensions of human life. Hegel's state was the necessary condition for morality to be installed in consciousness. Mill, Wundt, and James— with all their glorifications of individualism—were still environmentalistic in their explanations of human values. Wundt and, to a certain extent Mill, left the question of personal *character* up in the air, and James's account of "great men" (their *initiative* notwithstanding) finally depended on the roll of the genetic dice. But character and heredity aside, all of them looked to the external world, the real world of society for an explanation of why we hold to certain values, why we prize certain ends. Again, James could invoke evolutionary notions in accounting for this without going to the excessive lengths of a Spencer. Thus, he could retain evolutionary theory for psychology with the distractions of Darwinism omitted. But in the externalization of morals, the four carried on the war on substantialism and caused the self to recede further from the shores of psychological concern. Hegel had so idealized it as to exempt it from empirical treatment. Mill and Wundt got it lost in the bedlam of perceptions. James kept it, but only as the "passing present Thought" which, as such, was as impersonal as any other thought. Excluding Hegel, the Absolute Ego was transformed into the mere ego and this into no more than several measurable mental processes. It is no wonder that James thought of the new *humanism* as but the old Absolute Idealism in new dress. What humanism required was not so much the abandonment of empiricistic psychology as the recognition that all these experiences hang together in an actual *person* who must be comprehended in the deepest personal terms. Humanism, that is, called for a restoration of the *self* in psychology; not that introspecting, experimenter-self that looks at mental processes as if they were objects in the outer world, but the existential self that endures intact throughout the tides of experience.

I have several times here and in the previous chapter noted James' commitment to eliminate Hegelian notions from the new psychology and his great success in America. Today's reader may not understand the source of such missionary zeal, in part because James was so successful. In the essay "Monistic Idealism," which appears in his *A Pluralistic Universe*, James quotes lengthily from an essay by Professor Henry Jones, appearing in the *Contemporary Review* for 1907, and voicing alarm over the idealists:

For many years adherents of this way of thought have deeply interested the British public by their writings. Almost more important than their writings is the fact that they have occupied philosophical chairs in almost every university in the kingdom. Even the professional critics of idealism are for the most part idealists—after a fashion. And when they are not, they are as a rule more occupied with the refutation of idealism than with the construction of a better theory. It follows from their position of academic authority, were it from nothing else, that idealism exercises an influence not easily measured upon the youth of the nation—upon those, that is, who from the educational opportunities they enjoy may naturally be expected to become the leaders of the nation's thought and practice. . . . "The Rhine has flowed in the Thames" is the warning note rung out by Mr. Hobbhouse. Carlyle introduced it, bringing it as far as Chelsea. Then Jowett and Thomas Hill Green, and William Wallace and

Lewis Nettleship, and Arnold Toynbee and David Ritchie—to mention only those teachers whose voices now are silent—guided the waters into those upper reaches known locally as the Isis. John and Edward Caird brought them up the Clyde, Hutchison Stirling up the Firth of Forth. They have passed up the Mersey and up the Severn and Dee and Don. They pollute the bay of St. Andrews and swell the waters of the Cam, and have somehow crept overland into Birmingham. The stream of German idealism has been diffused over the academical world of Great Britain. The disaster is universal. (*A Pluralistic Universe*, pp. 53–54)

This, written less than a decade before the outbreak of World War I, helps a later generation to understand what is meant by the claim that a war might be fought between "Hegelians of the left and Hegelians of the right." Power was more focused a century ago. What the major universities were teaching in the 1880s was very likely to surface as national policy a decade hence. It was also likely to determine which books were published, which authors sought. There were, of course, far fewer universities and a more homogeneous enrollment. Once the "old boys" got it in their heads that something was right, it wasn't long before their untutored countrymen received it in the form of a "tradition."

I note all this not for the purpose of taking sides. Alas, today's psychology might obtain some animation from a "Hegelism" or two. And, in fact, the steady increase in the number of "humanistic," "existential," and "phenomenological" treatises would seem to indicate that contemporary psychology recognizes as much. My point, however, is that James and his disciples faced very poor odds when, in the closing decades of the nineteenth century, they struggled to keep psychology on a scientific course. Some might say that it took the First World War to complete the project, and there is surely a grain of truth in this. American Hegelianism was never as formidable a school as was the

British version, if only because American higher education has never had a truly national character. But in the midwest—in St. Louis and at the University of Chicago—and in any number of our smaller colleges, idealism was all the rage. It arrived at Harvard with Josiah Royce, but by then James' mission was well on the way toward completion, unhampered by the collegial friendship James and Royce formed. Under the influence of James and his following, the surviving idealism migrated toward departments of Philosophy and Religion, leaving academic psychology to its laboratories.

But before returning the nineteenth century to its shelf, we still must ask about that great divide that ruptures our sense of connectedness to its psychology. It is only necessary to thumb through the offerings of today's psychology departments in order to appreciate how far we have journeyed from the thoughts and programs of Mill, Hegel, Wundt, and James. But have we? This is one of those delightful questions which keep historians up past their bedtimes, and which no responsible scholar will answer with finality. If we examine only the titles of courses and inspect only the standard texts assigned to those who take them, the gap does seem wide and unbridgeable. James' "proofs" against the argument for the unconscious look frankly ridiculous to those tutored in the psychology of the post-Freudian epoch. So too does his speculation on nerve currents, to contemporary students of neurophysiology. Mill, though some will grant that he was on the right track, presents today's behavioristic psychologist with an associationism that could not even survive nineteenth-century criticism. Wundt, even accepting his historical standing, offers little that the current textbook writer is obliged to include. And Hegel, extirpated from the consciousness of Anglo-American psychology for nearly a century, is not simply dated but unintelligible to those who would now call themselves professional psychologists.

Let us go deeper now into the character of today's psychology; to layers of thought and commitment lower than what is revealed by texts and course titles. There is a strong and stable division of contemporary activity that can be generically identified as *experimental* psychology. Its subject matter is diverse and changing, but its (unexpressed) metaphysical foundation is constant. This division of inquiry is directly indebted to Mill and Wundt who provided the constant foundation, no matter how far off the mark their choice of topics may now seem. It was Mill's *argument* for an inductive and experimental science of mental processes and for a descriptive science of society that altered the conceptions of an entire generation of thinkers. And it was Wundt's lectures and books, his laboratory and his *Philosophische Studien* that disseminated the earliest findings from psychological research and that served as a point of intellectual fixation for those eager to keep abreast of the developments. Moreover, in their major works both Mill and Wundt preserved the essentially *psychological* character of this discipline at a time when developments in neurology and experimental surgery could quite easily have drawn the subject into biology. James' contribution here was just as great, if a bit later. He never denied the functional relationship prevailing between mental and neural processes, but he insisted on understanding them in their own terms. As he would not permit the wholesale fracturing of thought into pieces, he would not permit it to be drowned in neural pools. There were years when the summoning works of Bain, Maudsley, Ferrier, Charcot, Helmholtz, and others made it seem inevitable that the old introspective psychology of the philosophers would soon be incorporated into the sister disciplines of medicine and physiology. Mill, Wundt, and James have an unchallengable claim to the credit for preventing the assimilation.

Within experimental psychology's several branches and

across the range of current psychological specialties we also discover what can only be called a *functionalistic* perspective. In the clinical offerings this takes the form of concepts of "adjustment"; in experimental offerings, that of "adaptation" or, more specifically, "learning." This is, of course, in the patrimony of Darwin, but Darwin needed interpreters and defenders in psychology. His own psychological theses were too general, even too odd. William James was surely the first American psychologist to put the functionalist point of view to work on the widest range of psychological issues; to prepare psychology for the subtler aspects of the Darwinian legacy. But at the same time, he stripped this Darwinism of the unnecessary metaphysical baggage that Spencer had heaped on it; its implicit "mind-dust," its accidentalism, its boistrous monism. By the time James was finished with it, it had become pragmatism, with nearly all the theory removed and only the common-sense and experiential supports remaining. The larger projection and more formal pronouncements of Darwinism were preserved as working hypotheses which psychology was to test.

Today's curriculum is also enriched by any number of courses addressed to the nature and determinants of personality and to the relations this personality enters into with other personalities, with institutions, and with the *Zeitgeist* in which it finds itself. To this subject Mill, Hegel, Wundt, and James contributed equally, if differently. Hegel's philosophical system is, at least on one reading, an immense social science designed to explain the evolution of the world's personality through successive stages. This is a process accompanied and directed by rational energies facing the impediments of self-inflicted contradictions. Less spectacularly, Mill and James underscored the external sources of self-identity. Wundt brought focus to bear on the cultural architecture of every developed consciousness.

As I hope to have made clear throughout, these men did not stand alone. They are the especially influential representatives of an influential age. Theirs was a time when romanticism, idealism, materialism, radicalism, orthodoxy, elitism, environmentalism—when all the conceivable *isms* struggled happily on the limitless field of nineteenth-century intelligence. It was an age that was busy making the world we live in, and conscious of the many important tasks it would leave undone. A genuine *science of human nature* was one of these—a central one—which the nineteenth century, having made such a good start, thought that we could finish.

BIOGRAPHICAL
OUTLINES

John Stuart Mill (1806–1873)

Mill was born on May 20, 1806, in Pentonville, London. His *Autobiography* documents the interest James Mill took in his early education, which included the Latin and Greek classics and extensive study of British and world history. By the time he was eight years old, he had already begun to tutor his siblings. His serious studies of Aristotelian and Scholastic philosophy were undertaken in 1818, the year his father's *History of India* was published.

In 1820 and for about a year he stayed with the family of Sir Samuel Bentham in France, Sir Samuel being the brother of Jeremy. On his return to England and through his father's contacts he was able to read law with John Austin but, as always, not in a school but in his own home. Plans for a career in law were entertained but finally rejected and, in 1822, he began his employment with the India House, a term of employment that lasted decades.

It was at about the time of his first employment that Mill completed his reading of Bentham's *Treatise on Legislation*, a work that changed his life and numbered him immediately among the disciples of utilitarianism. Mill himself founded a Utilitarian Society as early as 1823, he then being seventeen! Within a year his career as a published author began with entries in the new and "radical" *West-*

minister Review. His episode of despondancy began, it seems in 1826 when, finally giving himself some time to reflect on the course his life was taking, he was shaken by sentiments of empty futility. It was the poetry denied him in his tenderest years that saw him through, and that for a time moved him in the direction of Romanticism.

Between 1826 and 1840, Mill's literary efforts were largely confined to the *Westminister Review* and the *London Review*. He was the first editor of the latter, which was founded in 1835 and merged with the former a year later. His first systematic and original work in Philosophy was his *System of Logic* (1843), which was to become something of the Bible for the experimental sciences. An *inductive science of the mind* was but one of the possibilities developed and defended in this work, and its author was an instant celebrity.

Mill's friendship of many years with the Taylors led to a romantic attachment with Mrs. Taylor that remained unrequited until the death of her husband. She and Mill were married in 1851, remaining sublimely happy until her death seven years later. Mill believed, and many will concur, that his best writing was occasioned by this relationship. He credits her with originating so much of *On Liberty* as to deserve to have her name on it. To this may be added *Utilitarianism, Subjection of Women*, and *Thoughts on Parliamentary Reform* as works in which Mrs. Taylor must certainly have had a hand. She died and was buried at their summer house in Avignon where Mill himself then chose to remain for the rest of his life, except for sporadic and abbreviated visits to England. The East India Company's loss of control in India resulted in its orderly collapse, and Mill retired with a pension in the year of his wife's death.

Throughout his adult years and ever more intensely after his marriage Mill devoted himself to the common cause. He aided in the founding of suffrage societies, defended the principles of socialism, concerned himself with the fate of freedom in an increasingly administered world divided into classes. Neither in life nor in print was he able to relax the essential tension between liberty and order, between the rights of the individual and the good of the whole. But no man ever presented his confusions with such clarity. He, with a handful of his countrymen, raised the essay to the level of an art, instructing the masses in a lesson that would be forgotten all too soon: A confident morality cannot excuse oppression.

Mill died on May 8, 1873 in Avignon and, by the terms of his will, was buried next to his wife.

Georg Wilhelm Friedrich Hegel (1770–1831)

Hegel was born on August 27, 1770, in Stuttgart. He learned Latin on his mother's lap, proceeding thence to Stuttgart's classically oriented Grammar School. His university studies began at Tübingen where his unhappy affair with theology led him quickly back to the Greek and Roman classics. Hölderlin and Schelling were friends of his in these years and, though he impressed them, his professors were not very positive in their estimation of his philosophical abilities. It was his friendship with Schelling and not his formal studies that attracted him to Fichte's works.

For a time after receiving his doctorate (1793) he worked as a private tutor in Switzerland, availing himself of the isolation to inquire into the *historical* Jesus and what young and active minds in every age call the meaning of life. Hölderlin's intercession made it possible for Hegel to return to Germany as a private tutor in Frankfort (1797) where he busied himself with the economic and political issues then engaging the German intellectual world. The small inheritance occasioned by his father's death (1799) gave Hegel just enough financial independence to leave Frankfort and take up residence in Jena (1801), the diadem of Weimar culture. Soon after his arrival, he and Schelling began the *Critical Journal of Philosophy* (1802). He earned appointment as *Privatdozent* with his dissertation on planetary orbits. Only with Schelling's exit from Jena do the days of Hegel's philosophical originality begin (1803), his *Phenomenology of Spirit* appearing in 1807. Insufficiently hostile to the victorious Napoleon, who took Jena in 1806, Hegel found the Weimar climate uncongenial. He took the position of rector at the far less prestigious gymnasium in Nuremburg where he remained until 1816. Then, in 1818, he was honored by appointment to the chair in philosophy at Berlin, succeeding no less a figure than Fichte. There he remained until the end, productive and influential, a figure of first national and then international standing. It was the Berlin years that found him completing his *Philosophy of Right, Reason in History, Encyclopedia*, and *Philosophy of Religion*. His *Science of Logic* was completed in the country where he had taken his family during the cholera epidemic in 1831, the epidemic to which he nonetheless succumbed.

Hegel's Berlin lectures are the source of most of his major publications. His close ties to the Prussian government added to his local and national influence, even though on no reasonable construal can his writings be judged as supportive of the democratic revolutions initiated by his adoring countrymen the year before he died. Then as now, one can find justifications for all sorts of convictions in Hegel's works; for nationalism and one-worldism, for democracy and statism, for moral absolutism and moral evolutionism. He died on November 14 and was buried, according to his instructions, next to Fichte.

Wilhelm Wundt (1832–1920)

This "senior psychologist in the history of psychology," as Boring called him, was born near Mannheim. His father was a Lutheran minister who saw to it that the boy's early education was directed by a young vicar, Friedrich Müller. Gymnasium study proceeded first at Bruschal, then at Heidelberg. After an initial year of university study at Tübingen (1851), he moved to Heidelberg where he distinguished himself in the physical and biological sciences. His choice of medical training seems to have been the best compromise in light of his father's death and his mother's very modest inheritance. As with James, however, the practice of medicine was not for him. His interests in physiology took him to the celebrated institute directed by Johannes Müller at the University of Berlin (1856). Returning to Heidelberg for his doctorate the same year, he stayed for another eight. His Heidelberg lectures in 1862 would appear in published form as *Lectures on Human and Animal Psychology*. His even more influential *Foundations of Physiological Psychology* was also composed and published during the Heidelberg years.

It was in 1875 that he was named to the chair in philosophy at Leipzig, accepting research space and facilities as part of the appointment. William James had not been sure whether his own psychological demonstrations began at Harvard in 1875 or 1876, so again this useless question of priority may haunt our unproductive moments. In any case, there certainly was a psychology laboratory by 1879 and, within two years, Wundt had seen to it that there was a journal prepared to publish its findings—the *Philosophische Studien*. His students in the new experimental psychology included Cattell, Külpe, Klemm, Titchener and, as we have seen, even William James at least as a auditor. Psychology, however, was not his single concern, nor the purpose behind his initial appointment. He respected the latter with textbooks in logic, ethics, and philosophy during the 1880', subjects he continued to work on throughout his prolific career which ended on August 31, 1920.

Like Hegel, Wundt was honored by his government and

his countrymen. He had served as a medical officer in the Franco-Prussian War (1870–1871) and as rector of his university (1900). He taught his classes until he was eighty-five, nearly blind but still intellectually vital. It has been often observed that Wundt's early tiltings with death—his serious illness in 1856 and the premature death of his father—had worked on his religious upbringing to forge an essentially spiritualistic outlook. This, in turn, has led some historians of psychology to wonder how intellectually committed he was to philosophy. Not having access to Wundt's private motivations, we need only observe that the university professor in nineteenth-century Germany was absorbed into a deep and revered tradition of philosophical scholarship and that the absorption was complete when the professorship itself was in philosophy. Wundt seems to have adhered to the Leibnizian approach to "moral science" as he adhered to the Helmholtzian approach to natural science and the Hegelian approach to historical-cultural science. Like so many of his fellow scholars in the nineteenth century, he was busy working things out, trying to preserve the hopefulness of Enlightenment rhetorical science by developing methods and perspectives suitable to real science. Since his early experiences were unique but his life's commitment was not, we are on safer ground attributing the latter to the broad cultural traditions that were his and that surrounded his every effort.

William James (1842–1910)

Ralph Barton Perry's *The Thought and Character of William James,* cited in chapter 5, is still the best brief biography, ideally supplemented by Henry James' *Notes of a Son and Brother* (1914).

Henry James the elder was a man of catholic interests,

eccentric religiosity, and aggressive tolerance, at least in the forging of the intellects of his children. He had turned away from official religion and adopted Swedenborgianism, then something of a rage in the fashionable spheres of American intellectual life. Although neither Henry Jr. nor William adopted this faith, both benefited from their father's defense of it and his careful scrutiny of what seemed to be the inconsistencies and hypocricies of the widely accepted alternatives. The grandfather, William Sr., had made a fortune through investments in the Erie Canal, and it was this fortune that gave Henry Sr. the time to develop his raw powers— and his friendships; Oliver Wendell Holmes Sr., Ralph Waldo Emerson, Charles Dana, George Ripley, even Thomas Carlyle.

Our William James was born on January 11, 1842, at the family residence in New York City. He was two when his father discovered Swedenborg, but discovered no consuming passion of his own for many years. At the age Mill was when he organized a Utilitarian Society, William James was still thinking of a career as an artist. He traveled much and often, giving less than full concern to the completion of his studies. But he did enter Harvard and went all the way through to the medical degree (1869), thereupon suffering an invalid existence on and off for three years. His Harvard days had put him under the tutelage of some famous men and got him on one of Louis Agassiz' (1865) expeditions to South America. He found the trip grueling, the work tedious, Agassiz facinating.

It was while in Europe in 1867 that his thoughts turned toward psychological problems within the context of physiology, causing him to journey to Berlin where Helmholtz and Wundt were holding forth on such issues. But by 1870 he was again medically and psychologically debilitated, a state of malaise finally relieved by Renouvier's works. With Renouvier's example before him, he is found picking himself up in the spring of 1870, resolving that his "first act of free will shall be to believe in free will" (Perry, p. 121).

James' first teaching appointment at Harvard was in 1872. Within three years he began to lecture on what we would now call physiological psychology, but within the curricular context of philosophical studies. It was in 1878 that he agreed to write a psychology text for Henry Holt, thinking that he could complete it within two years. A dozen years later the two volumes of his *Principles* appeared and established James as America's premier psychologist. For James, however, 1878 involved a more significant relationship than the one he had with Holt; it was the year of his marriage to Alice Howe Gibbens, whose effect on his life and general well-being mirrored that wrought by the remarkable Mrs. Taylor on John Stuart Mill.

With fame came official productive travel to a man whose youth was often aimlessly charted on distant soil. His Gifford Lectures at Edinburgh (1901–1902) were published as *The Varieties of Religious Experience* (1902); those given at Columbia appeared as *Pragmatism: A New Name for Some Old Ways of Thinking* (1907); and the Hibbert Lectures at Oxford as *A Pluralistic Universe* (1909). He also accepted a visiting lectureship at Stanford just in time to witness the earthquake that ruined San Francisco (1906). Fatigue and failing health forced his resignation from Harvard in 1907, whereupon he and Mrs. James planned what was to be his last trip abroad. He became seriously ill in Nauheim and was brought quickly to the family's country house in New Hampshire where he died on August 26, 1910.

The pragmatism lectures, given first as the Lowell Lectures in Boston and then again at Columbia, surprised James by their reception. He became nearly a cult figure to his eager young audience at Columbia, as he had for some time been a father figure to leaders of thought on both sides of the Atlantic.

NOTES

1. The Nineteenth Century

1. Thomas Carlyle, "Signs of the Times," originally published anonymously in the June 1829 issue of *Edinburgh Review*.

2. *Ibid*. Here Carlyle is referring to Pierre Cabanis' *Rapports du Physique et du Morale de l'Homme*. English translations of his Preface to this important work and of his long *10th Memoire* have been furnished respectively by Francine S. Robinson and Margaret Heliotis in series E, vol. 4 of *Significant Contributions to the History of Psychology*, D.N. Robinson, ed. (Washington, D.C.: University Publications of America, 1978–1980).

3. The history of psychological materialism in modern times in reviewed in ch. 9 of my *An Intellectual History of Psychology* (New York: Macmillan, 1976).

4. These notions appear in a number of Descartes' works and especially in Articles 17, 23, 24, 30, 31, 32, 35, 37, 39, and 41 of his *Les Passions de l'Ame*, translated as *The Passions of the Soul* by E. Haldane and G.R. T. Moss in *The Philosophical Works of Descartes* (New York: Dover, 1955).

5. *Ibid*., pp. 433–34.

6. This passage appears in Voltaire's *The Ignorant Philosopher*.

7. Translated as *Man: A Machine* by M.W. Calkins (New York: Open Court, 1912).

8. From Holbach's *The System of Nature* (1770). The passage comes from the selection translated by Peter Gay, *The Enlightenment: A Comprehensive Anthology* (New York: Simon & Schuster, 1973).

9. Thomas Carlyle, "Signs of the Times.

10. As Locke says in his Introduction to *An Essay Concerning*

238   1. THE NINETEENTH CENTURY

Human Understanding (1690), "I shall not at present meddle with the physical consideration of the mind . . . and whether those ideas do, in their formation, any or all of them, depend on matter or not." (Chicago: Regnery, 1956.)

11. John Locke, ch. 9 of *An Essay Concerning the True Original, Extent, and End of Civil Government* (1690). In *Social Contract* (New York: Oxford University Press, 1960).

12. David Hume, *Essays Moral and Political* (1748), containing his critique of "contract" theories in the essay, "Of the Original Contract." In *Social Contract* Jean-Jacques Rousseau, *Du Contrat Social* (1762). Consult the edition by C.E. Vaughan, *The Political Writings of Jean-Jacques Rousseau* (Cambridge: Cambridge University Press, 1915).

13. Shelley's *Defense* is widely anthologized now although it was not published in any form until Mary Shelley's 1840 edition, nearly twenty years after it had been written.

14. Wordsworth informs the reader of the aim of his poems thus: "to illustrate the manner in which our feelings and ideas are associated in a state of excitement." *The Preface to "Lyrical Ballads"* (1800), published in many editions.

15. Immanuel Kant, *Critique of Pure Reason*, Norman Kemp Smith, tr. (London: Macmillan, 1929). See particularly the *Transcendental Deduction* (B), B167, B168.

16. *Ibid.*, A21:B35.

17. *Ibid.*, A22:B36.

18. William Hazlitt, *Table Talk* (Essay 5: "On Genius and Common Sense"), first published in 1821.

19. Edmund Burke, *Inquiry into the Origins of the Sublime* (1756).

20. Jean Le Rond D'Alembert, *Preliminary Discourse to the Encyclopedia of Diderot* (1751), R.N. Schwab, tr. (Indianapolis: Bobbs-Merrill, 1963), p. 7.

21. David Hume, *A Treatise of Human Nature* (1739), L.A. Selby-Bigge, ed. (London: Clarendon Press, 1973; reprint of 1888 ed.)

22. *Ibid.*, book 1, part 3, sec. 15.

23. I refer here to Shaftesbury, Hutcheson, Butler, and others whose major works can be found in *British Moralists*, L.A. Selby-Bigge, ed. (2 vols.; New York: Dover, 1965).

24. Jeremy Bentham, *An Introduction to the Principles of Morals and Legislation* (1789), ch. 10, sec. 11.

25. I. Kant, *Critique of Pure Reason*, A:381.

26. For this explanation of supernatural naturalism vs. natural supernaturalism, consult ch. 8, book 3 of Carlyle's *Sartor Resartus*.

27. Fichte's *Characteristics of the Present Age* and several other important works are discussed in my preface to "Fichte," *Significant Contributions to the History of Psychology*, series A, vol. 2.

2. John Stuart Mill

1. *John Morley: Nineteenth-Century Essays*. Selected and with an introduction by Peter Stansky (Chicago: University of Chicago Press, 1970). The quotation is taken from "The Death of Mr. Mill" (1873), p. 102.

2. *Ibid.*

3. We learn this much from his *Autobiography*, but associationism had a wide circle of patrons even before the elder Mill stood as its champion.

4. Alexander Bain, *James Mill: A Biography* (London: Longmans, Green, 1882), p. 32.

5. J.S. Mill, *Autobiography* (1873), Jack Stillinger, ed. (Boston: Houghton Mifflin, 1969).

6. Burke, too, was unsparing in his efforts to convey to his countrymen the principled arguments of the colonists, but he subjected Price's preachments to scorn and denunciation in his *Reflections on the Revolution in France*. The subtitle of the essay is "And on the Proceedings in Certain Societies in London relative to that Event." Dr. Price had urged that the King be reminded, by the very means of addressing him, that he was the servant of the people, and not their master. Burke replies, "The law, which knows neither to flatter nor to insult, calls this high magistrate, not our servant, as this humble divine calls him, but '*our soverign lord and king*'; and we, on our parts, have learned to speak only the primitive language of the law, and not the confused jargon of their Babylonian pulpits" (p. 294). *Reflections on the Revolution in France* in B.W. Hill, ed., *Edmund Burke on Government, Politics, and Society* (Glasgow: William Collins & Sons, 1975).

7. See, for example, his "Speech on Conciliation with the Colonies" in *Edmund Burke on Government, Politics, and Society*, pp. 159–87.

8. A measure of its power is the frequency with which later political writers find it necessary to condemn or applaud the work. As a statement of Burke's overall political philosophy, *Reflections* is somewhat anomalous, unless one takes the view that he was in fact a closet Tory all along. Writing in our own century, Leslie Stephen thought that *Reflections* placed Burke at least once "on the side of the oppressors," but it was clearer to Stephen than to Burke who the "oppressors" were in 1790.

9. *Reflections*, p. 353.

10. *Rights of Man*, part 2, p. 147 in *Paine: Common Sense and Other Political Writings*, edited, with an introduction by Nelson F. Adkins (Indianapolis: Bobbs-Merrill, 1953).

11. *Ibid.*, part 1, p. 89.

12. *Ibid.*, part 2, p. 119.

13. *Ibid.*, part 1, pp. 88–89.

14. This is a persistent maxim in Paine's essays and his favorite device for exposing what he judges to be the fallacy in Burke's argument. As a purely empirical or historical claim, it is certainly true that the past cannot hold the future hostage to a document. But it is equally true that the very constitutional government for which Paine pleaded so successfully is a government of law which commits later generations to obedience. The power of amendment is exercised only within the framework of the document and, to this extent, is a power limited by those now dead.

15. David Hume, *A Treatise of Human Nature*, L.A. Selby-Bigge, ed., (New York: Dover, 1965), book 1, part 1, sec. 1.

16. Thomas Paine, *Rights of Man*, part 2, pp. 115–16.

17. The most accessible treatment in English however is the translation by J.H. Bridges of Comte's *A General View of Positivism* (New York: Robert Speller, 1957). As Comte says in the first footnote of this work, the multivolume project was called a *Course* "because it was based upon a course of lectures delivered 1826–1829. But since that time I have always given it the more appropriate name of System" (p. 2).

18. Comte, *The Catechism of Positive Religion*, Richard Congreve, tr. (3d ed. rev.; London: Kegan Paul, Trench, Trubner, 1891), p. 114.

19. Comte makes the place of women central in all of his social and political writings, but he would scarcely qualify today as a

2. JOHN STUART MILL

feminist. His position is that women excell in *affection* and the social sympathies, notwithstanding their limitations in the purely speculative realms. Their place is very much in the home, with their children.

20. Comte, *A General View of Positivism*, p. 234. On the same page, he goes on to say, "If there were nothing else to do but to love, as in the Christian utopia of a future life in which there are no material wants, Women would be supreme. But life is surrounded with difficulties, which it needs our thoughts and energies to avoid; therefore Man takes the command, notwithstanding his inferiority in goodness."

21. *A General View of Positivism*, p. 110.

22. See, for example, pp. 174–76 in *The Catechism of Positive Religion*.

23. Tocqueville's *Democracy in America* became something of a standard reference in British Victorian circles, providing amunition for both Whigs and Tories. The restraint so usual in Mill's discussions of religious issues was, no doubt, indebted to Tocqueville's analysis of the role of relegous life in the American democracy. It was Tocqueville, too, who drew the lines of tension between liberty and equality, recognizing that the pursuit of the latter could only be at the price of the former. The broad consensualism preached by Paine during the revolutionary years was fit for its special context. By Mill's time, however, it had already matured into forms of social intolerance not entirely different from the British version.

24. In Bain's biography, we find James Mill writing of his years at Edinburgh: "All the years I remained about Edinburgh, I used, as often as I possibly could, to steal into Mr. Stewart's class to hear a lecture, which was always a high treat. . . . I have never heard anything nearly so eloquent. . . . The taste for the studies which have formed my favourite pursuits, and which will be so till the end of my life, I owe to him." (*James Mill: A Biography*, p. 16.) Stewart was never happy with Reid's term "common sense," because it suggested an appeal to vulgar criteria of truth. His recommended alternative, appearing in all of his major works, was "the fundamental laws of human belief." But J. S. Mill, as we shall see, judged locutions of this sort to be as mischievous as "common sense."

The past decade has hosted a much needed revival of scholarly interest in the "Scottish School" and specifically in the works of Thomas Reid. It is even more misleading than usual to apply the term *school* to philosophical positions as varied as those defended by Reid, Stewart, Thomas Brown, James Mill, and James Beattie. The closest affinity is between the first and last on this list, but Beattie was at best a popularizer and parrot of the Reidian philosophy. The April 1978 number of *The Monist* is devoted to Reid and may be consulted for contemporary interpretations.

25. There are now at least two standard editions of Reid's later essays and one recent edition of his first major critique of Hume: *Essays on the Active Powers of the Human Mind* and *Essays on the Intellectual Powers of Man* with an introduction by Baruch Brody have been republished by M.I.T. Press (Cambridge, 1969). The edition edited and discussed by Sir William Hamilton has been reproduced in two volumes: *Philosophical Works of Thomas Reid* Harry Bracken, ed., (Hildesheim: Georg Olms, 1967). The most recent edition of Reid's *Inquiry* is edited by Timothy Duggan (Chicago: University of Chicago Press, 1970). All references in this chapter are drawn from the first American edition of *The Works of Thomas Reid* (Charlestown: Samuel Etheridge, 1815).

26. *The Works of Thomas Reid*, vol. 2, (ch. 6 of *Inquiry*).

27. It was the draft of this chapter which Hume claimed in a letter to Reid to have some trouble following, an unfortunate difficulty in light of the fact that "The Geometry of Visibles" was central to Reid's rebuttal of Hume's entire epistemology. For a fuller discussion, consult my "Thomas Reid's *Gestalt* Psychology" in *Thomas Reid: Critical Interpretations*, Stephen Barker and Tom Beauchamp, eds., Philosophical Monographs (1976), 3:44–54.

28. "Inquiry," ch. 2, sec. 6. The full quotation is as follows: "If there are certain principles, as I think there are, which the constitution of our nature leads us to believe, and which we are under a necessity to take for granted in the common concerns of life, without being able to give a reason for them, these are what we call the principles of common sense; and what is manifestly contrary to them, is what we call absurd."

29. For Hume's discussion, see his *A Treatise of Human Nature*, Book 1, part 1, secs. 1 and 4.

30. This form of argument proceeds from Reid's thesis on the

irreducibility of *persons*. He took "self" to be a fundamental entity—what the medievalists would call a "substance"—admitting of no metaphysical analysis or logical proof. Reid's entire theory of causation depends upon the actions of an intending and intelligent being. Hume, of course, dismissed the "self" as simply a "bundle of perceptions" joined together by contiguity, resemblance, and causal relations. For a discussion of this issue, see "Personal Identity: Reid's Answer to Hume," D. N. Robinson and T. L. Beauchamp, *The Monist* (1978), 61(2):325–39.

31. *Essays on the Active Powers*, essay 3, p. 181.

32. John Stuart Mill, *An Examination of Sir William Hamilton's Philosophy and of the Principal Philosophical Questions Discussed in His writings*. All references are to the edition edited by J. M. Robson and introduced by Alan Ryan (Toronto: University of Toronto Press, 1979), vol. 9 of the *Collected Works*.

33. *The Works of Thomas Reid, Collected, with Selections from His Unpublished Letters: Prefixed, Stewart's Account of the Life and Writings of Reid. Preface, Notes, and Supplementary Dissertations by Sir William Hamilton* (Edinburgh: Maclachlan & Stewart, 1846; *The Works of Dugald Stewart* (11 vols.), Sir William Hamilton, ed. (Edinburgh: Maclachlan & Stewart, 1854–1856).

34. Descartes protested that he never subscribed to the theory of "innate ideas," only to the inference that those notions which cannot be traced to sensation and memory must proceed from a natural inclination or primitive conception.

35. Even on the assumption that these are, somehow, "sensory," then these must be taken as "ultimate and simple." This is especially so on the phenomenalistic doctrine which requires that sensations be other than duplications of real material entities "out there." If our perception is not a copy of what is "out there," but is the effect of it, then it is clear that it must be "ultimate and simple."

36. In this it may be said that Mill did both an injustice. Neither Reid nor Kant adopted the view that our mere inability to imagine something was proof of its impossibility. Reid's "common sense" principles, as gifts of nature, worked in the interest of survival in the real world. The point here is not that we cannot even conceive of other principles, but that we would judge as absurd that which is contrary to the principles of

common sense. Even here, however, I say too much for these principles. In our daily commerce, we neither judge of their validity nor weigh alternatives to them. Rather, they are the ground or context for all thought and deliberate action, and similar principles operate in behalf of nature's other creatures as well. Kant's a priori Categories of the Pure Understanding are only functionally, not logically equivalent to Reid's principles of common sense. The Kantian categories are *necessary,* whereas Reid's principles, as built into our very constitution, are *contingent.* A world much different from own would call for different principles of common sense.

37. The relevant work here is Herbert Spencer's "Mill *versus* Hamilton," *Fortnightly Review,* 1865 (July 15), pp. 536–39.

38. *The Active Powers of the Human Mind,* essay 4, pp. 282–83.

39. *Ibid.,* essay 3, p. 61.

40. *Ibid.,* essay 5, p. 319.

41. John Stuart Mill, *A system of Logic Ratiocinative and Inductive, Being a Connected View of the Principles of Evidence and the Methods of Scientific Investigation* (1843). All references are to the edition of 1900 (London: Longmans, Green, 1900).

42. Named after Robert Owen (1771–1858) the British cotton magnate who promoted socialism in the abstract but who did so much to reform the conditions of factory workers and their families. At one point (1813) he formed a company whose profits were to be kept at 5 percent in order to improve further the benefits of his workers. His partners in this short-lived venture were the Quaker, William Allen, and none other than Jeremy Bentham. Frustrated by British inertia, he established the commune of New Harmony on a 30,000-acre plot in Indiana (1825). It lasted about three years and cost Owen much of his fortune.

43. *Active Powers,* essay 3, p. 74. Reid's emphasis upon the future-oriented nature of moral actions was intended to underscore their rational as opposed to their hedonic origin.

44. *Active Powers,* essay 4, p. 284. In this, Reid thought of himself as conforming to the spirit of Newtonian "natural philosophy." In all of his three major essays, Reid avoids metaphysical speculation and strives for the most parsimonious explanation required by the facts of the case. He takes historical linguistic usage as one of the most reliable guides to an understanding of

the human mind, and is ever on guard against those corruptions of language philosophers are so eager to introduce. Had he lived long enough to study Mill's Universal Law of Causation, he probably would have rebuked the author for treating the law as something other than a set of rules fathomed by observers who have noted certain regularities. In this, his position is similar to Berkeley's vis-à-vis Newton's gravitational laws; Berkeley claimed that, when he examined these vaunted laws, he could find nothing but the effects themselves.

45. *Active Powers*, essay 4, p. 284. Note that Reid is not opposing determinism here, but insisting that moral beings determine their actions. He does not allow himself to be caught in an infinite regression on this point, however, because—as noted above—he takes such beings (persons) to be irreducibly individual.

46. John Stuart Mill, "Utilitarianism," in *The Utilitarians* (New York: Dolphin Books, 1961), ch. 2, p. 415.

47. *Ibid.*, p. 434.

48. *Utilitarianism*, p. 434. We have in this passage—and there are many such as these in other works by Mill—a sign of Owenite sympathy; a pervasive optimism regarding human nature when it is freed from artificial social burdens and oppressive environments.

49. This is the title of the second chapter of his *Examination* and is the core-element in his phenomenalistic epistemology. This is how he expresses the doctrine: "All the attributes which we ascribe to objects, consist in their having the power of exciting one or another variety of sensation in our minds ... our knowledge of objects, and even our fancies about objects, consist of nothing but the sensations which they excite, or which we imagine them exciting, in ourselves."

Mill notes that one or another form of this doctrine is embraced by "idealists" such as Berkeley and by such "transcendentalists" as Kant. Mill, however, subscribes to neither of these forms, but to a third—the doctrine as understood by David Hartley and James Mill, and more recently by his close friend, Alexander Bain (Examination, pp. 9ff.).

50. Perhaps his uncharacteristic lack of discernment here was grounded in his belief that all forms of intuitionism finally yield similar *political* consequences, no matter how they might differ

in the subtler metaphysical ways. In writing about his motivation to undertake the *Examination*, Mill offers a revealing passage in the last chapter of his *Autobiography*:

"Now, the difference between these two schools of philosophy, that of Intuition, and that of Experience and Association, is not a mere matter of abstract speculation; it is full of practical consequences, and lies at the foundation of all the greatest differences of practical opinion in an age of progress. The practical reformer has continually to demand that changes be made in things which are supported by powerful and widely-spread feelings . . . and it is often an indispensible part of his argument to show, how those powerful feelings had their origin. . . . There is therefore a natural hostility between him and a philosophy which discourages the explanation of feelings and moral facts by circumstances and association, and prefers to treat them as ultimate elements of human nature; a philosophy which is addicted to holding up favourite doctrines as intuitive truths, and deems intuition to be the voice of Nature and of God, speaking with an authority higher than that of our reason."

Again, however, Mill fails to make instructive distinctions. Reid, for example, would take our reason to be very much "the voice of nature," and would show how this very reason leads to an indubitable confirmation of those intuitive truths which Mill would have originating in "circumstances."

3. Georg Wilhelm Friedrich Hegel

1. Peter Gay's translation of Kant's "Was Ist Aufklärung" (1784) is given in Peter Gay, ed., *The Enlightenment: A Comprehensive Anthology* (New York: Simon & Schuster, 1973), pp. 384–89.

2. Immanuel Kant, *Fundamental Principles of the Metaphysics of Morals*, Thomas K. Abbott, tr. (New York: Bobbs-Merrill, 1949).

3. The translation is by Anna Swanwick and is taken from the 1901 limited edition of Goethe's *Works* (in 10 volumes) published for the Anthological Society by J. H. Moore & Co., London.

4. *Versuch einer Kritik aller Offenbarung* (Königsberg, 1792). This work was dedicated to "the Philosopher" and supplied something of a "religious imperative" to human nature complementing the Categorical Imperative of Kant's ethics.

5. Two volumes of Fichte's *Popular Works* were translated in the nineteenth century by William Smith (4th ed.; London: Trübner, 1889). The works cited in this chapter have been collected recently in a single volume, series A, vol. 2 of *Significant Contributions to the History of Psychology*, D. N. Robinson, ed. (Washington, D.C.: University Publications of America, 1978–1980).

6. Fichte's "transcendental nationalism" was scarcely unique in the Weimar of the early nineteenth century. The threatened Napoleonization of Europe promised to eliminate from the German people nothing less than their culture. Fichte was persuaded not only that this was worth preserving but that the proposed (and imposed) alternative was notably defective.

7. Friedrich Schelling arrived at Weimar's celebrated University of Jena in professorial dress at the remarkable age of twenty-three. Though younger than Hegel, the latter may be said to have begun as something of Schelling's philosophical junior. The two jointly edited Jena's *Critical Journal of Philosophy* in the years 1802–1803. The most Fichtean of Schelling's efforts—but even this shows signs of independence—was his *Vom Ich als Prinzip der Philosophie, oder über das Unbedingte im menschlichen Wissen* (1795). This translates as *The Ego as a Principle of Philosophy; or, On the Unconditioned in Human Knowledge*. But in the *Ideen* we learn that the *natural* world enjoys existential parity with Ego and is inescapably the source of Ego's content.

8. Friedrich Schelling, *The Philosophy of Art: An Oration on the Relation between the Plastic Arts and Nature*, A. Johnson, tr. (London, 1845).

9. The quote is taken from John Watson, *Schelling's Transcendental Idealism: A Critical Exposition* (Chicago: S. C. Griggs, 1892). p. 1.

10. *Ibid.*, p. 188.

11. Oscar Wilde, *Epigrams* in *The World of the Victorians: An Anthology of Poetry and Prose*, E. D. H. Johnson, ed. (New York: Scribner's, 1964), p. 495.

12. G. W. F. Hegel, *Encyclopedia of Philosophy*, G. E. Mueller, tr. (New York: Philosophical Library, 1959). The quotation is from p. 1.

13. G. W. F. Hegel, *Science of Logic* (in 2 vols.), W. H. Johnston and L. G. Struthers, tr. (London: Allen & Unwin, 1929), p. 20.

14. G. W. F. Hegel, *The Phenomenology of Mind*, J. B. Baillie, tr.

(2d. ed.; London: Allen & Unwin, 1949). Baillie's comment appears in the prefatory note to the second edition.

15. Bertrand Russell, *A History of Western Philosophy* (New York: Simon & Schuster, 1945), p. 730).

16. *Enclyclopedia of Philosophy*, Preface, p. 64.

17. *Encyclopedia of Philosophy*, p. 54.

18. G. S. Hall, "Notes on Hegel and his Critics," *Journal of Speculative Philosophy* (1878), 12:93–103. This was the official journal of American Hegelianism in the closing decades of the nineteenth century.

19. See, for example, John Dewey's *My Pedagogic Creed* (New York: E. I. Kellogg, 1897). And on imported Hegelianism in general, consult *The American Hegelians: An Intellectual Episode in the History of Western America*, William H. Goetzmann, ed. (New York: Knopf, 1973).

20. G. W. F. Hegel, *Reason in History: A General Introduction to the Philosophy of History*, R. S. Hartman, tr. (Indianapolis: Bobbs-Merrill, 1953).

21. The relevant passage appears in W. C. Dampier, *A History of Science*: "[Hegel's] Philosophy of Identity was bolder. It started with the hypothesis that not only spiritual phenomena, but even the actual world—nature, that is, and man—were the result of an act of thought on the part of a creative mind, similar, it was supposed, in kind to the human mind. ... The philosophers accused the scientific men of narrowness; the scientific men retorted that the philosophers were crazy." W. C. Dampier *A History of Science* (Cambridge: Cambridge University Press, 1966), pp. 291–92.

22. Hegel, *Science of Logic*, 2:365.

4. Wilhelm Wundt

1. E. G. Boring, *A History of Experimental Psychology* (New York: Appleton Century, 1951), p. 345.

2. I need only cite here the fine recent studies by Arthur Blumenthal and especially his "A Reappraisal of Wilhelm Wundt," *American Psychologist* (1975), 30:1081–83.

3. J. F. Herbart's *A Text-Book in Psychology* appeared first in

English in the translation by Margaret K. Smith and was published by D. Appleton in 1891. A facsimile edition, with my own introductory comments, is provided in series A, vol. 6 of *Significant Contributions to the History of Psychology*, D. N. Robinson, ed. (Washington, D.C.: University Publications of America, 1978–1980).

4. Gustav Theodor Fechner, *Elemente der Psychophysik*; translated by Helmut E. Adler as *Elements of Psychophysics* (New York: Holt, Rinehart & Winston, 1966), p. 46.

5. Wundt's *Lectures* are reproduced in series D, vol. 1 of *Significant Contributions to the History of Psychology*. The edition is the English translation by J. E. Creighton and E. B. Titchener (London: Swan, Sonnenschein, 1894). As Wundt notes in his preface to the second edition, his *Lectures on Human and Animal Psychology* had been at the center of his thoughts and teaching for nearly thirty years. It may be safely concluded, then, that they stand as the products of Wundt's mature and stable positions on the issues discussed in this chapter. So prolific a writer could not avoid over the years stating such positions in a variety of ways, some of them seeming to contradict each other or suggesting a radical departure from earlier ones. But what was most consistent in Wundt's long career is what is found in the *Lectures*.

6. G. W. von Leibniz, *Monadology* (#17) in *Leibniz—The Monadology and Other Philosophical Writings*, R. Latta, tr. (Oxford: Oxford University Press, 1898).

7. *Monadology*, #79.

8. G. W. F. Hegel, *Reason in History*, R. S. Hartman, tr. (Indianapolis: Bobbs-Merrill, 1953), 3:2.

9. Wilhelm Wundt, *Völkerpsychologie*, 1912. Translated as *Elements of Folk Psychology: Outlines of a Psychological History of the Development of Mankind*, E. L. Schaub, tr. (London: Macmillan, 1916), p. 3. Page references are to the English edition.

10. Condorcet, *Sketch for a Historical Picture of the Progress of the Human Mind*, June Barraclough, tr. (New York: Noonday, 1955).

11. J. F. Herbart, *A Text-Book in Psychology*, pp. 190–91.

12. Perhaps the best review of how the present views the past in the matter of Wundt's program is Richard Littman, "Social and Intellectual Origins of Experimental Psychology," in *The First Century of Experimental Psychology*, Eliot Hearst, ed. (Hillsdale,

N.J.: Lawrence Earlbaum, 1979), pp. 39–86. In the same volume, Richard F Thompson and I have attempted to review the narrower context of biological science within which Wundt fashioned his "physiological" psychology: Richard F. Thompson and Daniel N. Robinson, "Physiological Psychology," pp. 407–54.

13. Alfred Binet, *On Double Consciousness* (Chicago: Open Court, 1980), p. 12. This work has recently been republished in series C, vol. 5 of *Significant Contributions to the History of Psychology*.

14. George Romanes' *Animal Intelligence* was first published in 1882. The edition of 1883, published by D. Appleton is now available in series A, vol. 7 of *Significant Contributions to the History of Psychology*. The work was heralded by many as the first systematic attempt to apply Darwinian principles to the full sweep of psychological processes as displayed by the lower organisms; C. Lloyd Morgan's classic is *An Introduction to Comparative Psychology* (London: Walter Scott, 1894), the facsimile edition of which appears in series D, vol. 2 of *Significant Contributions to the History of Psychology*.

15. Throughout this chapter I have made use of some of my own recent lectures given as part of the centennial programs of the past few years. These include "Mind, Body, and Spirit at the Dawn of Experimental Psychology" (Annual Convention of the A.A.A.S., Houston, Texas, 1979); "The Metaphysics of Wundt's Psychological Psychology and Its Effects on Praxis" (Annual Convention of the Eastern Psychological Association, Philadelphia, 1979); "Minds, Brains, and Selves" (87th Annual Convention of the American Psychological Association, New York, 1979).

5. William James

1. The record was made no clearer when G. Stanley Hall, who had been James' student, later published (October 1895) in the *American Journal of Psychology* a retrospective appreciation of those who had put experimental psychology on the American academic map. James was not cited at all! Writing to Hall on the matter, James reminded Hall that Hall had received his first instruction in the subject from James when "there was no other place but Harvard where during those years you could get" such training.

Extracts of the letter are given in Ralph Barton Perry, *The Thought and Character of William James* (Cambridge: Harvard University Press, 1948), p. 182.

2. His contract with Henry Holt for the book was executed in July 1878. See Perry, p. 186. The authorized edition of James' *Principles of Psychology* published by Henry Holt was reissued as a facsimile edition (New York: Dover, 1950). Volume 1 ends with ch. 16 and volume 2 with ch. 28.

3. Perry, p. 85.

4. This famous statement by Huxley appeared in his unsigned article, "On the Hypothesis that Animals Are Automata, and Its History," *Fortnightly Review* (1874), vol. 16.

5. *Essays in Radical Empiricism* first published in 1912 and *A Pluralistic Universe* first published in 1909 appear together in the edition of 1947 published by Longmans, Green, New York. All references in the text are to this edition.

6. Mach's differences with James and vice versa do not figure centrally in the matter of epistemology. James would not confine psychology to the laboratory as would Mach, however, and his own *pluralism* could not, of course, tolerate Mach's single-minded positivism, his "empirio-criticism." James and Mach met in the summer of 1882 during one of James' European journeys. Years later he would write (in this case, of Ostwald), "I don't think I ever envied a man's mind as much as I have envied Ostwald's—unless it were Mach's." (Perry, p. 236). James was closer to Mach, however, than to what would become the Machian school, though it is not clear how close Mach himself would have been to the latter.

7. This is one of the essays in the collection, *The Will to Believe and Other Essays in Popular Philosophy* (Cambridge: Harvard University Press, 1979). "Great Men and Their Environment" first appeared in the *Atlantic Monthly*, October 1880.

8. "Great Men and Their Environment," Harvard edition, p. 175.

9. There are passages in his *Essays in Radical Empiricism* which seek to apologize for this breach of the faith. In one long note, for example, he expresses his debt and loyalty to Renouvier and insists that "the only 'free will' I have every thought of defending is the character of novelty in fresh activity-situations," (p. 185).

But here we have the right to remind James of "Midshipman Easy." This character of novelty, called by any name, is a breach of the determinist's peace, even if a small one.

James' intellectual debt to Charles Renouvier (1815–1903) borders on the clinical! It was during a period of deep despair, while studying in Europe, that James began to pour over Renouvier's *Science of Morals*, a work that argued forcefully for the coequal unprovability of determinism and moral freedom. Renouvier was as much the "pluralist" as James was to become, and was ever on guard lest the unique value of the individual person be submerged by sociological thinking.

10. From *The Importance of Individuals* (originally published in 1890 by Open Court as a reply to those who had criticized "Great Men and Their Environment") in *The Will to Believe and Other Essays in Popular Philosophy* (Cambridge: Harvard University Press, 1979), p. 144.

11. There are now several careful studies of the phenomenological aspects of James' Psychology. Especially cogent is Bruce Wilshire's *William James and Phenomenology: A Study of "The Principles of Psychology"* (Bloomington: Indiana University Press, 1968).

12. Perry, *The Thought and Character of William James*, p. 279.

13. Charles Sanders Peirce, *Collected Papers*, vol. 5, Charles Hartshorne and Paul Weiss, eds. (Cambridge: Harvard University Press, 1965), p. 297.

14. *Ibid.*, p. 1.

15. There is, however, all the difference between the claim that the meaning of a concept is no more than its method of measurement and the *pragmatic* claim that ties meaning to practical consequences.

16. Cited in Perry, p. 132.

17. *A Pluralistic Universe*, in *Essays in Radical Empiricism, and A Pluralistic Universe* (London: Longmans, Green, 1947), p. 322.

INDEX